D1320190

The Baltimore School
of Urban Ecology

The
Baltimore School *of*
Urban Ecology

*Space, Scale, and Time
for the Study of Cities*

J. MORGAN GROVE,

MARY L. CADENASSO,

STEWARD T. A. PICKETT,

GARY E. MACHLIS, and

WILLIAM R. BURCH JR.

Foreword by Laura A. Ogden

Yale UNIVERSITY PRESS/NEW HAVEN & LONDON

Published with assistance from the foundation established in memory of Calvin Chapin of the Class of 1788, Yale College.

Any opinions, findings, and conclusions or recommendations expressed in this material are those of the authors and do not necessarily reflect the views of the National Science Foundation (NSF) or the USDA Forest Service.

Yale University Press books may be purchased in quantity for educational, business, or promotional use. For information, please e-mail sales.press@yale.edu (U.S. office) or sales@yaleup.co.uk (U.K. office).

Set in Minion type by Integrated Publishing Solutions, Grand Rapids, Michigan.
Printed in the United States of America.

Library of Congress Control Number: 2015932952
ISBN 978-0-300-10113-3 (cloth : alk. paper)

A catalogue record for this book is available from the British Library.

This paper meets the requirements of ANSI/NISO Z39.48-1992 (Permanence of Paper).

10 9 8 7 6 5 4 3 2 1

Contents

Color plates appear following page 108

Foreword

Laura A. Ogden

This is a book that offers a way for us to think about cities and their social, political, and ecological complexity, as well as a work that charts a path toward the possibility of more sustainable cities in the future. Social theorists have thought long and hard about the ways cities are utterly distinct even while they are emerging and changing through their connections with other places. For example, Raymond Williams in his 1973 classic, *The Country and the City,* shows how the "country" and the "city" come into being as contingent forms of social life during the transition to capitalism in Europe. At the end of the book, Williams argues that cities are the catalyst for an emerging international economic system, an argument that anticipates contemporary theorists, such as Saskia Sassen, who offer compelling insights into the role of cities in the making of the global.

Yet the authors of *The Baltimore School of Urban Ecology* extend our understanding of cities considerably by treating cities as historically constituted social-ecological forms. At best, cities are sites characterized by shifting intensities—where beings, goods, and ideas saturate and reconfigure the boundaries between the social and the natural. *The Baltimore School* uses Baltimore, one of the most richly compelling cities in the United States, as a kind of productive template for the creation of ideas. These ideas help us understand the ways the city's social and

ecological life are inseparable modes of existence, dynamically produced
in space and time. In the process, J. Morgan Grove, Mary Cadenasso,
Steward Pickett, Gary Machlis, and William R. Burch Jr. significantly
transform the discipline of ecology. Their approach is necessarily interdisciplinary and experimental because cities challenge boundaries of all
kinds.

On maps, city boundaries appear legible and discrete. Although this
characteristic can be quite comforting, as we all know, cities resist this kind
of containment. Spend time in Baltimore, and the fluidity of these boundaries becomes self-evident. In April, for example, chimney swifts settle in
Baltimore after spending their winters in the Amazon. On the ground, bird
lovers cluster together, their faces upturned in hopeful anticipation, as the
swifts create soaring vortexes in the sky before exhaustedly roosting in
Baltimore's abandoned smokestacks. Simultaneously, e-birders around
the country monitor the swifts' arrival in Baltimore, an event that looks
a lot like storm clouds when captured by satellite imagery. Swifts, often
described as flying cigars, are less showy than the Baltimore oriole. Of
course, sighting a Baltimore oriole actually *in* Baltimore itself would be
an ornithological rarity. Yet the Baltimore oriole, like Poe's raven, per-
meates the city's iconographic landscape. These birds, too, traverse the
globe, troubling the boundaries between city and country, the real and
the imaginary, nature and society.

We can map other lines of flight as well. Each day thousands of
federal workers commute to Washington, D.C., from Baltimore, reflecting the shifting geography of housing, labor, and governance. Con-
versely, about a third of the people working in Baltimore, at any given
time, actually live in the suburbs. Yet, when you are in the suburbs, there
is a good chance that the person working at the strip mall or restaurant
has triumphed over the reverse commute. This means that life in the
city, for people at least, is lived as routinized mobility. We often think
of time spent in transit as lost time, life on the periphery of real living.
But as the French anthropologist Marc Augé has shown us, traveling
these transit routes is a practice of history and memory. Instead of life
lost, the commute is life unfolding at the stop-and-go pace of a crowded
bus line. Along the way, monuments to the city's collective history spark
personal, individualized memories as well. As we pass, for instance,

Camden Street's Babe Ruth statue, we may recognize one of baseball's greatest players. Or we may wonder, if we do not know *his* history, why there is a statue of Babe Ruth in Baltimore anyway. In those same fleeting moments, as the bus rolls along, perhaps the memory of a childhood trip to a ball field floods our senses. On the commute, the past and the present intermingle in barely recognized flashes of illumination, all in the time it takes to glance up from the morning newspaper.

The city's boundary-defying network of commuting workers reflects the realities of Baltimore's post-industrial productivity as well as the political economy of urban housing markets. Once, the production of goods, particularly steel, tied Baltimore's ports and workers to the rest of the world. During this era, Frederick Douglass, the country's most famous abolitionist, worked as a child at the docks in Baltimore, a time he considered crucial to his political awakening. Douglass's coming-of-age occurred in Fell's Point, now an upscale neighborhood gentrified with restaurants, bars, and tree-lined row houses. A few miles from here stands Frederick Douglass High School, established in 1888 as one of the first integrated public high schools in the United States. In the short commute between these two sites, Douglass's message of racial and social equality has been muted by decades of uneven urban development. Urban development has effaced other forms of liberation as well. Hundreds of miles of streams are now hidden beneath the city's surface, forming a secret aquatic world. Occasionally, these streams erupt through the pavement, leading to collapses in the city's infrastructure. In other places, these streams quietly leave the city, sometimes carrying the city's detritus into Chesapeake Bay.

In this book, what we used to call *nature* is not just the environment, a mode of life separate from society. Instead, the Baltimore School insists on a research practice that seeks to understand urban *social-ecological relations* and *processes of change,* as opposed to an approach to studying ecology "in a city." Central to this approach is an examination of the messy social and ecological patchiness that characterizes the urban landscape. Although patchiness is a spatial and temporal lens, it is important to note that these scholars do not shy away from the political. Instead, patchiness becomes a prism for understanding the processes that create variation, including those leading to social and racial inequality in Baltimore. While the authors focus on Baltimore, the work is an exemplar of patch dynamics in urban ecology more broadly.

Although this is a book of paradigm-shifting significance for those interested in urban ecology, the authors also insist that *understanding* cities is insufficient. Today, most of the world lives in cities. Urban living has become the norm for what it means to be human and, by extension, it has become the norm for other forms of life as well. For the past fifty years, this normalization of urban life has continued at an exponential pace around the globe, while rates of inequality for urban communities of all kinds (human and nonhuman) keep pace. This context motivates the Baltimore School's urgent commitment to use science to develop new visions for urban stewardship. Of equal importance, the school's science emerges out of long and careful collaborations with communities and activists who call Baltimore home. This is a book about Baltimore's past, present, and future, but its resonance reverberates to all the far-flung places we all call home.

Preface

This book tells the story of nearly two decades of social and ecological studies in Baltimore. We choose to tell this story now for many reasons, both global and personal. One important reason is that the majority of the world's people lives in urban areas. In the United States, it is a super majority, with more than 80 percent of Americans living in cities or suburbs. But the urban condition is not constrained to a country or continent; it is a global trend. Most of the urban growth by 2050 will occur in cities that have not yet been built. The twenty-first century can already be conceived of as "the urban century."

The second reason for this book is the increasing ecological knowledge about urban areas following from the growing scientific investments in the study of cities as urban ecological systems since the mid-1990s. Indeed, there is growing appreciation that urban areas are social-ecological systems and can be studied as such. An important step forward for the study of urban areas was the funding of two long-term ecological research (LTER) projects by the U.S. National Science Foundation (NSF) in 1997: the Baltimore Ecosystem Study (BES) and the Central Arizona–Phoenix (CAP) LTER projects.

But there is also an important practical motivation for our focus on urban areas. Urban areas are increasingly engines of innovation to mitigate and adapt to local, regional, and global social and environmental challenges. Urban areas are attempting to simultaneously address a diverse range of issues, including human migration, public health, economic restructuring, water supply, sea-level rise, and increasing temperatures. The complexity and interdependence of these issues have become apparent as urban areas develop and implement plans to increase their sustainability and resilience. Advancing the sustainability and resilience of cities and urban regions is of local, regional, and global importance.

New approaches are needed for generating ecological knowledge about urban systems. Of course, we are excited to satisfy basic scientific curiosity about cities and urbanization. We marvel at the vitality of cities and seek to understand how they work as complex social-ecological systems. New approaches are also needed because many seek to make cities more sustainable and resilient in terms of people (social), place (environment), and prosperity (economy). Equity is part of this triumvirate. All three of these motivations—scientific curiosity, social-ecological system complexity, and the multifaceted nature of sustainability and resilience—require new approaches for studying the city: its regions, global connections, and internal changes.

This book is about an interdisciplinary approach for meeting new needs for the study of cities: patch dynamics. In this book we advance patch dynamics as an approach to integrate science disciplines and practices in order to address the spatial, organizational, and temporal complexity of urban areas. We do not propose patch dynamics as a theory. Rather, we present patch dynamics as an approach toward building theories, developing methods, and advancing practice. Although patch dynamics is most familiar from ecology, we believe this approach will resonate with many other disciplines and professions.

Because we consider patch dynamics to have broad relevance, this book is intended for ecological and social scientists, for students who are interested in studying cities or working across disciplines and professions, and for practitioners—policy makers, planners, designers, managers, and community activists—who confront complex and interdependent urban issues. Finally, this book is intended for scientists and practitioners who work in urban areas and seek to improve the connections between science and decision making. Increasingly, people recognize that complex urban issues require comprehensive approaches and understandings that involve multiple disciplines and account for space, scale, and time. Our goal is that readers of this book will gain new perspectives on how they can study, build, or manage cities.

We feel it is important to acknowledge what this book is not. This book is not a textbook about urban ecology. It does not try to account for and synthesize every idea, approach, or tradition. Rather, it is about the development of an approach—patch dynamics—that has served as the basis for the Baltimore Ecosystem Study since its beginning in 1997. Thus, this book reflects our experiences, growth, and history of developing an urban ecology research program and, frankly, our passion for all the nobility, quirks, venality, resilience, and beauty that is the history and future of the city of Baltimore, its region, and the Chesapeake Bay.

The Chicago and Baltimore Schools of Urban Ecology

We use the term *Baltimore School* for our evolving approach to urban ecology and as shorthand to highlight differences in theoretical content and ambition from the Chicago School. Urban ecology has been used to describe the work of the classic Chicago School of sociology. The Chicago School of sociology was a pioneering approach in the 1920s that attempted to establish a general theory of urban social systems. It employed ecological concepts such as competition, succession, and spatial patchiness, but it did so using analogies rather than mechanistic models.

The Chicago School is problematic for several reasons. First, the 1920s Chicago sociologists did not fully reflect the contemporary ecological thought of their time. They were unaware of the theoretical controversies associated with key ideas they had adopted from ecology. For example, the nature and causes of ecological succession and climax communities were already being hotly debated as early as 1917. The Chicago School also assumed that village or rural life was the ideal, and cities fell far from that state of grace. The Chicagoans established a tradition of emphasizing the pathologies they saw in cities, a habit continued by many contemporary environmental scholars who have also assumed that cities are a blight on the land. In sociology, the Chicago School has long since been replaced and its critics have established other disciplinary approaches for the study of cities as social systems. However, the ecological approach represented by the classical Chicago School has yet to be replaced by more contemporary ecological approaches to the study of cities as social-ecological systems.

The Baltimore School is a contemporary approach to understanding urban ecological systems and for increasing the practical capacity to solve urban ecological problems. It is based upon four propositions, which emphasize (1) the integrative use of contemporary social and ecological concepts, theories, and methods and data; (2) the complexity of cities in terms of space, scale, and time; (3) the use of midrange theories; and (4) the linkages between science and decision making. Further, in contrast to the Chicago School, we do not assume that cities and urban systems should necessarily be viewed in negative environmental terms. There are certainly costs of density and contagion in cities. But there are also efficiencies of scale, savings in energy and materials, and benefits of innovation and interaction that accrue to urban systems. Our concern is not to judge cities but to understand how they are structured, how they work, and how they change as integrated social-ecological systems over time.

Structure of This Book

We have structured this book to describe the essential dimensions of the patch dynamics approach to urban ecology, progressing from the conceptual to practical applications. In chapter 1, "The Baltimore School of Urban Ecology," we introduce and describe the four key propositions that define the Baltimore School. These four propositions are recurring themes, implicitly and explicitly, through the remainder of the book.

In chapter 2, "Standing on the Shoulders of Giants: Intellectual Challenges in the Ecology of Cities," we discuss the historical connections between biophysical ecology and social science approaches to urban ecology. To provide context to these historic connections, we first provide a contemporary overview of ecology and its subdisciplines. We then describe the Chicago School of urban ecology and the critiques of its approach. We locate the Chicago School in the context of four dominant biological perspectives that social scientists have used to study the city. We conclude by framing this historical narrative in terms of spatial and organizational complexity for the study of urban ecological systems.

In chapter 3, "Expanding the Landscape: Applying Patch Dynamics to Social-Ecological Systems," we define and describe the contemporary form of patch dynamics from ecology, how it can be joined with the social sciences, and how it can be applied to urban ecological systems. An important facet of this approach is to be more inclusive of different types of temporal complexity than addressed by the Chicago School, and indeed even by the ecology of the late twentieth century. We discuss how a patch dynamics approach can be a useful and well-developed conceptual tool for integrating contemporary perspectives from both the biophysical and social sciences in order to address spatial heterogeneity at multiple levels of organization and different types of change over the long term.

In chapter 4, "From Baltimore to Bangkok: Interdisciplinary Issues and Strategies," we address the interdisciplinary challenges and opportunities that figure into our integrative pursuit. In this chapter, we consider the unique traits of urban ecological systems and their relevance to patch dynamics. We discuss the benefits, strategies, and mechanics for interdisciplinary patch dynamics in terms of problem recognition, theory, methods and data, analysis, and application. We use examples from Bangkok and Las Vegas to illustrate the challenges an interdisciplinary patch dynamics approach must be capable of addressing.

In chapter 5, "Pixels, Plots, and Parcels: Data Issues and Strategies," we address empirical issues and strategies for the transition from an ecology *in* cities to an ecology *of* cities. We expand upon the discussion in chapter 4 regarding methods and data needs for an interdisciplinary approach. Pixels, plots, and parcels are crucial building blocks of this approach. These building blocks are part of an overall strategy that includes an extensive-intensive data framework, ways of knowing, and midrange theories.

In chapter 6, "Cholera in London and Urban Tree Canopy in Baltimore: Linking Science and Decision Making Through Patch Dynamics," we present two examples to illustrate the utility of a patch dynamics approach to decision making. London's cholera epidemic of 1854 and

Baltimore's urban tree canopy goal and sustainability plan provide one historical and one contemporary case. We have also chosen these examples because they illustrate two important inflexion points in how we conceive of cities: the Sanitary City that emerged in the late 1800s and the Sustainable City that has been hoped for since the late 1900s. In order to clearly connect our examples to a patch dynamics approach, each illustration is described in terms of the story, the ways of knowing, the data framework used, and the advances in practice and science.

In chapter 7, "Metacities and an Urban Land Ethic," we consider how ideas of space, place, and ecosystems have threaded through the course of the book. We introduce the idea of metacities: the concept that cities may consist of a variety of mosaic landscapes, each of which reflects particular perspectives on urban structure and functioning. A patch dynamics approach can bring together the diverse perspectives of a metacity in order to envision and bring about desirable urban futures. Finally, just as Aldo Leopold saw the roots of ecology as the basis for a land ethic, we consider how an ecology *of* cities and a patch dynamics approach to space, place, and time may provide the seeds for an urban land ethic and more equitable and resilient cities in the future.

You can access all of the figures in the book at http://beslter.org/landing -Baltimore-Urban-Ecology-book.html, where the figures are available to view and share.

Acknowledgments

This book is the result of support and collaborations in Baltimore since 1989. It is understandable that there are many organizations and persons to recognize. We thank Jackie Carrera, director of the Parks & People Foundation, and her wonderful colleagues Guy Hager, Mary Washington, and the Parks & People staff who have facilitated and smoothed our way in Baltimore. None of us would have worked in Baltimore were it not for the Parks & People Foundation, and BES would not exist without that essential partnership. The Urban Resources Initiative (URI) was an important precursor to BES. The URI board had the vision and patience to support the idea of urban ecological research, education, and training in Baltimore. We thank Sally Michel, Laura Perry, Van Stewart, Ted Wiese, Lynne Durbin, Alma Bell, Calvin Buikema, and Gennady Schwartz.

The Yale School of Forestry and Environmental Studies (F&ES) was a leading member of URI. John Gordon, Jared Cohon, Joyce Berry, and Leigh Shemitz helped URI survive in its early days. We especially thank Gordon Geballe, Colleen Murphy-Dunning, and Shawn Dalton for their creativity, obstinacy, and zeal, which allowed URI to prosper in Baltimore and New Haven, Connecticut, and to become an essential part of F&ES.

Staff members from local agencies were more than our "decision maker" partners. They taught us about the region, provided direction many times, and offered insights and interpretations in our research results. We thank Beth Strommen, Kimberly Grove, Anne Draddy, Bill Stack, Don Outen, Michael Galvin, Rob Northrop, and Jeff Horan.

Insights from the Baltimore Ecosystem Study, Long-Term Ecological Research program, supported by National Science Foundation grant DEB 1027188, and from the Urban Sustainability Research Coordination Network, supported by grant DEB 1140077-CFDA 47.074, have contributed to the ideas presented in this book. Several persons from NSF were helpful guides and thoughtful supporters in the early days of BES. We thank Scott Collins, Tom Baerwald, and Henry Gholz for their essential roles.

Support from the USDA Forest Service has been crucial to our joint work in Baltimore as well. We thank Robert Lewis, director of the Northeastern Research Station during the first few years of our work in Baltimore and, more recently, Michael Rains, director of the Northern Research Station and Forest Products Laboratory, for his inspired leadership in public service and education, and his facilitation of our best efforts. Tom Schmidt, Mark Twery, Lynne Westphal, Ann Bartuska, and Beth Larry enabled the Baltimore project to grow and prosper within the Forest Service. In urban ecology, one has to "think outside the box *and* the pipe," and we have been supported in doing so by the Forest Service.

We thank Dr. Freeman Hrabowski III, president of the University of Maryland, Baltimore County, for his enthusiastic and continued support of our intellectual partnership with his university. His example in the pursuit of greater inclusiveness in the research community and his personal encouragement have meant a great deal to us.

The Central Arizona–Phoenix LTER project has been our urban LTER twin. We have survived and grown together. Nancy Grimm, Chuck Redman, and Dan Childers have shared the pains and joys of running an urban LTER project and contributed to our development.

Laura Ogden has been the gentle and supportive intellectual companion to this book. She has helped find invisible doors when we have painted ourselves into intellectual corners.

Amy Grove, Jarlath O'Neil-Dunne, Dexter Locke, Michele Romolini, Chris Boone, and Neil Bettez created the illustrations for this book. A patch dynamics approach without illustrations of maps and relationships is unimaginable. Our gratitude for their work is profound. Jonathan Walsh has cared for us in all our Web endeavors.

We thank our editor, Jean Thomson Black, for her guidance, care, and patience in the development and realization of this book.

Finally, we thank our family and friends for their support and tolerance during the writing of this book and our work on the Baltimore project. For some of us, it has been a labor of more than twenty-five years, and our work in Baltimore has been accepted as another member of the family.

The Baltimore School of
Urban Ecology

Urban systems have seemed to most ecologists to be so drastically different from the places they were trained to study that any work in urban areas has often been done with hesitation. This hesitation may have also been the result of not having social scientists to collaborate with and share the journey. Whatever the reason, ecologists have generally conducted research in cities in specific locations that were analogs of the kinds of rural places where they were accustomed to working. These urban studies tended to focus on ecologically familiar places and compared urban and nonurban areas: parks as analogs of rural forests and vacant lots as analogs of fields or prairies. Urban streams and remnant wetlands were the object of ecological studies similar in scope and method to those conducted in nonurban landscapes. The standard tool kit of ecology worked in such urban-rural comparisons with little modification. Sometimes it may have been necessary in urban areas to mark research plots in inconspicuous ways, and research may have had to be scheduled to avoid conflicting or unsafe activities in some locations. By and large, however, urban ecology prior to the 1990s sought out familiar kinds of places within various urban contexts. This approach can be labeled an ecology *in* the city.[1]

Since the mid-1990s, a significant transition in urban ecology has occurred, focusing on a strikingly different research ambition and agenda. In Baltimore, we have wanted to move beyond the traditional ecological comfort zone and examine the ecological structure and functioning of all kinds of habitats and areas within the metropolitan region. Furthermore, we have sought to promote interactions among biophysical and social scientists. As a result, we have developed an ecology *of* the city as a complement to an ecology *in* the city. This approach has proven widely useful. Yet it is important to recognize that both research approaches—ecology *in* and ecology *of*—are necessary and indeed complementary for a full understanding of the ecology of urban social-ecological systems.

Our approach to the ecology of urban social-ecological systems is based on four essential propositions. First is that *the ecology of cities addresses the complete mosaic of land uses and management in metropolitan systems,* not just the green spaces as rural analogs that were the focus of ecology *in* cities. Our approach to urban ecology requires that we understand urban mosaics as integrated ecosystems consisting of biotic, physical, social, and built components (figure 1.1).[2] This proposition is fully compatible with the definition and use of the ecosystem concept in mainstream contemporary ecology. Indeed, Tansley's original discussion of the ecosystem concept in 1935 emphasized the role of humans.[3] While the basic definition of the ecosystem as a biotic complex interacting with a physical context in a specified spatial frame can apply to urban systems, it has proven useful to explicitly include the social and built components to avoid any confusion about whether physical and biotic complexes include or exclude social systems and human infrastructure within urban areas. A major aid to our efforts to integrate the biophysical and social sciences is the human ecosystem framework developed by Machlis and others in order to incorporate social structures and interactions within the scope of the ecosystem.[4] With this perspective, we see humans and their institutions as a part of the ecosystem, not external to it.

Our second proposition is that *the urban mosaic is complex in terms of space, scale, and time.* Spatial heterogeneity, expressed as gradients or mosaics, is critical for explaining interactions and changes in the city. Since the middle of the twentieth century, ecology has become increas-

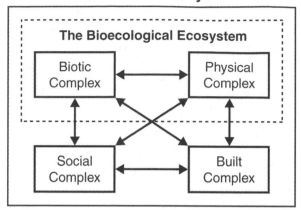

Figure 1.1. The human ecosystem concept, showing its expansion from the bioecological concept of the ecosystem as proposed originally by Tansley inside the dashed line. The expansion incorporates a social complex and a built complex, which includes land modifications, buildings, infrastructure, and other artifacts. Both the biotic and the physical environmental complexes of urban systems are expected to differ from those in nonurban ecosystems.

ingly aware of the need to understand spatial heterogeneity.[5] Gone are the days when ecosystems could be considered uniformly mixed and the system to be in equilibrium.[6] Landscape ecology, metacommunity ecology, and metapopulation ecology, emerging from developments in island biogeography and population genetics, have made spatial heterogeneity a core topic of ecological research and application.[7] This awareness has prepared ecologists to examine the fine-scale heterogeneity so often encountered in urban systems, where turning a corner might reveal a new patch defined by contrasts in biotic, social, or physical structures—or, more likely, all three. The functional significance of such a patchwork has been an irresistible research topic, resonating with both urban reality and new thinking in the ecological and geosciences. Spatial heterogeneity, the changes in heterogeneous patchworks, and the fluxes across patch boundaries and entire patchy mosaics is the purview of the theory of hierarchical patch dynamics.[8] This concept has provided a bridge for comparison with other urban areas, notably the Central Arizona–

Phoenix LTER,[9] and as a bridge to linking with the theory and practice of urban design, which itself is acutely tuned to spatial heterogeneity.[10]

Spatial heterogeneity can be examined with increasing levels of analytical complexity (figure 1.2 and plate 1).[11] Complexity increases as the analysis moves from patch type and the number of each type to spatial configuration and to changes in the mosaic over time.[12] At the simplest level of spatial complexity, systems can be described in terms of a set of spatial patch types. Richness of patch types summarizes the number of patch types making up the set. Analytical complexity is increased when the number of each patch type in an area is quantified. This measurement is expressed as patch frequency. How those patches are arranged in space relative to each other increases the complexity of understanding the spatial heterogeneity and structure of the system.[13] Finally, each patch can change over time. Which patches change, and how they change and shift identity constitutes a higher level of spatial complexity. The most complex characterization of system heterogeneity occurs when the system is quantified as a shifting mosaic of patches or, in other words, when the patch dynamics of the system is spatially explicit and quantified. Although the passage of time is an element at the highest level of spatial complexity, this is distinct from temporal complexity, where the function of phenomena such as lags and legacies is examined.

Organizational complexity relates to the interactions within and among social and ecological scales of organization (figure 1.2). For instance, humans organize and interact at multiple social scales, from individuals to households, neighborhoods, and complex and persistent government jurisdictions. Organizational complexity can be examined with increasing levels of analysis, reflecting the increasing connectivity of the basic units that control system dynamics within and among scales of social and ecological organization. Within organizational hierarchies, causality can move upward or downward.[14] Organizational complexity drives system resilience, or the capacity to adjust to shifting external conditions or internal feedbacks.[15] Following our structural approach (figure 1.2), we return to a spatial patch as an example of the basic functional unit of a system to explain organizational complexity more fully. The simplest level of organizational complexity is within-patch

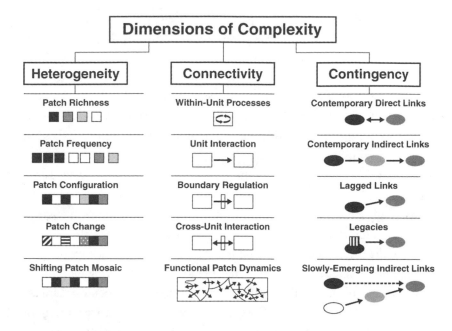

Figure 1.2. Framework for complexity of social-ecological systems. The three dimensions of complexity are spatial heterogeneity, organizational connectivity, and temporal contingency. Components of the framework are arrayed along each axis, increasing in complexity from top to bottom. A more complex understanding of spatial heterogeneity is achieved as quantification moves from patch richness, frequency, and configuration to patch change and the shift in the patch mosaic. Complexity in organizational connectivity increases from within-unit processes to the interaction of units and the regulation of that interaction to functional patch dynamics. Historical contingency increases in complexity from contemporary direct effects through lags and legacies to slowly emerging indirect effects. While not shown in the figure, organizational connectivity can be assessed within and between levels of organization. (See also Plate 1.)

processes. When the interactions among patches are incorporated, analytical complexity increases. Understanding how interactions may be regulated by the boundary among patches constitutes a still higher level of complexity. The analytical complexity increases further by examining whether patch interactions are controlled by features of the patches themselves in addition to the boundary. Finally, the highest level of analytical complexity on the organizational axis is the functional significance of patch connectivity for patch dynamics, both of a single patch and of the entire patch mosaic within and between scales.[16]

Temporal complexity addresses the historical contingencies that include legacies, path dependencies, and temporal lags in urban ecological systems.[17] The historical distribution of physical environmental conditions, soils, and biota can influence contemporary and future ecological and social conditions. The built environment is itself a legacy in many urban systems. Certainly this is the case in Baltimore, which was established in 1792. The persistent template of the old market roads as well as the newer road networks present a powerful legacy. The clashing street grids, with their alteration of hydrology and demarcation of neighborhoods, and the partially implemented Olmsted Brothers parks and parkways plan are another form of legacy. Social legacies include the legal segregation of African Americans during the Jim Crow era and the later "redlining" by the federal Home Owners' Loan Corporation. Such social legacies have environmental and social consequences today. The historic distributions of social groups, economic classes, and housing characteristics affect different aspects of contemporary vegetation in residential parcels.

Temporal complexity refers to relationships that extend beyond direct, contemporary ones. Historical contingency includes the influence of indirect effects: legacies or apparent memory of past states of the system, the existence of lagged effects, and the presence of slowly appearing indirect effects constitute increasing historical complexity (figure 1.2).[18] To illustrate the analytical levels of this axis, we start with the simple or contemporary ones. Contemporary interactions include those interactions where element A influences element B directly. Indirect contemporary interactions involve a third component, C, to transmit the effect of A on B. An interaction is lagged if the influence of element A on element B is not immediate but manifested over some time period. A higher level of temporal complexity is invoked by legacies. Legacies are created when element A modifies the environment and that modification, whether it be structural or functional, eventually influences element B. At the high end of the temporal complexity axis are slowly emerging indirect effects. These types of interactions occur when the apparent interaction of elements A and B is illusory and element B is actually influenced by some earlier state of element A and that influence is mediated through an additional element, C.

Our third proposition is that *an ecology of cities is an integrative pursuit.* We have already identified Machlis and colleagues' human eco-system framework as an integrative frame for urban ecology (figure 1.3).[19] This framework requires concepts, theories, methods, and data from the social and biophysical sciences. We recognize that the social and biophysical sciences writ large can be further categorized in terms of disciplines such as psychology, anthropology, geography, sociology, political science, economics, physics, chemistry, geology, biology, mete-orology, and ecology, and that these disciplines can be further catego-rized into subdisciplines. We recognize too that some disciplines include spatial dynamics in their questions and explanations while others do not. Some disciplines tend to focus on one level or scale of organization over another. And some disciplines tend to focus on long-term changes measured in centuries to millennia while others address changes meas-ured in seconds to days. Thus, an ecology of cities needs to be open to and capable of integrating diverse disciplines across the urban mosaic in terms of spatial, organizational, and temporal complexity.

We purposefully use the term *pursuit* in our third proposition to signal a goal. Ultimately, our goal for an ecology of cities is to move beyond the comparative understandings associated with urban-rural analogs from an ecology in cities. With an ecology of cities, our goal is to pursue a more general scientific understanding of urban ecolog-ical systems and increase the practical capacity to comprehensively and systematically solve urban ecological problems. Such a general scientific understanding might take the form of a "general systems theory." This goal recognizes that currently there is no comprehensive theory of urban ecological systems, much less of social-ecological systems as a whole.

Although there is no comprehensive theory of urban ecological systems, we have a diversity of theories from the social and biophysi-cal sciences from which to build. We suggest that these theories might be best described as midrange theories. The idea of midrange theory comes from the sociologist Robert Merton.[20] Merton proposed the idea of midrange theory in 1949 in his essay "On Sociological Theories of the Middle Range" because he was concerned ultimately with the develop-

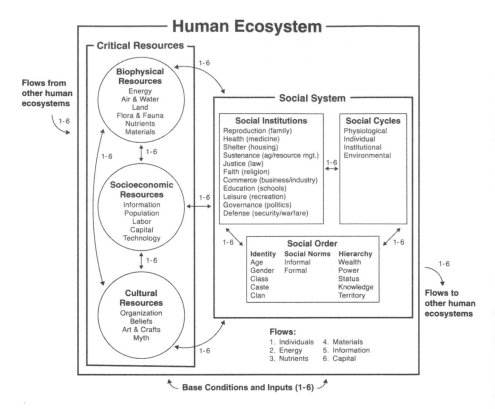

Figure 1.3. The human ecosystem framework: critical resources, social system, and flows. Social identities and hierarchies can play a significant role in the inequitable distribution of critical resources.

ment of a unified, or general systems, theory of sociology. This interest paralleled the concern in other disciplines at that time to develop, for instance, a unified theory of physics or a unified theory of biology.

Merton cautioned his sociological colleagues that it was premature to expect to have achieved a general systems theory of society. Rather, he recommended that sociologists should focus on theories of the middle range, which could be located between "the minor but necessary working hypotheses that evolve in abundance during day-to-day research and the all-inclusive systematic efforts to develop a unified theory that will explain all the observed uniformities of social behavior, social organization, and social change."[21]

Critical to theories of the middle range is that they point to distinctive theoretical problems or questions, suggest specific hypotheses that can be empirically tested, and can be generalized to new phenomena or conditions. Thus, Merton asserted in the case of sociology that middle range theories are intermediate and distinctive from general systems theories that "are too remote from particular classes of social behavior, organization, and change" to be empirically and conclusively tested. Merton was careful to emphasize that although middle range theories involve abstractions, those abstractions could be empirically and conclusively tested. Middle range theories are also intermediate and distinctive from the "detailed, orderly descriptions" of minor working hypotheses that cannot be generalized to other conditions or phenomenon.[22]

Merton's concept of midrange theory is relevant to our third proposition in two ways. First, although the term *midrange theory* emerged from sociology, it is appropriate to other disciplines in the social and biophysical sciences. In his essay for instance, Merton draws parallels to Gilbert's theory of magnetism, Darwin's theory on the formation of coral atolls, and Boyle's theory of atmospheric pressure. Merton describes how each of these theories could be understood as a midrange theory. The disciplines needed for our integrative pursuit have many theories that may be fruitfully understood as midrange theories. Our preceding two propositions suggest some potential directions for enhancing and combining midrange theories from diverse disciplines. For instance, midrange theories may have variables in common, although the same variable may be the independent variable for one theory and the dependent variable for another. Furthermore, midrange theories may be linked and enhanced by shared or complementary assumptions about spatial, organizational, or temporal complexity. Or midrange theories may be linked by their relevance to a common practical problem. Moreover, it remains premature to declare that we have achieved a general systems theory of urban ecological systems. The field is in a developmental stage and theories of the middle range are our building blocks. We are most likely to advance a general systems understanding of urban ecological systems by developing, integrating, and consolidating theories of the middle range.

Our fourth proposition is that *an ecology of cities can be useful to link and advance both decision making and urban ecology science.* The typical types of questions that decision makers ask in order to address a problem are: what to do, where, how, how much, by whom, when, and for how long? These types of questions can be seen as components of the decision maker's solution and correspond to our propositions. For instance, the decision maker's questions "what," "how," and "how much" are questions about the parts of the system. "Where" corresponds to spatial complexity. "Who" matches to organizational complexity. "When" and "for how long" correspond to temporal complexity. Further, these types of questions are not exclusive to "environmental problems"; they are characteristic of many issues faced in urban areas such as public safety, health, recreation, urban design, and community and economic development.

The context for asking these decision-making questions has shifted subtly but significantly since the 1990s. Historically, issues associated with public safety, health, recreation, and community and economic development were addressed in isolation by decision makers, much as the analogs from an ecology in cities were treated in isolation from the complete spatial mosaics of an ecology of cities. However, decision makers increasingly ask how these issues can be addressed comprehensively and systematically in terms of urban sustainability and resilience. These individual issues and their associated public agencies and NGOs are increasingly entangled and are to be understood not in isolation but as interdependent problems requiring interdependent solutions. This decision-making shift requires understanding and addressing problems in terms of multiple and interacting social and biophysical drivers and outcomes, connectivity across space and among levels of organization, and short- and long-term trends and solutions.

Our experience in Baltimore suggests that there can be dynamic feedbacks between decision makers and scientists to help decision makers address the new context they face and to build a more general understanding of urban ecological systems (figure 1.4).[23] Our generic illustration begins with the separate disciplines of traditional ecology, economics, and social sciences incorporated into a management or policy concern. A management or policy action (Action$_z$) results. Management monitors the practical outcome to evaluate whether the desired result was achieved. Contemporary urban ecology, which includes so-

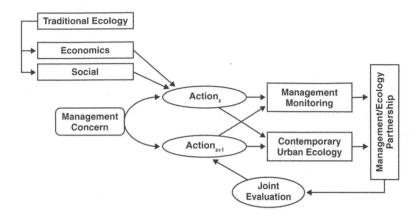

Figure 1.4. Dynamic links between science and decision making: an abstracted cycle of interactions among scientists and decision makers.

cial sciences and economics, is then available to conduct research that recognizes the meshing of natural processes with management and policy actions. Combining an ecology of cities with the concerns of managers can generate a partnership to enhance the joint evaluation of management actions. New or alternative management actions can result to address additional management concerns (Actions$_{z+1}$).

The dynamic feedbacks between decision making and science in figure 1.4 illustrate the potential for advancing the scientific understanding of urban ecological systems. But what kind of science is most likely to be advanced? We have already made the case for a midrange theory perspective. Another perspective is to think of science as either basic or applied. Given the potential dynamic connections we see between decision makers and scientists, we advance the perspective of midrange theories in the context of what Stokes calls "Pasteur's quadrant" (figure 1.5).[24] Three of these quadrants are of particular interest for urban ecological research. The two most familiar quadrants may be the first and third. Stokes defines the first quadrant, "pure basic research," as science performed without concern for practical ends. This quadrant is labeled "Bohr's quadrant" since physicist Nils Bohr had no immediate concern for use as he worked to develop a structural understanding of the atom.

In this quadrant urban ecologists work to understand physical, biological, and social laws that advance our fundamental understanding of
the world. For instance, urban systems can be useful end members for
understanding the effects of altered climates, organismal components,
substrates, and landforms, or changes in livelihoods and lifestyles on
consumption, social institutions, identity, and status. The third quadrant, "pure applied research," is defined as science performed to solve
a social problem without regard for advancing fundamental theory or
scientific methodology. Stokes labeled this "Edison's quadrant" since in-
ventor Thomas Edison never considered the underlying implications of
his discoveries in his pursuit of commercial illumination. In this quadrant urban ecologists work to develop solutions to specific problems,
such as bio-retention systems for removing pollutants from stormwater
or social marketing to increase household participation in tree-planting
programs. Stokes defines the second quadrant, "use-inspired basic," as
science that is designed to both enhance fundamental understanding
and address a practical issue. This quadrant is labeled "Pasteur's quadrant" because biologist Louis Pasteur's work on immunology and vac-
cination both advanced our fundamental understanding of biology and
saved countless lives. In this quadrant urban ecologists work to advance
scientific theories and methods while addressing practical problems.
For example, how do households' locational choices affect ecosystem
services and vulnerability to climate change, or how do ecological structures and social institutions interact over the long term to affect urban
resilience and sustainability? While some of our work in Baltimore can
be located in each of these three quadrants, most of our research in Baltimore is use-inspired basic.

In summary, our ambition in Baltimore since the mid-1990s has
been to develop a new approach to urban ecology: an ecology of cities. Our approach to an ecology of cities is based on four propositions.
First, the ecology of cities addresses the complete mosaic of land uses
and management in metropolitan systems. Second, the urban mosaic
is complex: spatially, organizationally, and temporally. Third, an ecology of cities is an integrative pursuit utilizing midrange theories and
is often designed to both enhance fundamental understanding and ad-

Quest for fundamental understanding?	Yes	Pure Basic Research (Physicist Bohr)	Use-Inspired Basic Research (Biologist Pasteur)
	No	--	Pure Applied Research (Inventor Edison)
		No	Yes
		Considerations of use?	

Figure 1.5. Stokes's Pasteur's quadrant. In Pasteur's quadrant, Stokes categorizes four different types of research. Most research associated with our work in Baltimore would be located in the quadrant of use-inspired basic research.

dress practical issues. Ultimately, our goal is to develop a more general scientific understanding of urban ecological systems and to increase the practical capacity of decision makers to address the complexity and interdependence of urban ecological problems. Fourth, an ecology of cities can be useful for linking and advancing both practice and science.

Patch Dynamics: A Contemporary Approach for an Ecology of Cities

The Baltimore School of urban ecology employs a patch dynamics approach for several reasons. First, a patch dynamics approach is useful for making the transition from an ecology in cities to an ecology of cities. It provides a structural approach for addressing mosaics, complexity, and social-ecological integration in ways that are useful to both science and decision making. Further, although patch dynamics initially comes from ecology, it privileges neither the biophysical nor social sciences, nor theories, methods, or data from any particular discipline. Indeed, we believe a patch dynamics approach has a sufficient number of conceptual and empirical hooks that it resonates with a variety of disciplines and professions.

The remainder of the book describes the essential dimensions of a patch dynamics approach to urban ecology, progressing from the conceptual to practical applications. To set the stage for the contemporary approach of patch dynamics and urban ecological systems, we first trace the historical connections between biophysical ecology and the social sciences in urban ecology in the next chapter.

Standing on the Shoulders of Giants

Intellectual Challenges in the Ecology of Cities

So That We May See Further

A city is many things. As the introduction of the old *Dragnet* television series (and the radio series that preceded it) had it: "There are 8 million stories in the naked city." This referred to the complexity that was New York City at the time and prepared the audience for the week's episode, which would tell one tale in the search for and capture of nefarious criminals. But there are many stories about any city. And there are many ways to conceive of these stories.

We have found that the rich and creative growth of intellectual themes for the study of cities from the social sciences and urban design have occurred independently of the development of biophysical ecology. We recognize that for much of its history, biophysical ecology has avoided studying the city, with a few notable exceptions. Despite this avoidance, ecological concepts and theory have influenced the development of urban thought in other disciplines. Although many works in the social sciences draw upon ecological literature, we note that much of the ecology incorporated in these efforts predates the new layers and perspectives that have emerged in contemporary ecology. In other words, most of what has developed historically as urban ecology from the social sciences has occurred without being informed by the contemporary ecology of its time.

In this chapter we weave together the development of perspectives about city form and function from the fields of sociology and biophysical ecology. We cannot be exhaustive. Instead, we trace some parallel trajectories and highlight reciprocal influences. Our narrative is guided by focusing on themes that resonate among disciplines and uses a concern with spatial pattern and process as a synthetic node around which to integrate this discussion. Spatial patterns and processes of spatial change have emerged as a central theme in contemporary biophysical ecology over the past several decades. Similarly, spatial pattern has been both central and controversial in social approaches to studying cities. Indeed, spatial pattern and change are two of the most conspicuous attributes of urban systems to specialists and casual observers alike. In order to develop a synthesis of contemporary biophysical themes with themes derived from various social sciences, we seek a way to organize and harmonize the "8 million stories" that have been told and are being told about the metropolis as an ecological system.

The goal of this chapter is to discuss the historical connections between biophysical ecology and sociological approaches to urban ecology. This historical narrative lays the foundation for linking the study of spatial heterogeneity in the social and economic sciences with the contemporary understanding of spatial heterogeneity in biophysical ecology that we discuss in chapter 3. We believe the true scope of contemporary ecology offers a much firmer foundation for linkages with the social and economic sciences than in fact most practitioners of those disciplines may realize.

To provide context to these historical connections, we first give an overview of contemporary ecology and its subdisciplines. We then describe the Chicago School of urban ecology and some of its critiques. We locate the Chicago School in the context of four dominant biological perspectives that social scientists have used for the study of cities. We conclude this historical narrative in terms of spatial and organizational complexity issues for the study of urban ecological systems.

A Contemporary Perspective on the Science of Ecology

Ecology originated in the late nineteenth century as a synthesis of botanical and zoological studies of the distribution and abundance of organisms. It was fueled by the rich biogeographic data that had accumulated during the voyages of "discovery" by European colonial powers and the explorations that followed those landings and treks. The physiological capacities, structural adaptations, and evolutionary histories of organisms were the early ecologist's stock-in-trade. In its early form, ecology was defined as the study of the interaction between organisms and their environment. In most cases the term *environment* was interpreted as the physical resources and constraints, along with habitat attributes, that organisms experienced. Notable in this definition is the focus on interactions. We believe this focus is unusual in the definitions of sciences, which more commonly emphasize the objects of study rather than the interactions between objects and their environments.

From this initial synthesis that defined ecology, additional layers of complexity were eventually addressed. Over time, ecology came to link with and help unify an impressive array of specialties. As the twentieth century unfolded, biophysical ecologists added a number of subdisciplines— animal population ecology, population genetics, plant population biology, ecosystem ecology and biogeochemistry, and landscape ecology—to highlight some of the more obvious growths of ecology (figure 2.1). In order to account for the new areas and concerns that these kinds of biophysical ecology have opened up, it is useful to state a broader definition of ecology. Although it maintains its traditional focus on organismal-physical environment interactions that the original definition established, *ecology is the scientific study of the processes influencing the distribution and abundance of organisms, the interactions among organisms, the interactions between organisms, and the transformation and flux of energy and matter.*[1]

This new definition broadens the traditional focus on interactions by adding interactions between organisms. However, the addition of organism-organism interactions, especially across trophic levels, has alerted ecologists to new types of interactions. Interactions between microbes and plants, between plants and consumers, between animals and disease organisms, between dispersers and pollinators and the plants and animals that depend on them for transport and reproduction have all become major types of study that were rare or absent during the first fifty years of the twentieth century. This addition of a complex set of interactions increases the evolutionary significance of ecological studies. Ecosystem ecology is an additional source of novelty. It has added the

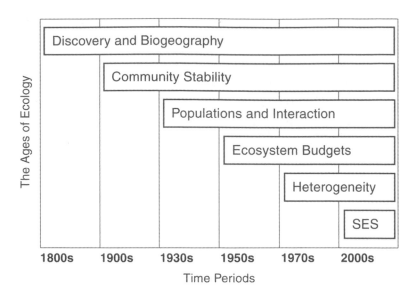

Figure 2.1. A diagram of the thematic history of biological ecology. The most recent development is a focus on social-ecological systems (SES).

study of transformations of matter and energy, expressed using a budgetary approach, to the work of biophysical ecologists.

　　Along with its new focus on biotic interactions and transformations, biophysical ecology has been altered literally by new viewpoints made possible by technological advances. With the increasing availability of remote sensing, such as aerial photography and satellite imagery, ecologists can encompass much more in a single view than the founders of the discipline could see. This expanded scope has invited new kinds of comparisons and alerted ecologists to the great spatial heterogeneity of the systems they study. The broader spatial scope is evident in the relatively new discipline of landscape ecology, which was codified in the United States in the mid-1980s,[2] although it emerged earlier in Europe and with stronger connections to planning and social concerns. Taking into account the increased spatial concern of ecology, which is not obvious in our earlier definition, gives a more complete sense of how ecology has evolved in the second half of the twentieth century to produce the contemporary view of ecology, which is broad, inclusive, and spatially aware

Box 2.1. A Brief History of Ecology and Description of the Science of Ecology

Ecology as a professional discipline was initially recognized in the first two decades of the twentieth century. However, ecology had its roots in the voyages of European discovery and the biogeographic insights that emerged from that global exploration in the late 1700s and 1800s. Alexander von Humboldt's travels, the explorations of the students of Linnaeus, and the voyage of the *Beagle* are some of the most famous and consequential of such travels. Ecology emerged from a combination of field botany, plant physiology, and field zoology to explain the patterns documented in the age of discovery. Perhaps the first explicitly ecological theory was that of vegetation succession, which emerged around 1900. Although it recognized that plant communities were dynamic, that dynamism was constrained by assumptions of equilibrium end points and the goal of community stabilization. However, this established the concern of ecology with community change, which nourished paleoecology, disturbance ecology, and later resilience ecology, for example.

Close on the heels of dynamic ecology was the ecology of animal populations. First pioneered by mathematical ecologists such as Volterra and Lotka in the 1920s, this field was primarily the province of animal ecologists and theoreticians. It shared a focus on competition with dynamic community ecology but added concerns of predation and processes of the niche, such as convergence and stable coexistence. This approach was the initial locus of incorporating evolutionary thinking into ecology in the 1960s, when plants were finally brought under the population tent as well.

After World War II and the spread of systems thinking from the cybernetics developed by the military establishment, ecosystem ecology emerged as a newly recognized ecological specialty. The concept of ecosystem had been introduced in the 1930s and first applied to field studies in the 1940s. However, it was the impetus of the postwar promulgation of systems thinking that finally facilitated a home in biological ecology for ecosystems. The aggregate metabolism of communities and their associated physical environments was and remains the core of ecosystem ecology.

In the 1970s, ecology began to turn its attention to factors that generated or maintained heterogeneity in the systems ecologists studied, in contrast with the earlier assumption or assertion of spatial uniformity. Landscape ecology had its birth in this decade, although the precedent of island biogeography dates to the late 1960s, and some theoretical and empirical pioneers had argued for the importance of spatial heterogeneity even earlier. Landscape ecology consolidated the concern with spatial heterogeneity and also helped reinforce a temporal perspective in ecology. The birth of landscape ecology coincided with an increasing concern for integration across scales and approaches in ecology and signaled a realization that human artifacts and activities were common components of ecosystems and regions in which they had often been ignored by biological ecologists. This realization ushered in the millennial age, in which synthesis of the evolving ecological concerns adopted the role of humans as both external and internal components of ecological systems. Hence, the current age is one of social-ecological systems (SES).

The contemporary conceptual frameworks of all the ecological approaches now operate under a nonequilibrium paradigm. Dynamics are seen as probabilistic rather than deterministic; the openness of systems (whether populations, ecosystems, patches, or landscapes) is recognized, as is the fact that open systems may be regulated in part by fluxes that originate outside their boundaries. Furthermore, the dynamics are not seen as aimed at single fixed stable end points, and disturbances are seen to influence system structure and function. Finally, humans—as social and engineering agents—are an undeniable part of ecological systems.

This quick and crude cartoon of ecological history slices a subtle intellectual and empirical tradition much too coarsely. However, it suggests that the relationships between the social sciences and the bioecological sciences will have had a dynamic and shifting base for relationship through time. The ages of ecology may be better described as approaches to ecological subjects, or as lenses of observation. The different approaches often have different scales and technologies of study, and often speak incommensurate conceptual languages. In addition, all of these approaches, in their evolved forms, continue to contribute to the whole of contemporary ecology. They do so under quite different conceptual rubrics than were dominant in the early years of each.

This overview of ecological history does not show the pervasive influence of the "proto-ecologist" Charles Darwin in establishing competition as a key ecological mechanism, nor does it suggest his influence in focusing biology and other disciplines, such as geomorphology and social science, on change. Furthermore, with the exception of the mention of cybernetics from the World War II effort, it ignores shifts in the cultural and political contexts of the science.

This cartoon also fails to show the unraveling and intertwining of knowledge, techniques, and questions as the approaches mature through time. Fortunately, contemporary ecology is much more like a braided stream than the separate roads illustrated here for graphic simplicity. Integration is the hallmark of pioneering work in all ecological approaches now.

(see box 2.1: "A Brief History of Ecology and Description of the Science of Ecology"). It is against this backdrop that an overview of key themes and the potential for cross-fertilization with disciplines beyond biophysical ecology can be considered for a contemporary urban ecology.

Intellectual Themes from Sociology and Parallels with Biophysical Ecology

To advance a contemporary urban ecology, we return to the past. We do this not to be bound by the past but to understand some of the ideas that have shaped the themes that continue to resonate today. Over the roughly one hundred years of sociological attention to the city, use of ecological concepts for the study of cities has evolved. A simple synopsis can be extracted from this complex history. Initially, human ecology emphasized the spatial dimension with few variables included, and most of those were from biophysical ecology. City growth was thought to be driven by collective action and was controlled from the top down. In reaction to this spatially determined theory, an aspatial alternative emerged. The second wave of human ecology emphasized behaviors rather than spatial relationships. In this approach, urban change was driven by individual action and emerged from the bottom up. During this phase, many additional factors were added to the explanatory tool kit. The current phase of urban social-ecological research attempts to integrate these two approaches by combining a spatial framework with different types of drivers of change. We will expand this brief synopsis and point to the influence of biophysical ecological concepts and theories at various stages.

THE FIRST STEPS IN HUMAN ECOLOGY AND THE CITY: THE CHICAGO SCHOOL AND CRITIQUES

The first set of themes we will summarize emerged from the Chicago School in the first quarter of the twentieth century. The Chicago School is relevant not only because of the themes that emerged from it but because its frequent label as a school of urban ecology may lead individuals new to urban ecology to believe that the Chicago School typifies urban ecology as a science today. Although there are connections between the birth of urban sociology in the Chicago School and the early science of ecology in America, the two are not the same. Our survey reinforces both these points.

The Chicago School is well represented in one of its seminal publications. Park, Burgess, and McKenzie's landmark publication, *The City: Suggestions for the Investigation of Human Behavior in the Urban Environment,* in 1925 formally introduced human ecology as a new research agenda for sociology and the study of cities in America.[3] For these sociologists, the emergence of the industrial city represented a major societal transition toward modernism—from a traditional and idealized agricultural and mercantile society, in which the production and trade of agricultural goods and commodities was paramount, to an industrial and chaotic society in which the production and trade of manufactured goods was the chief process. The Chicago School also focused on many of the social changes that had resulted at that time from the rapid expansion of America's urban areas due to the mass immigration of people from Europe and rural America. The explosive growth of the city, the confluence of people from diverse backgrounds, the breakdown of old ways, and the changes that were necessary for a viable new urban life caught the imagination of adherents of the Chicago School. Thus, there were complex and unprecedented urban problems that needed to be understood and solved.[4]

The Chicago School, founded at the University of Chicago and led by members of the first university department of sociology in the United States, initially focused on space and differentiation in the city. Important early developments in American ecology were also taking place at the University of Chicago, where the concept of vegetation succession was introduced and exemplified in the dune systems of Lake Michigan. An academic neighbor, the University of Illinois in Urbana-Champaign, was also an early center of American ecology, where important theories and methods of vegetation gradients, animal ecology, differential adaptation to environment, and quantitative sampling of communities were developed. Drawing on this biophysical context, the Chicago School established the city as a suitable topic for sociological study and sought patterns and regularities aimed at creating a general theory of urban areas.[5]

There were several important members of the Chicago School, including Robert Park, Ernest Burgess, and Roderick McKenzie. Robert Park was especially biologically aware.[6] He focused on the adjustment of human groups to the environment, just as biophysical ecologists were concerned with the adaptation of plants and animals. He viewed economic competition as a special case of the ecological interactions that humans added to the biotic precedent. Initially, Park included both cultural and biotic drivers for urban organization. Cultural drivers included such things as the organization of neighborhoods by ties of cooperation, shared values, and the similar backgrounds of residents. In contrast, the "biotic" drivers included competition and functional differences. Functional differences were considered to be such factors as social class and occupation. Even though there were identifiable driving factors, the mechanisms for the differentiation and distribution of the human population were not organized. The human sorting was not premeditated or prescribed. Rather, different areas took on characteristics of their inhabitants. It was in this sense that social organization took place, not in some rational allocation of space in the city. But under Park's model, social organization drove the physical organization of the city. In addition, social organization was considered to serve industrial purposes. Ultimately, Park dismissed the cultural components of social organization, leaving only the competitive and spatially functional ones, the ones he had identified as "biotic."

Ernest Burgess focused on the growth and subsequent differentiation of the city.[7] He proposed an influential spatial model in which the city was divided into distinct concentric rings (figure 2.2). In early-twentieth-century Chicago, these rings included the central business district ("the Loop"), a transitional zone, a zone of workers' homes, a residential zone, and a commuter zone. These rings were seen as ways in which social organization was expressed in space.

Differentiation for Burgess was in terms of land uses, social roles, and jobs. For example, within the transition zone, various enclaves of recent immigrants were present. The transitional zone also accommodated new invasions of business and light industry. Within the residential zone were included single-family dwellings, residential hotels, and apartment houses. The differentiation of the city in terms of concentric ring land uses was considered to increase with growth. Class, cultural, and recreational variation were possible sources of differentiation.

The Chicago School was interested in signs of social disorganization, which its adherents attributed to rapid growth and the assembling of people in the nontraditional social milieu of the city. Burgess combined methods of spatial mapping and case studies to examine pockets of social disorder such as vice, disease, crime, suicide, and other indices of social disorder. The Chicago School's studies of gangs exemplify this concern. Gradients of these disordered factors were expected to exist, centering on the urban core and dissipating toward the suburbs. Animal crowding studies were taken as evidence for the ecological reality of some of these disorganizing factors. Such analogies seem quaint at best after eighty years, and prejudicial and misleading at worst.

Burgess emphasized the successional invasion of one ring by another as the city grew. The successional change component of this model was taken from the science of biophysical ecology, which had undergone a radical synthesis and theoretical flowering in the subject some ten years earlier. The succession model that Burgess drew upon

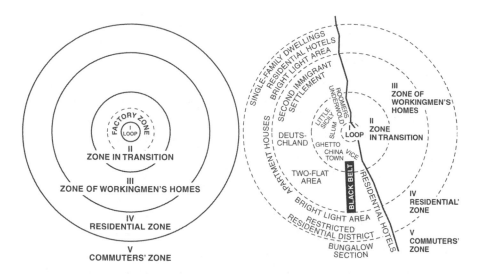

Figure 2.2. E. W. Burgess's zonal model: (left) the idealized pattern; (right) its application to Chicago.

from ecology was unidirectional and deterministic. Indeed, succession was seen as inexorable, with pioneer communities replaced by later successional communities and ultimately replaced by the one community best adapted to the regional environment—the so-called climax community. It is notable that this simple, unidirectional view of succession has not survived either the empirical test or the conceptual critique afforded by some one hundred years of biophysical ecological research. In Burgess's work, succession was equally deterministic of inner rings replacing outer rings. He did acknowledge a decentralization process as sub-business centers were established and presumably accompanied by localized rings of work, residence, and vice associated with them. Although this would seem to foreshadow a multinucleate view of the city that was later proposed by Harris and Ullman,[8] Burgess's fame rests on the ring-like model of sectoral succession.

The environmental mechanisms suggested by the ringlike model of sectoral succession were developed further by Roderick McKenzie.[9] Unlike Burgess's exclusive focus on the city, however, McKenzie thought that his processes should be found in any settled area throughout the urban region. McKenzie proposed an ecological approach to the study of human communities based upon plant ecology and in terms of selection, distribution, and accommodation. First, like plant ecologists of the time, McKenzie identified different types of human communities. These communities supported the economic functions of the city. McKenzie's communities were those of (1) primary service, agricultural and resource extraction; (2) commodity distribution, which connected agricultural, forest, mineral, and marine resources with consumers and manufacturers; (3) industrial manufacturing; and (4) secondary service aimed at supporting the commodity and industrial functions, including recreation, education, punishment, and administration.

McKenzie sought to understand succession within these community types in which ultimate crisis and reorganization occurred when the community reached a certain size and, subsequently, suffered disorganization. The state of maximum development was a type of fixed "climax," just as the plant ecologists had erroneously proposed. A plant community was considered to be at its climax stage when it reflected the community type expected to exist within that specific climatic zone.

The social climax could be disturbed, just as the biophysical climax could be. According to McKenzie, disturbance might include two major kinds of phenomena: innovation or invasion. Innovation resulted from new transportation technologies or new modes or rates of communication. Such novel connections could disrupt a community's access to knowledge and ease of mobility, which might alter the social structure of that community. The second major type of disturbance was invasion of a community. Invasion could occur when the use of land within a human community changed from agricultural to industrial, for instance. Invasion could also occur when transportation routes changed or buildings became obsolete and were replaced by new uses or residents. New industries could invade, accompanied by changes in movement, pollution, economic impact, and so on. Similarly, changes in real estate markets could result in invasion of a community. Finally, McKenzie recognized redistribution of income as a source of disturbance. After innovation or invasion events, communities could be reset on a new successional trajectory toward a supposed climax associated with the new structure and resource flows.

In all cases of human community succession, McKenzie proposed deterministic trajectories toward increased complexity and differentiation, just as he understood the botanical precedents to experience. At the same time, the dominant type of social organization for each community type was hypothesized to resist invasion by other types of community. As a community developed, it was thought to become better accommodated to its environment, and hence better able to resist invasion.

CRITIQUES OF THE CHICAGO SCHOOL: CONCEPTS AND METHODS

The Chicago School has been abundantly criticized. One recurrent criticism is that conceptually, the Chicago School focused too narrowly on spatial explanations to the exclusion of other potential organizing factors. Hawley complained that the Chicago School made human ecology synonymous with the study of spatial distributions.[10] Firey stated that Burgess and his associates were spatially deterministic and ignored the cultural significance of space.[11] Gottdiener and Hutchinson extended this complaint to encompass a more general fallacy of environmental determinism and succession toward a climax community.[12] Another significant complaint was the limited set of drivers that the Chicagoans considered, relying almost exclusively on competition.[13] Finally, the Chicago School failed to address the entire urban region in its general approach. This last complaint has helped clarify that the simple ring models of the Chicago School failed to account for the networked and multinucleated nature of the city that was emerging even in the early twentieth century.

The mounting complaints about the Chicago School were accompanied by a search for a more satisfactory approach to urban ecology from a sociological perspective. These researchers included Louis Wirth, Walter Firey, and Amos Hawley. The first wave of critics brought culture back into what had been a spatial and biotic pursuit. Ironically, one of the leaders of this movement, Wirth, was himself a member of the University of Chicago's Department of Sociology. He proposed a theory of urban life: what was uniquely urban emerged from the size of urban settlements, their human density, and the heterogeneity of backgrounds of people in the city.[14] Wirth's methods depended upon a statistical approach rather than the case studies used by the Chicago School. Although Wirth disagreed with his colleagues in his department on the causes of urban differentiation and their case study approach, he shared certain assumptions with them. He continued to be concerned with the huge changes that Chicago and other industrial cities in the United States were experiencing and he continued to focus on the pathological side of urban life. He also shared the conviction that urban life differed from life in villages and small towns.

Firey argued that the Chicago School's simple spatial models did not correspond to the empirical evidence. The rings of the Chicago School failed to appear in other cities. Indeed, there was evidence of idealization in the maps Burgess produced for Chicago, such that they glossed over important social heterogeneity within rings and land uses. Firey proposed several factors that prevented such idealized city forms from appearing. First, in contrast to the ring model, economic values are insufficient for explaining the entire distributional complexity of space in cities. Second, cultural values ascribed to space can drive choices about the use of land. Indeed, symbolic and sentimental uses of land may sometimes override economic values. Finally, influences from beyond a metropolitan region can drive the allocation and uses of land within a region.[15] If anything, Firey's critiques of the Chicago School alerts us to the deep significance of heterogeneity within cities and the need to link cultural understandings with spatial relations.

The shift from the Chicago School to alternative explanations was driven not only by emerging subdisciplines in sociology but by the changing nature of the American city itself. The end of World War II signaled an acceleration in the expansion of suburbia, a deconcentration of business and commerce, and a focus on networked nodes of urbanization. The alternatives to the Chicago School saw space as a cultural phenomenon[16] and the significant influence of external economic and policy drivers.[17] However, these critiques of the Chicago School were limited as well. For instance, Hawley advanced a technologically deterministic view that shifts in transportation and communication were driving the changing social organization evident in the post–World War II American city. Space itself was not the organizing concern; it was important only insofar as space had economic and social meaning and cost and in that different locations were technologically linked.[18]

RECENT ADVANCES IN SOCIOSPATIAL APPROACHES TO URBANISM AND CONNECTIONS WITH BIOPHYSICAL ECOLOGY

In *The New Urban Sociology,* Mark Gottdiener and Ray Hutchinson have synthesized a new approach to the sociology of urban areas.[19] Overall, their synthesis is a combination of culture, in the largest sense, and space as a culturally infused environment. Gottdiener and Hutchinson point to five major insights of the contemporary sociospatial approach to urban sociology. First, the metropolis has a regional and global context. In particular, human settlements are connected to the worldwide system of capitalism. Second, conflict leads to spatial segregation by class, gender, and race. Conflict between such groups is driven not only by economics but by other resources in which people and institutions are interested. Third, the sociospatial approach integrates political, economic, and cultural factors in its analyses. No single realm is considered to be dominant in and of itself. Fourth, special attention is given to "pull" factors of real estate investment. The real estate complex of businesses and industries is an especially effective force, which integrates aspects of economics and culture. Pull factors are supply factors that entice or encourage people and institutions to relocate from older neighborhoods and central cities to suburbs and exurbs. Along with this, government interventions shape regional pushes and pulls that affect real estate investment or disinvestment. Push factors are disamenities, threats, expenses, or risks that are perceived to exist in older neighborhoods and central cities. Push factors create a demand for new development outside established urban sites. Finally, the spatial configuration of the contemporary conurbation is recognized to be multicentered. Therefore, a regional approach to cities in connection with suburbs and exurbs as a networked system is emerging.[20] In many of these features, the sociospatial approach resonates well with the approaches of contemporary biophysical ecology.

The sociospatial approach has two particular features. First is the quantification of social differentiation across a metropolitan region. An initial attempt to measure social differentiation was the social area analysis approach developed by Shevky and Bell.[21] Shevky and Bell invented social area analysis to explain how a metropolitan region becomes socially differentiated. Their analysis relied on three dimensions of social structure: (1) population density, (2) social status, and (3) family status. Social status was derived from occupation, income, and education, while family status was defined by the nature of the dwelling unit, the presence and characteristics of children, and whether the adult female member of the household worked outside the home. From these features of social structure, social area indices were derived to delineate and classify the social characteristics of an area.[22] Shevky and Bell had preselected the factors expected to be important. Berry built upon their approach by employing multivariate approaches to assess the relative importance among the many variables that may influence the location of different social groups.[23] Berry's multifactorial method represents a systems approach that is capable of more integrated understanding of urban structure and change than its predecessors.[24]

A second feature of the sociospatial approach is its emphasis on generalizability and integration of theory and methods. This characteristic extends the sociospatial approach beyond the tradition introduced by the Chicago School, which focused on individual case studies. Examples of generalizations include the discovery that segregation is a universal feature of American cities and that technology is not the primary driver in urban evolution.

FOUR ECOLOGICAL PERSPECTIVES AND URBAN SOCIAL THEORY

Martin Melosi contends that the Chicago School and Gottdiener and Hutchinson's sociospatial approach can be classified in terms of four ecological perspectives of urban social theory.[25] Melosi points out that much of the history of urban social theory has labored under the erroneous assumption that people, and hence cities, are separate from nature. He provides a framework for classifying the history of urban social theory in terms of this assumption. Melosi's critique is based upon three assertions. First, cities must be viewed in their environmental context. Here, Melosi's meaning of "environment" is similar to that of a biophysical ecologist: landform, climate, disturbance regimes, and so on. Second, he asserts that understanding the role of nature in human life requires that the place of nature in cities be recognized. Finally, Melosi argues that built infrastructure is a cultural expression *and* influences and is constrained by nature. These three assertions are consistent with the "design with nature" perspective of architecture, landscape architecture, and urban design and planning.[26]

Melosi proposes four ecological perspectives: (1) organic theory, (2) city as modifier of nature, (3) ecological theory of the Chicago School, and (4) systems theory. Organic theory analogizes the city with the body of an organism. This is a powerful metaphor but, like most metaphors, it is only partially true. The image of a city as an organism suggests the integration and interdependence of human communities and environments within settlements. Integration within cities is a strong implication of the organic theory. One way to conceive of cities as organic entities is to see them as transformed combinations of resources. According to Havlick, cities are second-order resources for humans and societies.[27] Perhaps more anthropogenic is the view of Harvey, who views cities as a human-derived resource system that creates structure and differentiation of space.[28] Adding human experience to the city as a derived resource system highlights not only that the city is a resource system made by people but also that it is transformed and experienced by people.[29] Cities in this view become an interaction between space, resources, and society. This interaction leads to a new kind of ecosystem that is open to fluxes with the outside world.[30]

Cities are necessarily connected to the outside world. This view is echoed by Cronon, who labels cities as "second nature," accumulating raw materials from vast resource catchments and transforming them within.[31] The suite of themes that can be brought together in the organic theory views cities as dynamic, rather than static backdrops for human and natural activity. Cities, like many organisms, are seen as ever-mutating systems. Shane advances the concept of "recombinant urbanism" to describe a particularly dynamic view of the metropolis.[32] This is a useful metaphor but not a literal organic one. Recombination refers to the genetic mixing of preexisting elements or of new mutations to produce new biological structures and functioning. Shane suggests that cities are comprised of generalizable elements that are repeated and reorganized to form different cities.

Biophysical ecologists must add a caution to the organic theory approach. Organisms are often homoeostatic systems, driven by evolved functions, and frequently acting with purpose. Optimization or maximization models can be carefully used in such situations, where natural selection can act as a mechanism yielding optimal structure or function within a limited environment. The organism metaphor has been problematic in many urban applications because the targets of that application are manifestly not evolved via natural selection, or homeostatically regulated by tight physiological and hormonal feedback systems. In addition, they lack the brains and central nervous systems that mediate optimization behavior in higher animals. Contemporary biophysical ecologists are loath to use the organic metaphor because of its teleological and homoeostatic implications. Such behaviors are best treated as hypotheses about systems rather than foregone conclusions that are derived by analogy.[33]

A second major perspective is the conception of the city as modifier. In this view, the built structures of cities modify basic physical processes. For instance, the hydrological cycle is modified by cities through the construction of streets, gutters, drains, and impervious surfaces such that they produce greater runoff, reduce ground water infiltration, and lower soil moisture content relative to nonurban areas in the same region.[34] Thus, the city as modifier perspective seeks to understand how cities alter and transform environmental conditions, both internally and externally, over time. Biophysical ecologists are discovering a rich array of significant and unexpected patterns and processes in urban ecological systems. Ecological patterns and processes may be thought of as ecological "facts." Ecological facts may be social facts, too, having economic value and social meaning, and reflecting power and status, for instance.[35] There is much to do still in this arena.

The Chicago School's "ecological theory" is a third ecological perspective. We noted earlier that the ecological theory used by the Chicago School is quite different from contemporary biophysical ecology. Nevertheless, it is worth summarizing again the core tenets of that theory and tracing some of the threads that followed from it. The Chicago School concentrated on factors determining urban spatial patterns and their social impacts. The spatial arrangements were concentric around the core, distinctive, and depended upon competition as the primary driver for this spatial differentiation. Their impacts on social order and disorder were central to the Chicago School. Whether social order or disorder best characterized the city was highly controversial. Descendants of the Chicago School also tried to explain the relationship between population size and the organizational structure of cities. Hawley suggested that as the population of a city increased around the periphery, the organizational function of the urban core increased.[36] Schnore and Duncan identified four complexes to build a model of urban change. Their complexes included population, social organization, environment, and technology (POET). The "POET model" extended the purview of urban sociology beyond the city line and pointed toward the integration of diverse factors.[37]

Melosi's fourth ecological perspective is systems theory. Brian Berry is credited with introducing this important idea to urban sociology.[38] Cities can be analyzed as systems in comparison with other systems. That is, models of cities or parts of cities would specify a boundary for the purposes of the study and then specify the components of the system, the interactions among them, and the kinds of dynamics that the system could experience. In addition, generalizations may emerge from studying cities in just the same way that they have emerged from the study of other kinds of systems. The same kinds of conceptual constructs and models should apply to cities as well as to those systems models within the physical, chemical, biological, and cybernetic sciences. Like other systems, cities can be studied as structural, functional, and dynamic entities. The systems approach is especially important because of its nested hierarchical nature. Cities can be disaggregated into component systems, or may participate in the structure and functioning of larger systems that include them. The development of systems theory since Berry first promoted its use in urban sociology has progressed from focusing exclusively on closed, self-regulating systems to effectively addressing open systems.

Summarizing the Past, Looking to the Future: Spatial and Organizational Complexity

Not only are urban areas conceivable as systems, they are usefully thought of as complex systems. We identify two dimensions of complexity that must be addressed to understand the structure, process, and change in urban systems. These two kinds of complexity will reappear throughout the book.

SPATIAL COMPLEXITY

It should be clear that space has had a controversial history in urban ecology. The founders of the Chicago School based their theoretical and empirical apparatus on the discovery of spatial patterns and the explanation of those patterns using concepts from biophysical ecology current in the early 1900s. Critics of the Chicago School questioned the significance of space in urban ecological theory and focused instead on other explanations of social differentiation and change in the metropolis. Innovation and technology were key factors that were advanced in place of space in these new theories. In part, these critiques reflected the changing form of the American city from its industrial, bull's-eye form to its postindustrial networked form. The current generation of urban sociologists has established a more integrated theory. In the new view, urban theory deals with the complexities of mosaics and networked space along with the multiple social, cultural, economic, and policy drivers. What seems missing to us is the act of extending this integration from urban social theory to include the best of contemporary ecology. We propose that a focus on spatial heterogeneity can facilitate the integration of biophysical ecology and urban social ecology.

The study of spatial heterogeneity recognizes contrasts in a system of interest, and describes the origin and changes in those contrasts. Spatial heterogeneity can be the result of contrast in any structure or process of interest. Contrasts, for example, can exist in the three-dimensional architecture of a site, in the density of structural elements, in the concentration of materials or energy, in the processes transforming energy, materials, or information, in visual stimuli, or in meaning. Although such contrasts can be visualized as maps, it is important to recognize that contrasts in the material world are three-dimensional. Translating these abstract examples, researchers might discriminate patches of coniferous versus deciduous forest, density of migrant workers in one area versus another, wet patches of soil versus dry areas, hot spots of the breakdown of organic matter versus areas where organic matter in the soil breaks down only slowly, the evening bustle of a bright-light district versus a shuttered business block, or a boundary area tagged by several gangs versus core turf tagged homogeneously. Much more will be said about the structure and change of patches in chapter 3. It is important to realize that spatial heterogeneity can appear as discrete patches or as gradual surfaces of change. The basic concepts and causes of spatial heterogeneity apply to both the discrete and continuous forms of contrast. Merely the representation differs.

Spatial heterogeneity can be assessed with increasing levels of complexity, as we noted in chapter 1 and figure 1.2.[39] It may seem counterintuitive, but the most basic measures of spatial heterogeneity are actually "aspatial." These measures include the types of contrasts, the number or richness of contrasts, and the frequency of contrasts. Analysis of spatial heterogeneity becomes spatially explicit when the spatial configuration of contrasts is examined. Configuration may be presented as a map, but in the real world, configurations are three-dimensional arrays. The spatial configuration of an area can change over time, which anticipates both internal *change* within each node of contrast and change in the entire nexus of contrasts. Exploring these dimensions of spatial heterogeneity in both biological and social terms is the subject of the next chapter. However, it is important to introduce both aspatial and spatially explicit approaches to spatial heterogeneity because it helps clarify the integration that is possible with new spatial approaches in urban social theory that recognize a diversity of causal factors, agents, and scales of organization.

ORGANIZATIONAL COMPLEXITY

Many causal factors have been introduced, measured, debated, and replaced through the history of urban ecology. We suggest that three types of drivers of organizational complexity have emerged: (1) top-down and bottom-up control, (2) outside influence and internal control, and (3) individual and collective action. All three types of drivers provide alternatives for the controls and processes for either an entire urban patch mosaic or an individual patch within the mosaic. Thus, these drivers are scale neutral and can be used to describe the dynamics of a variety of spatial units, such as neighborhoods, urban districts, and exurban settlements.

The first type of driver addresses whether the control of structure and process within an urban patch emerges from large institutions and grand policies or from the behaviors of smaller institutions and a diversity of actors. A top-down institutional control might be, for instance, government transportation or tax policy. An intermediate level of control might be the differential willingness of a city's banks to sell home mortgages in redlined neighborhoods versus other neighborhoods. Such control is from the top relative to the different types of neighborhoods. Highly disaggregated, bottom-up control emerges from the decisions of individual households concerning their purchase and management of homes and land, for example.

The second type of driver concerns control that arises within or external to an urban unit of interest. Outside control may reflect shifts in global business, such as when a business closes its manufacturing plant in one city and opens a new plant in another country where operating costs are less expensive. Inside control is illustrated by the organizing activities of a neighborhood or community association to demand better city services or influence the city's zoning decisions.

The final type of driver contrasts individual and collective action. The individual approach recognizes that actors such as persons, households, firms, and neighborhoods are not necessarily working in partnership with other actors. Actors may in fact follow a few rules of behavior, leading to complex emergent patterns and processes. For instance, urban areas can become highly segregated if individual households follow a selection rule, in which case they simply choose where to live based upon the similarity of neighbors in terms of race, ethnicity, or lifestyle. In contrast, early urban sociology aimed to understand how immigrant groups adapted to the new environment of the changing American industrial city. Emphasis was on the collective activities and successes or failures in assimilation by newly arrived immigrant groups. Spatial emphasis was on the succession of groups through time in such areas as the transition zone adjacent to the urban core (figure 2.2).

Moving On

In the next chapter, we will lay out the concept and framework for a "patch dynamics" approach, an approach to spatial and organizational complexity that can accommodate the range of causes and agencies that urban social theorists have confronted since the 1920s in America. While the patch dynamics concept emerges from biophysical ecology, we believe it will resonate with a broad range of urban social theory. Patch dynamics can provide a tool for synthesis among the biophysical and social sciences aimed at understanding the how and why of spatial pattern and change in regional metropolitan systems, and their component districts and neighborhoods. Patch dynamics applies equally to built, green, and hybrid patches, and appears consistent with the multiple causality associated with the sociospatial approach to urban sociology. Patch dynamics is a contemporary, ecological approach, which urban sociology has been seeking since critiques of the Chicago School emerged. When coupled with the broad framework that encompasses the breadth of social, economic, and cultural drivers affecting the metropolis, patch dynamics can help explore emerging urban frontiers.

Expanding the Landscape

Applying Patch Dynamics to

Social-Ecological Systems

Reassessing Patch Dynamics

Patch dynamics emerged in ecology as an approach to under-standing spatial heterogeneity.[1] Though ecology is its original disciplinary home, patch dynamics resonates with contemporary urban social theory, particularly with the sociospatial approach advanced by Gottdiener and Hutchinson.[2] Consequently, a patch dynamics approach can serve as a critical node of synthesis between contemporary social and ecological approaches for an ecology of cities. In this chapter, we will define a patch dynamics approach and briefly review its contributions to describing and quantifying patterns and changes in spatial heterogeneity of bioecological systems. We will then apply patch dynamics to urban systems and demonstrate how it addresses the drivers of urban systems identified in earlier chapters.

Defining Patch Dynamics in Biophysical Ecology

Ecologists have emphasized homogeneity in their fine-scale studies or theoretical systems for a long time.[3] Such a strategy was important for extracting patterns from the "noise" of observations in the real world. Working with simple systems that could be assumed to be internally homogeneous, and working with theoretical systems that followed the simplifying assumptions allowed by mathematical formulations, ecologists were able to significantly advance their young science.[4] For example, core theories of population growth and limitation, or of competition and predation, all assume the obvious differences in size, behavior, or genetics of organisms to be unimportant for explaining the basic issue. Population limitation operates in spite of the manifest differences in sex, age, genetics, and nutrition in an animal population, for instance. Of course, on other levels of detail, variation is important. If concern was with the evolution of a population, of course genetic differences, such as those brought about by mutation or recombination, or differential mating success based on sex-linked traits, make a difference.[5] For certain ecological approaches, heterogeneity among organisms and heterogeneity among biotas were found to be important. But by and large, for explaining the structure and functioning of ecological systems observed at the scales of tens of meters to kilometers, uniformity was an important assumption.[6]

In the last third of the twentieth century, ecologists began to take seriously the differences within their fine- and medium-scale systems.[7] Communities of plants could not be adequately explained using the principles developed for entire climatic regions. The details of successional turnover during a span of several years could not be understood using the coarse-scale expectation of the development of a climax.[8] Animal populations were sometimes regulated by external events rather than the density dependence expected in uniform environments.[9] These and many other realizations led ecologists to finally admit that the local and regional heterogeneities of their systems might be functionally important rather than being mere "noise" that could be brushed aside to fit simple, idealized theories of uniform behavior or structure.[10]

Patch dynamics was one of the major developments within biological ecology to describe and quantify heterogeneity in all its dimensions. The concept was synthesized from several precedents in biogeography and ecology during the mid-1970s.[11] Island biogeography theory was one of the theories that was developed originally to explain different levels of species richness on oceanic islands of various sizes and distances from continents. Oceanic islands are characterized by discrete boundaries and are embedded in a matrix that is completely hostile to terrestrial life, forming a difficult barrier for colonization. Island biogeography invited application to island analogs on continents. Such analogs included lakes, caves, and mountaintops. Patch dynamics extended the perspective of island biogeography to any discrete continental habitat type and did not assume that the matrix was completely hostile. In fact, the matrix of any focal island analog or "patch" could be a mosaic of different kinds of habitats differing in diverse ways from the focal one. Patch dynamics therefore considers mosaics of habitat types or ecosystem types rather than a two-phase system of islands in a hostile matrix.[12]

The gradient approach to environmental heterogeneity complements the patch approach and can ultimately be combined with it. The gradient approach is a theoretical approach that was also maturing during the 1970s.[13] Although the gradient approach had been introduced in the early twentieth century by Henry Allen Gleason,[14] it was considered to apply to two-dimensional transects or models by most ecologists. Gradients of many factors, often combined into environmental complexes, were recognized by ecologists to explain patterns of diversity and species interaction along transects of elevation, moisture, or resource availability.[15] This approach began to open the eyes of ecologists to heterogeneity at a variety of scales. Robert Whittaker generalized gradient theory to three-dimensional concerns by introducing the idea of gamma diversity to deal with the differentiation in species and habitats over landscapes or regions.[16] Patch dynamics accommodates the nodes of heterogeneity within three-dimensional landscapes.[17] Hot spots of structure or process, separated by either gradients in architecture or function, can be arrayed as fuzzy patches across many different scales of interest to ecology.

What, then, is patch dynamics? First, patch dynamics is a branch of ecology that describes and quantifies spatial heterogeneity by dividing a specified area into different spatial units.[18] A large space can be divided into patches that differ in a structural feature or a kind of process of interest to a researcher. For instance, a marine intertidal zone can be divided into patches dominated by mussel beds of different species, or patches recently bared by wave action or battering by wave-tossed logs.[19] The different algal or mussel species present contrasting three-dimensional architectures, depending on the size of individuals and their density. These inhabited patches clearly differ in architecture from bare patches, which are characterized by the unoccupied rock surface. In a terrestrial system, a functional patch delineation might be based on a process such as litter deposition. For example, in fields undergoing succession following abandonment from agriculture, forest-field boundary zones have different amounts and kinds of litter deposition than patches closer to field centers. The exact nature and amount of litter deposition in different patches near the forest-field boundary depend on the identity of the neighboring tree species—oaks with their recalcitrant thick litter versus maples with their labile thin leaves, for instance. Such differences between patches affect which old-field species succeed in each kind of patch.[20]

Patch dynamics uses the differences in structure or function of different areas as a tool to quantify spatial heterogeneity. There are three initial aspects of patch quantification.[21] First, the number of patches is one kind of quantification. Second, the number of different types of patches is another, more sophisticated look at spatial heterogeneity. This measure is called patch richness. Once the kinds of patches are differentiated, the number or frequency of each type of patch can be assessed. This adds an additional layer of analytical complexity to the understanding of patch quantification. These three basic features of patches say nothing about their spatial features. The sizes and shapes of different patches and patch types may be added to the roster of quantitative descriptions of patches. The next level of complexity is the actual configuration or spatial arrangement of patches within a specified arena (figure 1.2).

These various features of patches divide into two broad categories: spatially inexplicit and spatially explicit. The spatially inexplicit features aggregate the nature of patches within a landscape without specifying exactly where the patches are. Richness, frequency, and average size and shape are spatially inexplicit parameters. Spatially explicit features of a patch array specify which patches are adjacent to one another, and how the patches fit together in the landscape of interest.

It is important to remember that patch dynamics incorporates temporal changes in spatial heterogeneity. While some patch arrays or some patches within an array may persist unchanged for long periods of time, recognizing that both individual patches and the entire patch mosaic can change is an important insight of patch dynamics.[22] For instance, patches can maintain their identify and change in size, shape, or location within a mosaic. Alternatively, patches can mutate into other patches or disappear as new patches are created or spread into their territory. Specifying what kinds of changes are to be observed in a system is an important research decision.

Putting all these characteristics of patch dynamics together shows it as a model of the spatial heterogeneity of ecological systems that (1) differentiates three-dimensional patch bodies from one another based on structural or functional criteria; (2) quantifies patch features in terms of number, richness, frequency, size, shape, and configuration; (3) recognizes the connections and interactions among patches within and among levels of organization based on fluxes of energy, matter, organisms, or information; and (4) allows individual patches and the entire mosaic of patches to change.[23] Thus, a patch dynamics approach is essential for examining and understanding the spatial and organizational complexity of urban systems.

The remainder of this chapter places the patch dynamics perspective at the service of integrating the bioecological perspective with social perspectives in order to understand urban systems as spatially heterogeneous and dynamic integrations of biophysical and social phenomena. The complexity and dynamism of urban systems are arguably their most important features.[24] This is especially true now that urban systems are experiencing such global growth and alteration and are becoming the most common home of humankind.[25]

Defining Urban Systems

We began this chapter on patch dynamics by exploiting its forty-year history in biophysical ecology. However, our ultimate goal is to use the concept to help integrate the social and biophysical perspectives necessary to understand the full complexity of urban ecological systems. In order to move toward this goal, we must say what is meant by an "ecological" system and an urban system.

The basic concept of a system is that of a unit or entity that is composed of a specified set of things linked by a set of interactions, all existing together within some boundary.[26] Systems theory recognizes a system and an external environment. The elements of a system can be tightly or loosely linked and can be persistent or temporary.[27] Similarly, systems can be relatively isolated from their environments or pervious to environmental influence. Systems theory is broad and can be applied well beyond the physical or military engineering realms in which it was initially developed. Indeed, Brian Berry was a leader in applying systems theory to urban areas in the 1970s.

With the introduction of the concept of the ecosystem by Tansley in 1935, ecology adopted a systems approach.[28] An ecosystem is the interaction of an organismal complex with an environmental complex in a specified, bounded area. The term *environment* in the definition of an ecosystem is in contrast to whatever biological complex is chosen. Tansley intended it to refer to the soils, waters, and air with which a community of organisms interacted. Note that this still leaves the general systems theory perspective of environment intact. An ecosystem is embedded, as all systems are, in a larger environment outside of the specified boundary of interest.[29]

Now ecologists can speak of ecological systems to include various ecological entities, from groups of genetic variants within a population or within a species to individual organisms to populations of a given species to communities of plants or collections of animals in an area to landscapes to ecosystems.[30] All share the fact that some biotically derived complex is in interaction with some physical complex within a specified spatial arena.

How can this general systems view and its specific instance in terms of ecology be related to cities and urban regions? Fortunately, the link is close.[31] We only have to specify what "urban" consists of and to indicate the kinds of relationships and boundaries urban areas might possess. The concept of the ecosystem is a good place for us to start.

If we were to define urban systems in a form parallel to the ecosystem, two basic components are essential. One is a biotically derived complex and the other is a relevant physical or environmental complex. Clearly, however, to specify an urban system from the basic definition of the ecosystem, something has to be added to the plants, animals, and microbes, and to the soil, air, and water from ecology.

Is it enough to add people as organisms? If this were sufficient, ecologists would use their familiar approaches from population biology and study the people of urban systems in terms of birth, death, population structure, age and sex differences, immigration and emigration, and evolution.[32] This approach undoubtedly leaves social scientists cold. What would *they* add?

The largest additions would perhaps be such things as cultures, institutions, and economies: in other words, the specifically human tools for dealing with resources, problems, exchanges, and meanings in life.[33] More will be said about the vast richness in each of these categories in chapter 4.

As important as these social features of urban systems are, they are not enough. Humans, through their individual, aggregate, institutional, economic, and culturally derived actions, build new physical structures and modify the biophysical environment. They dam rivers, plow fields, build highways, develop neighborhoods, pipe water, flush sewage, and transport waste. In other words, they construct vast infrastructure and modify the lands and ecosystems of the areas they inhabit or manage.

These types of human tools and actions add two complexes to ecosystems that parallel the ones recognized by Tansley and generations of ecologists since his landmark paper.[34] We interpret the added human features of urban systems to constitute (1) a social complex and (2) a built complex.[35] Thus, urban ecosystems contain not only biotically derived complexes such as parks, street trees, wildlife, soil microbes and decomposer fungi on leaf litter, soil invertebrates and insects, and the presence of humans as biological organisms that eat and void waste, live and die in cities, but they also include humans as families, neighborhoods, community groups, religious congregations, clubs, gangs, companies, government agencies, industries, and so on. They also include such things as human knowledge, norms and rules, capital, fashion, greed, status symbols, and economic devices that drive and limit exchange.[36] Not only does an urban ecosystem include the rivers, bays, estuaries, landforms, soils, rocks, groundwater, and air of the metropolitan region, but it also includes the streets, interstates, malls, water supply, sewers, houses, mosques, churches, synagogues, libraries, parking lots, rail yards, factories, junkyards, brownfields, and back lots that arise due to human design, neglect, and accident.[37] It is amazing and daunting to consider the breadth and importance of these components of urban ecosystems.

The urban ecosystem and its complexes—physical, biological, social, and built—have three important dimensions (figure 1.1). First, the urban ecosystem has an abstract definition, consisting of a kernel of meaning. Second, it can be specified or applied as a model to a wide variety of different situations and uses. Finally, the urban ecosystem can be represented by metaphors or images of the nature of a system with connotations that are used for a variety of noble or base goals. Metaphors of the urban ecosystem can be used to help generate new scientific insights, promote public understanding, sell widgets, advance conservation and sustainability, motivate progressive regulations, confound the public, or intrigue professionals across disciplinary boundaries. The three dimensions shared by the urban ecosystem concept are thus meaning, model, and metaphor.[38] As we have discussed earlier regarding the ecological perspective alone, these three dimensions constitute the core definition, specification through models, and images to visualize the concept. The definition is fundamentally abstract, free of scale, and neutral with respect to such features as closure, self-regulation, equilibrium, dynamics, and the presence of disturbance. The modeling strategy and exemplary kinds of models can be diagrammatic, conceptual, mathematical, computer simulations, or physical representations such as mesocosms and field experiments. Finally, the metaphors can be figures of speech or images used to generate or summarize technical insights. We argue for the neutrality, scale-independence, and open-endedness of the core definitions of all ecological concepts.[39] We admit that the specification via models can range from narrow and normative to broad and descriptive. However, one of the values of models is that they must, through their very specificity, admit and expose the assumptions that motivate them so that the values they harbor are clear in the scientific disciplinary, interdisciplinary, or public dialog in which they are used.[40]

Just as the biophysical ecosystem can be applied to a broad variety of situations, so too can the urban ecosystem concept. In the science of biological ecology, an ecosystem can refer to the entire tall grass prairie biome of the American Midwest, or it can refer to the interacting biotic and physical complexes in a rotting log on the floor of an Amazonian rain forest, or it can refer to a strip of riparian woodland and the surface stream and groundwater with which the trees and associated organisms interact. The prairie biome is a subset of the larger ecosystem of all the contiguous grasslands in America. The rotting log can be subsumed into a larger ecosystem of a rain forest patch of, say, a square kilometer in extent, and the strip of riparian ecosystem can be considered to be a part of a larger ecosystem delimited by the catchment upstream of it. All of these ecosystems are open to the fluxes of matter and energy from outside them while processing large amounts of nutrients and energy internally. All have important regulating factors that arise from outside their borders as well as controlling interactions that exist internally. All exhibit probabilistic changes and can encompass internal disturbances.

The urban ecosystem is similarly diverse in its specification, although there is much less experience in applying this concept scientifically.[41] "Urban" can refer to a central business district, the old, dense residential neighborhoods in cities that arose before the hegemony of the automobile, or a streetcar suburb. At a coarser scale, "urban" can refer to the entire West Coast megalopolis of the United States, the networked conurbation of the Netherlands, or the exploding new megacities of Asia, Africa, and South America. Under different cultural contexts, it can refer to a genteel district with tree-lined streets and tidy houses with manicured back gardens, or it can refer to the ad hoc shanty towns confined to the margin of an old colonial African city. Urban ecosystems may exist as forested or desert parks, stream corridors, or remnant green or rocky patches within the urban boundary. Sometimes such open spaces are manicured and managed, and sometimes they are neglected due to a lack of interest or lack of financial and human resources. An urban ecosystem may just as well refer to the vacant lots and brownfields of postindustrial cities as to the disused transportation corridors and neglected public rights-of-way with their scrappy, ruderal vegetation. Urban ecosystems may refer to the strange concentrations of buildings, infrastructure, energy, and attitude perched on a mountainside in the form of a popular ski resort. It may refer to the "footprint" or resource catchment and waste-processing hinterland of a major settlement.[42]

The immense variety of kinds of urban ecosystem models implied by the list above is important. There is no singular urban ecosystem in terms of model or meaning. Like the biophysical concept of ecosystem, the urban ecosystem concept can be applied to the entire range of eco-systems devoted to human settlement and resource management. How-ever, even focusing on cities in the broadest sense results in an extensive and diverse spectrum of models and expressions of what is urban. All of these are fair game for our further consideration.

The city is a new kind of ecosystem and one that we seek to exam-ine using the open-ended and inclusive approach of patch dynamics to understand the many layers of its social orders, resources, interactions, and built structures and managed landforms.[43] The great challenge is to take the four complexes of urban systems as equal partners: biotic, physical, social, and built. One thing we can offer in this chapter is to correct some of the misinterpretations of ecology that we have discov-ered in the social science literature, which we pointed out in chapter 2, so that the intellectual equality of the social and biotic components of the urban ecosystem concept is better met. There are important ideas and theoretical "hooks" from contemporary studies of the social and built complexes that can be combined effectively with what we know to be the key ideas of contemporary ecology to generate a new way to understand urban ecological systems.

Defining Urban Patches

Patches, as we have seen, require criteria of contrast to extract them from the welter of difference that typifies urban landscapes. Three kinds of criteria of contrast exist in cities and, when used together, can spec-ify integrated patches in the human ecosystem. These three criteria are physical, biological, and social. The order in which they are listed is un-important, since they are all required to fully appreciate and quantify urban heterogeneity. We treat the built complex as the result of the in-teractions among these three contrasts.

Physical heterogeneity is based on the soils and topography within an urban ecological system.[44] Soils may range from those that have sur-vived the process of urbanization to those that have been paved over to those whose basic structures are entirely human-made. Even in remnant soils, human activities in the settlement will affect the chemical properties, through pollution, for example, and the biotic properties, through the introduction of exotic invasive species, for example.[45]

Topography, or the underlying lay of the land, is an important feature of urban ecosystems and hence a criterion for discriminating patches within them. Cities are often founded at some topographically defensible site, on a sheltered harbor, or at the point where navigation in a stream is no longer possible. Industrial age cities often mark the intersection of transportation routes, as do postindustrial cities at a larger scale. Topography may mold the street patterns of a city or provide rhythm and impose inconvenience on a colonial or imperial grid. Even in recognizing that topography discriminates hillcrests, convex shoulders of slopes, concave toe slopes, and valley bottoms, each with their own microclimate, water regime, soil depth and quality, risks of exposure to different natural disturbances, and so on, the role of human modification of topography must also be recognized. Since the Middle Ages, geologists estimate, humans have become the dominant movers of earth on the planet.[46] Little urban development now occurs that does not level sites, shape topography, bury or attempt to move streams, and cut new paths for roads. All these kinds of topographic contrasts can be used to discriminate one patch from another patch.

Biological contrasts also exist within urban ecosystems. Organisms respond to position on slope, exposure of slopes to different directions, or to different wind patterns. Therefore, the distribution of plants, animals, microbes and the differences in their abilities to produce biomass, store carbon, moderate microclimate, and regenerate themselves differ from place to place in an urban region.[47] In some cities, riparian habitats along streams support distinct vegetation and microbial communities in sites where the water economy remains intact; hillcrests that remain unwatered typically support different species of trees or individuals that are relatively stunted compared to their conspecifics lower on slopes: pines on hilltops, hemlocks in ravines, oaks on slopes, and maples in protected coves.

Spatial clustering of activities and social groups, social "patchiness," is not exclusive to humans and can be an adaptive behavioral strategy for other social species as well. One of the more fruitful patterns observed across species is the tendency of behaviors, functions, and specific groups like drone bees or retailers to cluster in well-defined spatial patches within larger landscape mosaics. Social patchiness in cities, suburbs, and exurban development is legendary.[48] Spatial patterns are often associated with temporal cycles. Human ecosystems in urbanized regions have highly predictable patterns of behavior: rush hours and slack hours, school and sports seasons, and so on.

Ethnic enclaves have been documented in the ancient cities of the Middle East. Chinese coastal cities of the nineteenth century exhibited divisions based on trade interests. The delta cities of Southeast Asia such as Bangkok have districts defined by canals and waterways.[49] The immigrant cities of the industrial world collect and segregate migrants from different varieties of "the old country" or different places "down south" in specific neighborhoods.[50] Even in the walking cities of the early industrial era, American cities such as Baltimore were segregated: the managers and owners on the exterior of blocks while slaves, freed persons of color, and immigrant workers lived in the more modest housing stock along alleys in the interiors of neighborhood blocks. Shopkeepers lived above their stores in other neighborhoods, or in corner buildings supporting mixed uses.[51] The experience of tourists or urbanists in turning a corner and encountering a shockingly different social structure is a common one.[52] Such fine-grain differences in urban pattern are often related to when construction occurred, style of architecture, degree of maintenance of infrastructure, availability of municipal services or of community action, commercial activity, and so on. Demography, ethnicity, family structure and age, age of housing stock, landscaping fashion, among many other social attributes, all contribute to the patchiness of urban places.

This variety of urban patches can be recognized in several ways. Originally, patches were recognized using a "bottom-up" method. That is, close, fine-scaled observations of the physical and social urban fabric yielded data on the elements that discriminated patches from one another. Block-by-block or street-by-street observations or social surveys generated the differences upon which patches could be based. Some of these data were collected by the U.S. Census Bureau or by insurance companies in order to set premium rates in specific areas, for example.

Detection of physical patchiness can be made with methods developed in Europe and Asia in which the detailed cover elements of patches are composed and combined into different patch types, or "ecotopes."[53] Vegetation, pavement, building, and infrastructure are the major categories of cover used in ecotope measurements.[54]

Top-down methods for discriminating patches have been available since the advent of aerial photography and other remote sensing methods. Aerial photographs can be interpreted by expert observers, and the newer technology of satellite images, composed of pixels and bands of radiation, can be classified into patch types using their spectral signatures. These methods are considered top down because they take a complex representation of a large area and divide it based on the contrasts discerned from above. Both human operators and computer-assisted methods are available for this purpose.

Patches of social and biophysical heterogeneity require some sort of boundary or gradation in their delineation.[55] Boundaries are conveniently represented by lines on maps, but in reality they exist as zones of different widths. Often the structure of boundaries is itself functionally important and the structural or functional gradients they contain can govern the movement of materials, energy, information, and people and other organisms between patches. It is important to recognize that the idea of gradations across boundaries can be extended to an entire model of heterogeneity so that a surface or field of contrasts rather than a discrete patchwork may be used to represent heterogeneity.

In urban ecological systems, boundaries can often be associated with different types of social territories and behaviors. Territories can vary in terms of their organization. Some territories are "fixed" in that they are delineated geographically and attached to an entity that has formal legal rights and responsibilities. These legal rights and responsibilities are supported by laws and courts. Property parcels are an important example. Some boundaries are "situational." Although a situational boundary is associated with the fixed structure of a place, whether publicly or privately owned, the establishment of the boundary occurs in the form of claimed goods while-in-use. Situational boundaries can be measured in seconds, minutes, or hours, informally exerted, and raise questions as to when the claim begins and ends. Park benches and restaurant tables are examples. Finally, there are "egocentric" boundaries, which move around with an individual or group. Egocentric boundaries are examples of personal space and its ability to regulate spatial behavior.

Patch delineation can be based on both structural and functional criteria. Structure of urban heterogeneity may exist in terms of the physical, biological, and built complexes: topography, soils, ruderal vegetation, architecture, landscape architecture, infrastructure, and so on.[56] Functional patchiness can exist in terms of processing and storage of nutrients, water, materials, energy, productivity or in terms of the actions of individuals, households, organizations, agencies, commercial and business concerns, and levers of governance. Both the structure and function of patches can be either persistent or transient. Importantly, the movement of materials, information, energy, people, and other organisms between patches may affect the structure and function of donor and recipient patches. Examples of these sorts of interactions appear later.

PATCH CREATION

Patches can be created by the actions and characteristics of organisms, including humans and their institutions, or by physical changes in the structure of systems. One kind of patch origin can be considered to be an alteration of metabolism in a system and the second can be considered a kind of structural disruption or disturbance. Before proceeding, however, it is important to emphasize that assessing either of these modes of patch creation requires an explicit model of the nature of the patches and, hence, a specification of the roster of potential causes of patch origin. Without a model of system structure, a discussion of the causes of patch origin is premature. We will exemplify the two kinds of patch origin below: (1) organismal and institutional patches and (2) disturbance patches.

Organismal and institutional patches. The organismal origin of patches presents a broad array of potential agents. These include human individuals, human institutions, the disease organisms that can cause changes in human action or organization, and other nonhuman organisms. Essentially, organismal causes of patch origin may include any kind of wild,

cultivated, or naturalized organism as well as the complex manifestations of human populations and cultures.

Human individuals are relatively weak agents of patch creation.
Usually patch creation is the result of humans acting in the aggregate or
in concert. Not always is that action intentionally coordinated. A powerful example of patch creation is the generation of burned patches in
various landscapes resulting from the management actions of preindus-
trial humans or of people now acting with little or no industrial and
fossil fuel subsidy.[57] Indeed, fire is one of the oldest and most pervasive
causes of patch creation that humans have at their disposal. In urban
settings, the purposeful use of fire is viewed as a breach of the social
contract when it is employed for revenge, profit, or excitement.[58] Ac-
cidental urban fires have a long history of being significant creators of
patches in cities, such as those in Baltimore in 1904 or more recently in
the heavily wooded hills of Oakland, California, in 1991.

Human institutions create patches through various actions. Households may manage parcels differentially and neighborhoods contrast
in their aggregate management as a result of the behaviors of groups
seeking to maintain a particular lifestyle.[59] Public lands may be managed differentially depending on the municipal department in charge or
based on the degree of political pressure applied by an adjacent neighborhood. Management may apply different amounts of water, nutrients,
or protection from stress or disease for plants in parks, boulevards, road
verges, and so on. Such differences in management may favor different
species of native plants, wildlife, and invasives or result in different individuals or stands of plants having different rates of productivity and
health, canopy heights, or degrees of canopy closure.

Disease organisms have affected the behavior of human populations directly, with differential risk of communicable or infectious disease driving patterns of settlement or migration.[60] The resulting patches
may reflect different levels of wealth or ethnic identity, for example.
Similarly, perceptions of other sorts of risks have determined areas that
are avoided or preferred by people.

Disturbance patches. Events that disrupt existing structures in an
urban ecosystem can be classified as disturbance. This definition emerges
directly from biophysical ecology, in which the concern is with events

that disrupt the structure of some ecological entity.[61] Not any change is a sudden disruption of system structure. Again, a clear specification of the structure of the system of interest is required in order to evaluate what is or is not a disturbance. It is important to recognize that "unpleasantness" is not a criterion for deciding what a disturbance is in a technical sense. Given these caveats, it is clear that disturbance can exist in the form of disruptions due to (1) economic events, (2) natural events, or (3) development in urban ecosystems. This range of sources of disturbance is intended to illustrate the breadth of the concept rather than present distinct causes. There may in fact be interactions among different potential causes of disturbance.

Economic events have great power to disrupt the structure of urban ecosystems. Some of those disruptions may be perceived by most people as good and other such disruptions may be perceived as bad. Economic disinvestment in certain inner-city neighborhoods is an example of an economic stress that leads to physical disturbance. There are many underlying social causes for such disinvestment, and the causal chain of events may be complex.[62] Redlining by lenders and insurance companies is one contributing kind of factor, as we will see in chapters 5 and 6. Lack of employment opportunities within the commuting radius of inner-city residents is another source of economic stress. A shift from owner occupancy to absentee landlords may also be associated with reduced investment in some neighborhoods. Ultimately, however, housing stock can deteriorate to the point at which abandonment occurs. This in itself represents a disruption of the demographic structure of the inner city, reflected in a decline in population. Many postindustrial-based cities have experienced such trends and events as these. Further physical disturbance results if a high threshold of abandonment is reached and demolition of housing stock ensues. Demolition converts a complete cover of row houses, for example, into a gap-toothed pattern in which short runs of vacant lots and individual row houses alternate. In row house neighborhoods near downtown Baltimore, demolition often occurs first on corners. These locations were typically occupied by buildings having a commercial storefront on the first floor and residential space on the two higher stories. With the shift of retail from its pre–World War II pattern of dispersion in residential areas to its postwar concentration in the first generation of shopping malls, these corner properties were among the first in the city to become economically untenable. Therefore, abandonment and subsequent demolition occurred on corners first.

Economic factors create patches through investment as well.[63] Turning again to inner-city neighborhoods in a precarious position, the case of Federal Hill in Baltimore is a useful example. Swaths of this neighborhood near Baltimore's Inner Harbor were slated for demolition to accommodate the construction of Interstate Highway 95, a major motorway serving the East Coast megalopolis of the United States. However, stiff community opposition ultimately blocked the aboveground highway and a tunnel was built instead. In the meantime, the houses in Federal Hill had been condemned and vacated in preparation for demolition. Reinvestment in the neighborhood was stimulated by an innovative homesteading program in which the houses were sold for $1 to new homeowners, who were bound to renovate and then occupy them for one year. This was the first program in the United States to renovate a neighborhood in this way. The subsequent investment of hundreds of owner-renovators created one of Baltimore's first redeveloped neighborhoods. The patch that resulted from this economic investment is socially distinct from the working-class neighborhoods that abut it and physically distinct in terms of the fittings and renovation of the housing and small-scale commercial stock it supports. The economic investments ultimately changed the physical structure of the neighborhood.

What a classical ecologist would call a "natural" event or disturbance is also important in creating patches in urban ecosystems.[64] In biophysically dominated ecosystems, typical events such as intense fires, severe windstorms, large floods, extreme droughts, and massive landslides can act as sources of disturbance. Not all such events are disturbances to all systems in which they occur. Again, it is important to specify a model of the system in order to evaluate whether a disturbance has in fact occurred.[65] However, given a model of an urban ecosystem or some subset of a large or complete urban region, we can evaluate whether these fundamentally biophysical events disturb the structure of the system.

There is a long history of catastrophic floods rearranging the physical and social structures of American cities. One is the flooding of New

Orleans as a result of the storm surge from Hurricane Katrina, a category 4 storm, in August 2005. The artificial levees, designed to resist the flooding calculated to result from a category 3 storm, were breached by the storm surge. Much of the city was flooded, especially the areas distant from the river, which were lower than the natural levees on which the older parts of the city were built. Other cities on the Gulf Coast of the United States were also damaged by the storm surge and high winds. However, the position of New Orleans, located on the Mississippi River and experiencing subsidence at the same time the river was building up its bed, placed it in perhaps the most threatening situation.[66]

Hurricane Katrina may still be too recent to fully evaluate its long-term effects as an urban disturbance. Loss of life was high and was visited in particular on minority areas and on the elderly, infirm, and others who were unable, or in some cases, unwilling, to evacuate. Already it is clear that in the short term many people who left New Orleans may not return. Social disturbance in the form of altered community social capital, shifts in employment base and type, and increases in the price of the remaining undamaged or repairable houses is the likely result. Large tracts of houses have been ruined by the flooding. Whether they will be replaced, repaired, or razed is still an open question. It may not be possible to tell what the patch structure of New Orleans will look like in the future. However, it is clear that a major disruption of the physical and social fabric of the city and its neighborhoods has occurred. While the shape of the future city is unclear, what is apparent is that perceiving cities to be permanent, unchanging entities leaves people and agencies unable to respond to the disturbances that will inevitably affect our metropolitan areas.

A catastrophic flood for which there is a long-term perspective of time is the Great Flood of the Mississippi in 1927.[67] This flood inundated the waterfront and downtown districts of many cities and towns in the Mississippi Delta region, which stretches from New Orleans to Cairo, Illinois. In addition to the expected shifts in building type and form in many flood-affected settlements, there were vast social changes that resulted. The exposure of African American sharecroppers in the Delta to the effects of the flood and to the risky work or shelter on the levees under the segregation dominant at the time stimulated a momentous migration of many blacks to the cities of the North, including Chicago. Thus, the "natural" disturbance of the flood rippled through local and distant social systems as a further kind of disruption. The social and human capital of the Delta and the northern cities both changed as a result. The poor treatment of African Americans during the flood was also a stimulus to social change in race relations in the nation.

The flooding in Baltimore during Hurricane Agnes in 1972 destroyed buildings in the floodplains of the three streams draining the city and cost nineteen lives in the state of Maryland. At the federal level, Hurricane Agnes was the impetus for requiring flood insurance for new construction in floodplains.[68] In Baltimore, the disruption of the physical fabric of the city and the human cost prompted a subsequent change in the zoning of floodplains, essentially prohibiting new development and relocating existing uses in the floodplains. This was a major reorientation of land use in Baltimore, a coastal city that had for centuries faced its streams because they were power sources.

Earthquakes, either alone or in combination with consequent events, have acted as powerful disturbances to urban areas.[69] The 1964 Alaska earthquake altered shorelines and destroyed buildings in Anchorage, for example.[70] In mountainous regions, landslides often accompany earthquakes and are the source of disruption of the built environment. Tsunamis, such as those associated with the South Asian subterranean earthquake of 2004 or the eruption of Karakatoa in 1883, have disturbed coastal settlements.[71] Depending on the distance of a coastal area from the source of tectonic activity and its buffering by reefs, wetlands, or dunes, the impact of the tidal waves may vary. Town and city structure, social networks, and fishing economies are examples of urban structures disrupted by these kinds of events.

It is important to recognize that the impact of these so-called natural disturbances on a particular location depends not only on the force of the natural event but on human modifications to the target environment.[72] The severity of huge floods on the Mississippi in 1927 and in 1993 were both affected by the presence of levees.[73] Indeed, the large historical floods of the Mississippi postdate the construction of continuous runs of levees along the river. The human and the natural combine to shape the catastrophic event. The severe fires in locations where chaparral areas interdigitate with housing in Mediterranean climates of the western United States, or in areas where residential areas have been built beneath canopies of forest types that periodically burn, are examples of hybrid disturbances.[74] The impact of the 1904 Baltimore fire, which destroyed sixty-four acres of the central business district, including masonry buildings that were thought secure, was greater than it would have been otherwise because the firefighting equipment brought from New York City and Philadelphia did not have fittings that could connect to the fire hydrants in Baltimore.[75] The fire was eventually extinguished only when the wind shifted and drove the fire to the banks of the Jones Falls stream, which acted as a firebreak.

Natural disturbances can reveal the social fault lines for which humans, not nature, are responsible. In the case of the Chicago heat wave disaster in 1995, Klinenberg examines and compares two adjacent residential areas with similar characteristics but sharp differences in death rates.[76] North Lawndale had nineteen heat-related deaths, a rate of forty per one hundred thousand residents, compared to South Lawndale, which had three deaths, a rate of fewer than four per one hundred thousand residents: a tenfold difference. However, these two communities had similar microclimates and numbers of seniors living alone and/or in poverty. Thus, the two communities naturally controlled for weather and the subpopulations of people that were thought to be most at risk of heat-related death.

Though these two areas were mostly composed of minority groups, the groups were significantly different. North Lawndale was 95 percent black, and South Lawndale was 85 percent Latino. Yet Klinenberg does not let that simple variation stand as the explanation. He digs into the underlying social-ecological patch structure, noting,

> Latinos in [South Lawndale] did not experience the particular constraints of ghettoization, the rapid and continuous abandonment of institutions and residents, or the arson and violence that contribute to the destruction of the local social ecology. The second reason is that . . . the area has become a magnet for Mexican and Central American migrants. . . . The continuous migration of Mexican Americans to this com-

munity area has replenished its human resources and regen-
erated the commercial economy of retailers and small local
businesses. . . . While North Lawndale lost more than half
of its population between 1979 and 1990, [South Lawndale]
grew by roughly 30 percent. . . . There are only a handful of
abandoned buildings and empty lots in the area.[77]

The result in terms of human health for North Lawndale and
South Lawndale was significant. In North Lawndale, the urban ecology
was one of weed-filled lots, vacant buildings, and widespread fear. In
North Lawndale, the seniors were confined to their homes in poorly
ventilated rooms and fearful to venture outside. In South Lawndale, the
active street life and functioning public and private places, such as shops
and supermarkets with air-conditioning, all made for accessible spaces
that the elderly did not need to fear. The linkage of trust and busy street
life sustained a sense of mutual protection in South Lawndale. This was
simply not the case in North Lawndale. In South Lawndale, the mutual
support and awareness reinforced on a daily basis created trust in the
safety of the busy streets and made that community far less dangerous
and more supportive in the heat wave crisis than in North Lawndale,
which did not have the same elements promoting social cohesion.

Klinenberg summarizes his social autopsy of the Chicago heat wave:

Previous studies of heat wave mortality have shown that
residents of places with high poverty, concentrated elderly
populations, poor housing and low vegetation are especially
vulnerable. . . . Several place-specific risk factors . . . such as
quality of public spaces, the vigor of street-level commercial
activity, the centralization of support networks and institutions, concern the social morphology of regions; others, such
as the loss of residents and the prevalence of seniors living
alone, concern population-level conditions. . . . The key reason that African Americans had the highest death rates . . .
is that they are the only group in the city segregated and
ghettoized in community areas with high levels of abandoned housing stock, empty lots, depleted commercial in-

frastructure, population decline, degraded sidewalks, parks and streets and impoverished institutions. Violent crime and active street-level drug markets, which are facilitated by these ecological conditions, exacerbate the difficulties of using public space and organizing effective support networks in such areas.[78]

Again, the ecological and the social conspire to shape the impact of a disturbance type normally thought of as natural and inexorable. Further, the impacts of a disturbance may vary among patch types. Some patch types might be more or less vulnerable and these differences may have significant consequences for the overall resilience of the patch mosaic.

Development in urban ecosystems has two direct physical impacts on urban structures. First, it may clear the existing physical urban fabric, as when land is cleared for urban renewal projects. Such land may remain unbuilt on for some time and introduce at least temporarily a new patch in the city. Within old urban areas, the land may be reclaimed by structures after a short or a long period. The demolition of unsuccessful public housing and the subsequent building of new convention centers, festival malls, hospitals, and schools are examples of development that first destroys and then adds new structures in cities. Second, development may add new structures in place of existing ones or on wild land that had not previously been developed. Agricultural land may also be converted to urban structures and infrastructure via development. Microclimate, biodiversity, hydrology, social structure, commuting patterns, and economic drivers may all change as a result of these kinds of development. Interestingly, the claim by development boosters that large projects such as sports arenas and conventions centers have an unmitigated positive effect within an urban area may not be well supported when all economic and social costs are tallied.[79]

Transportation infrastructure is one of the most conspicuous disturbance factors in the history of urban areas. In fact, urban historians commonly note the change in urban form that accompanied shifts in modes of transportation: from walking and horse to horse-drawn trams to cable and electrified trolleys to the gas-powered automobile.[80] The size and composition of urban patches shift along with these shifts in mode of transport. The development of subway or elevated mass transit lines in early twentieth-century cities was followed by new residential and commercial patches. More recently, the expansion of multilane freeways or motorways around relatively compact cities and the installation of exchanges on these highways led to the extension of suburban and exurban development.[81] Typically, patches of other infrastructure and modes of development, including office and industrial parks and regional shopping malls, follow the location of large intersections on controlled-access highways.

Development may extend to the planting of vegetation patches or establishment of open spaces within urban ecosystems.[82] Cities have been greatly affected by the establishment of large parks and parkways,[83] and then later by the conversion of some of these to high-speed transportation corridors or paved playgrounds. Patches created by ruderal vegetation can emerge in neglected yards and rights-of-way or in old disused industrial areas. The change in species composition, canopy closure, and canopy height are examples of within-patch change that can affect the surrounding areas through biophysical effects, unplanned beneficial or illegal use, and resultant social perception.

In all of these modes of patch creation, ranging from those controlled by humans or other organisms to natural physical disturbances, the time dimension is clearly important. How a particular disturbance impacts a system to create new patches or to change existing patches depends on the legacies of past conditions and events in the system. Similarly, how changes in the metabolism of an area can generate patches or drive patch change can be affected by prior conditions in the area. In cases of recent events, the effect of legacies may be clear. It is as though the implications of the event are unfolding in slow motion. In the case of Hurricane Katrina, the twin legacies of racial segregation and economic disadvantage clearly determined for whom and where the damage from flooding was greatest.[84] Careful historical analyses can unravel the telescoped legacies that affected past events, as John Barry does for the Mississippi flood of 1927.[85] He showed how politically and personally motivated engineering decisions concerning the use of levees alone to attempt to control flooding, and the social structures of the Delta, based so conspicuously on race and class, placed different groups in harm's way or in safe haven, or allowed different groups either to recover locally or to be encouraged to migrate. His analysis also exposes the institutional responses or failures to deliver promised remedies.

The current patch structure in cities can depend on legacies of metabolism or resource availability as well as on structures left by prior disturbances. The borders of certain developments in Baltimore reflect boundaries of colonial land grants.[86] The location of some of Baltimore's large parks reflects the locations of nineteenth-century industrialists' country estates. The correlation of toxic release inventory sites with white, working-class neighborhoods reflects the legacy of racial segregation and the amenity afforded Caucasians of living close to their manufacturing jobs.[87] Blacks were forced to live at greater distances from factories, resulting in lower correlation with toxic release inventory (TRI) sites in the present. Clearly, the existing patterns of de facto segregation in Baltimore is itself a legacy of past de jure patterns. Legacies are often, therefore, a part of the complex concatenation of events that create new patches in urban ecosystems.

For example, Kornblum examined the legacies of social institutions in his study of blue-collar communities in seven South Chicago neighborhoods.[88] He analyzed the shifting ethnic mixes over time and measured the flux from predominately Irish and Polish immigrants in 1900 to Polish in 1930 and Mexican, African American, and Polish in 1970. "In general, the entire South Chicago area is honeycombed by neighborhoods which differ according to ethnicity. Included among its residents are Serbians, Croatians, Poles, Italians, Scandinavians, Germans, Mexicans, and Blacks, who make up the main residential groups. . . . There is further segregation on the basis of generation of arrival in the city."[89] Kornblum found that this mix of ethnic groups was shaped by the social institutions established by prior generations. "In becoming involved in political contests, generations of South Chicago people have continually modified their definitions of who 'belongs' in the community. And through the negotiation of new primary groups in local politics, South Chicago people also create a blue collar culture which all local groups, even those who are initially the most feared, eventually come to share."[90] Thus, although ethnic groups may sustain their identity with their traditional religion, food, music, and language, the legacy of earlier political institutions promotes assimilation and development of shared identity and values.

PATCH ORGANIZATION

Patch dynamics is an important theoretical tool because it can accommodate the many ways in which elements of spatial heterogeneity interact with one another.[91] As we have said earlier, the organization of patches relative to one another can be treated as an aggregate, spatially inexplicit characteristic (richness, frequency, and average size and shape), or it can be treated as a spatially explicit configuration (adjacency and assembly). We will say more about how to quantify heterogeneity and patches in these two ways in chapter 6, using shared social and biophysical methods. However, it is important here to emphasize that patches constitute a mosaic, in which they may interact. Some processes will tie patches together in the mosaic, while other processes will be relatively confined to specific patches or patch types. Patch dynamics, although sensitive to the features and dynamics of individual patches, gains its real power in addressing the behavior of patch arrays or mosaics[92] interacting within and between levels of organization.

Patch mosaics and patches can be hierarchical models of social-ecological heterogeneity. In other words, a patch observed at a particular scale may be broken down into other, smaller patches that are resolved at finer scales.[93] Likewise, the original patch may be a part of a larger patch resolved at a coarser scale. A neighborhood that can be resolved at the scale of city blocks is made up of patches of individual parcels or groups of similar parcels. That same neighborhood may be one of several that make up a district in an urban ecosystem. This example is a spatially explicit hierarchy of heterogeneity. A specific mosaic of patches at a given scale is resolved into a mosaic of finer scale patches or becomes part of a coarser-scale mosaic. The spatial configuration of the patches is maintained throughout the hierarchy.

It is possible also to model heterogeneity as spatially inexplicit patch hierarchies. For instance, a city park system may be disaggregated into forest parks, soccer fields, baseball diamonds, meadows, arboreta, parkways, and boulevards. The spatial configuration is not necessarily maintained as different kinds of parcels are related to larger units. This kind of hierarchy is one of classification rather than one of content.

In spite of the fact that it is possible to model heterogeneity without regard to configuration, we find that models that retain information about the arrangement of patches are the most powerful. Such models can deal with the form and regulation of interaction of patches. This is because the nature of the specific contrasts between patches and the nature of the boundaries between them are crucial factors controlling the fluxes among patches and, hence, the flows throughout an entire mosaic.[94]

Patch contrasts within urban ecosystems can be based on a variety of factors. For example, topographic heterogeneity defines patches in some hilly cities, such as Pittsburgh, Pennsylvania, Cincinnati, Ohio, or Oakland, California. Even in Baltimore, the large forest parks are associated with the major stream valleys in the city. Classically, in Baltimore, the wealthy lived on higher ground, leaving the coastal fringes to the working class. Architecture and housing density differ between those patches.

Flows between patches are of several types and are regulated by different factors. Social flows may be regulated by convention and socially defined symbols such as dress and accent. Lynch's famous surveys of urban residents' mental maps in Boston illustrate the kind of social boundaries citizens respond to and how their perceptions define boundaries.[95] Biophysical flows may be regulated by differences in vegetation structure between two patches or by the nature of infrastructure. For example, as more and more wealthy Baltimoreans reside in patches of new developments on the waterfront, the accumulation of floating refuse from patches upstream via storm drains and receiving streams has become an economic and political concern.

These examples show the importance of joining a patch perspective of cities with a network perspective.[96] In biophysical ecology, the importance of certain patch types as conduits for flows is recognized. Such patches are sometimes called corridors because of their shape and demonstration or assumption of function.[97] What kinds of patch might serve as a corridor depends on the structure recognized and the function of interest. For example, a long narrow forest strip between two larger forest patches is for some organisms a connector. For other organisms, such as those that require shady, moist, and quiet forest interior, such a long narrow strip bordered by meadow or settlement is no corridor at all. In fact, for such organisms, it effectively does not exist because it is bright, dry, and invaded by the noises from outside, which either interfere with their communication or signal risk. Generalist species may well use the thin connecting patch as a corridor if they are unaffected by the environmental conditions that exist within it.

This narrow corridor between forests can act as a barrier between the two meadows on either side of it. Oldfield organisms may be confined to one side or the other. Children may be instructed not to go through the hedgerow to the threatening, unknown territory beyond. The point is that the configuration of patches, along with their structure, determines what function they actually perform in a mosaic.[98]

Long narrow connecting patches, or bypassing patches, are conspicuous parts of cities. Highways, sewers, train lines, and certain pedestrian pathways are important networks in urban areas. Like the biophysical corridors described above, they can function to connect certain patches and separate others. The street grid of a city established before the advent of private automobile commuting may be an integral part of the city's patch mosaic, while new transportation corridors may have a different relationship to the neighboring patches.[99] A rail trail through a metropolitan region may not actually connect effectively with the patches along it. Elevated motorways may sever neighborhoods and cut off residents from commercial or social amenities they once enjoyed. Service infrastructure also connects and disconnects patches in new, three-dimensional ways. Storm sewers and sanitary sewers are notoriously leaky structures. Since in many cities where stream valleys remain an important topographical feature, those valleys are the location of the storm and sanitary sewer trunk lines and exchanges of surface stream water, sanitary drainage, and storm drain flow may be important.[100] For instance, leakage from water supply pipes may define base flow in some urban streams. Subterranean leaks or manhole overflows can contaminate surface streams. Surface stream flow may disappear into adjacent storm drains, only to appear as a subsidy in downstream areas. Bypassing the surface stream and floodplain processes can rob these waters of an important mechanism for removing nitrate pollution,[101] as we will see in chapter 6. Exactly how the elements of the patch mosaic are arranged and how they are connected by patch types that represent networks are crucial elements of spatial heterogeneity.

In social mosaics, the flow of information or influence becomes an important functional connection between patches that reflects patch organization. Police departments with limited resources may classify regions of a city in terms of priority for answering calls. Green zones may be relatively stable and secure areas, in which all calls are answered in an effort to keep crime low. Red zones may be judged to be crime-ridden areas, in which only the most desperate calls are answered. Yellow zones may receive a priority based on what areas they border. A yellow zone abutting a green zone may receive greater police attention than a yellow zone bordering a red zone. Although this is manifestly an unjust allocation of urban resources, it illustrates the importance of patch configuration. Members of the real estate industry would, of course, refer to this feature of patch mosaics as their cardinal rule: "Location, location, location."

Depending on the function of interest, a patch may serve as a source of a thing or process, a sink, a conduit, or be neutral to the flow.[102] How a patch mosaic is recognized in an urban ecological system depends on these research decisions, or on the perspectives of the practitioners and residents. A city may be represented by many different mosaics, each with its own focal flow or structure.

An important tool for dealing with the heterogeneity that urban ecosystems often exhibit is patch classification.[103] There are many ways to classify patches in settlements. One of the most common is that proposed by Anderson and his colleagues.[104] This classification was established in contrast to the demographic- and human density–based classifications of geography, because the human-based classification did not permit natural resource managers to understand lands beyond cities. The classification divides patch types into those that are primarily vegetated and those that are primarily urbanized. Within the urban mosaic, Anderson-type classifications typically recognize residential, commercial-industrial, transportation, waste, barren, and water. Some modifications of the Anderson system recognize three different densities of residential. Forest land and agricultural fields are also classified within urban areas. The Food and Agriculture Organization (FAO) has

proposed a basically similar kind of classification for the entire world.[105]
The basic philosophy of separating vegetated from built patches is retained in the FAO classification.

Although these familiar classifications separate urban lands from
vegetated lands, they confound land cover and land use. This makes
them unsuitable for some research questions in which the relationship
between structure of land cover and various biophysical or social functions is to be examined. The need for a classification that can serve this
research need, while recognizing the fine grain of urban heterogeneity
and allowing researchers to "see" hybrid social and biophysical patches,
has stimulated a new approach to patch classification in urban systems.

Cadenasso and colleagues have proposed a radically different classification, based on a different theoretical assumption than the Anderson
and FAOs classifications.[106] Cadenasso started with the assumption that
in urban systems, patch types can in fact be a combination of built and
vegetated features. A tour through any variety of urban areas, especially
if the tour includes back gardens and interiors of blocks in addition to
streets and parks, reveals the poverty of the assumption that urban and
vegetated are incompatible, mutually exclusive categories. Street and
road margins, lawns, meadows and oldfields, scrubland, forest stands
in parks and on institutional grounds, community gardens, embedded
farms, and many other forms of vegetation cover, both low and tall, can
be found in cities and suburbs as well as in the countryside. Such vegetation includes planted, wild remnants, ruderal volunteers, and managed
components. Of course, such elements of vegetation will be adjacent to
or overtop buildings and paved areas. As green roofs become a more
common architectural element, the hybrid nature of urban patches will
become all the more obvious.

Cadenasso's classification is labeled high ecological resolution classification for urban landscapes and environmental systems—HERCULES
(figure 3.1). It consists of six axes along which any patch of urban land
can be characterized: (1) building type, (2) proportion of patch occupied
by building cover, (3) presence and proportion of woody vegetation, (4)
presence and proportion of herbaceous vegetation, (5) presence and proportion of pavement, and (6) presence and proportion of bare soil. Analyses reveal that the fine categorical resolution of HERCULES is highly

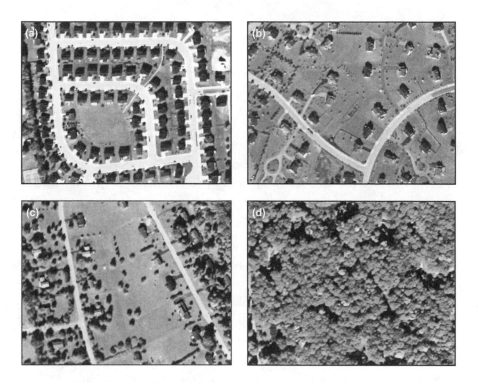

Figure 3.1. Examples of distinct HERCULES patches: (a) and (b) are differentiated by building density, although woody and herbaceous vegetation densities are the same; (c) and (d) are differentiated by density of woody and herbaceous vegetation, but building density is the same.

appropriate to the heterogeneity of urban lands. This heterogeneity is remarkably fine grained, and the Anderson-derived classifications fail to account for it even when applied to high spatial resolution imagery.[107]

HERCULES is a structural classification that does not make judgments about the use or social structure of the urban patchiness it recognizes. Social or political heterogeneity is best dealt with using data sets that are aimed specifically at these sources of heterogeneity. More will be said about these kinds of data and analyses in chapter 5. However, it is sufficient here to note some of the ways in which primarily social patchiness can be classified.

The classical way to deal with social heterogeneity in the United

States is through the major variables collected by the U.S. Census Bureau. Other countries collect similar demographic data. The major variables are population size, sex and age structure, ethnicity and national origin, education, income, home ownership, and employment. Variables are collected on the basis of households, but to protect people's privacy, data are aggregated and summarized with different units of analysis such as block groups, tracts, and more coarse units of analysis. Ancillary variables are associated with the census over various periods of its history. However, the core variables are essentially consistent through time.

New variables are available from other sources and are collected for different purposes than the census. Notable variables are collected by other institutions, such as the insurance industry or firms specializing in geographically focused market classification or segmentation systems based upon differences in household purchasing decisions, for instance. Insurance maps provide detailed data on housing age and building material. The marketing industry summarizes purchasing behaviors via point of purchase receipts and other survey methods.[108] These data are combined, along with information from the census, into descriptions of consumption behaviors and lifestyles that are present in different areas.[109]

The two major kinds of social data outlined above can be considered to be motivated by different social theories. The standard demographic data of the census relate to social theories of livelihoods and society as a productive entity. The census measures the human and social capital that can be applied to agricultural and industrial production. It is appropriate that this data set was mandated constitutionally by a new republic that was attempting to organize its resources and peoples to become a productive and viable nation on the world stage. Of course, other organizational tactics were applied to this problem, such as public education and the gridding and opening of federal lands to individual settlement, but the understanding of the basic human resources of the nation was a fundamental need. The basic theory is capitalism of industrial production and, of course, its Marxist response.

The second kind of data, that of the marketing cluster approach, is related to a different set of social theories associated with lifestyles and consumption. As the United States—and, indeed other industrial societies—has shifted to a service and consumption base, different kinds of data are required to fuel the models and predictions that business-people and policy makers desire.[110] Such models depend upon theories of capitalism based on consumption, with its corollary of geodemographic market segmentation, to generate interest in novel consumer products and services. The shift to a consumption economy was related to the spread of suburbanization, the growth of freeways, the establishment of the real estate industry as an economic force, the rise and identity of the middle class as opposed to the working class, the shift from factory to management and service employment, the growth of the personal automobile as the dominant mode of transit, the philosophy of obsolescence, and the increase in globalization.[111] This complex combination of causes, among others, signals a new way to think about and classify the organization of the social mosaic of the metropolis.

One level of social-ecological organization that frequently emerges is the neighborhood. Neighborhoods can be understood as villages and each village can be examined on its own and in relation to other villages. This is not to use the idealized "rural village" as a foil to the urban neighborhood as village. Rather, it is to use the concept of an urban mosaic of villages to advance the idea that urban neighborhoods may be usefully understood as villages in order to distill some essential properties of social behavior of urban neighborhoods. Unlike rural villages, however, which are separated by surrounding agricultural and forested lands, urban neighborhoods may be tightly packed, side by side. In addition, urban neighborhoods are an important intermediary unit between individuals and households and larger units of formal governance. The spatial structure of neighbors can be important for understanding the social dynamics of neighborhoods. Both Jane Jacobs and Steven Johnson have observed that emergent behaviors can result from thousands of individuals and a few simple rules of interaction that can create a familiar but complex choreography of interactions among strangers, producing routine social order, cohesion, trust, and safety.[112]

PATCH CHANGE

Patches change in several ways. They can change in structure or function. In biophysical ecology, patch change is due to the growth of the organisms that characterize a patch or the succession of communities from one kind to another. Patches can, as we have seen in the discussion of disturbance, change because of external influences as well, or when fluxes of materials or energy enter them from another patch and alter the resource levels or stresses present in a patch. Social succession is also a possible source of patch change, as are external influences and social fluxes. We will examine cases of urban patch change below.

Succession in urban patches can be due to the growth and senescence of vegetation, just as it can in biophysical patches. Trees and shrubs, either planted or migrating into patches on their own, can change patch structure. Such changes would be reflected in recognizing different patch types in the HERCULES classification, for example. Likewise, lawns change as thatch and soil organic matter increase with age.[113]

Social succession is illustrated by the maturation of families and the shifts of neighborhoods to predominance by empty nesters. Sometimes, social succession also occurs when new migrant groups move into a neighborhood or when factories close and employment and commuting patterns of residents change as a result. Succession in social processes can also be the result of changes in the "maturity" of institutions.[114] A neighborhood savings and loan may be purchased by a national or indeed international bank, and shift its role in a community as a result.

Social patch change can also reflect fashion. In Baltimore, the wealthy had traditionally lived on the higher ground. Now, however, as the city shifts from a working port and industrial economy and population sprawls out into the suburbs, some members of the upper classes are claiming the low ground as new luxury condominiums are being built along the shores of the harbor and warehouses are being converted into lofts and well-appointed apartments.

Infrastructural change also causes patch change. The deterioration over time of sewer and water supply systems and housing stock are examples. The old row house architecture of Baltimore was built to house factory workers, dock workers, and their managers and the merchants who served those industries.[115] A tacit assumption was that occupants would have the skills or wealth to maintain their homes. Now that most

Baltimore housing is occupied by professional residents, the middle class employed in service and administrative roles, or the poor, this assumption is no longer valid. Most people have neither the skills nor the resources to maintain the old housing stock in the city. In underserved neighborhoods, the added factor of absentee landlords has exacerbated the normal wear and tear on housing stock. A telling pattern of change in housing stock is seen in neighborhoods experiencing marginal investment. In such neighborhoods, the larger houses appear to be the first to decline to the point of abandonment. These are the first to be divided into apartments and occupied by renters rather than owners. Where once these houses were the jewels of the block, they are now the eyesores. Patch change often follows the decline of these buildings.

Industrial succession has a role to play in patch change as well. Again, using the example of Baltimore, an old harbor city, the use of dockside industrial sites has shifted over time. Baltimore's first deep-water port was established in the 1700s in Fell's Point. As the shipping industry shifted to larger vessels, this small area proved unsuitable to dock them. The majority of port activity shifted to other areas in the city. Ultimately, maritime industry abandoned Fell's Point, although the roots of the area in entertaining sailors ashore prepared it for the tourist and local entertainment businesses that now exist there.

Because so much of industrial activity is now globally rather than locally controlled, industrial succession in American cities usually means abandonment at this point. Although the port activity in Baltimore shifted to other patches in the city and county, accompanied by developing railroad and shipping technologies, many of the industries that now survive in Baltimore are based on generating and sharing academic and medical knowledge, providing medical services, and tourism. The kinds of structures and social relationships needed to drive those industries show themselves in developing patch structures in the city and county.

The examples of industrial succession illustrate the effect of both structural and functional changes in patch types. On one hand, the shift from shipping to entertainment in Fell's Point retains much of the physical structure of the neighborhood, although its social and economic function are now much different than two hundred years ago. On the other hand, the shifts from heavy manufacturing, such as steel, tanks, bombers, and autos, to the generation and delivery of medical knowledge have resulted in major physical patch changes. The conversion of brownfield and declining residential patches to medical research and hospital buildings and the replacement of low-income by middle-class housing to serve the research function are examples of physical patch changes.

Patches do not change in isolation. As we have noted before, they occur as mosaics in which they can interact and affect one another as well as the mosaic as a whole and organizational levels above and below. Changes in one patch within an urban matrix are often associated with changes in other patches, sometimes distant ones. The status of certain residential and commercial patches in the city center is tied to that of residential and commercial patches in the suburbs. Social theory recognizes this by citing both push and pull factors in explaining the changing status of suburban and central city patches.[116] The reduced investment in certain central city patches results from factors that push residents and investors out of some of those patches—poor schools, poor services, high crime. At the same time, certain suburban patches exert a "pull" on investors and residents, through factors such as availability of open space, schools with better reputations, proximity to nonindustrial employment, and so on. The whole mosaic of patches and patch types shows a shifting pattern as a result of these push and pull factors.

New patches are introduced in the form of such developments as transportation corridors and regional malls. Old patches, such as those that characterized rural villages now being subsumed into a growing suburb, are converted to new forms and uses. For example, residential structures on the village main street are expanded and converted to commercial use with new parking lots surrounding them, rather than the green yards and mature trees of their village incarnation. Agricultural fields, hedgerows, and woodlots give way to condos, tract houses, luxury estates, and the shopping, schools, and offices that accompany them. Contemporary urbanization is the very essence of change in a mosaic of patches.[117]

Patch change is driven by the same kinds of factors that create patches. These factors can be either metabolic—that is, they deal with the transformation of material, energy, and information in systems—or structural—that is, they deal with the way the components of a system are put together: system architecture. Abrupt structural changes to system architecture are known in biophysical ecology as disturbances. Origin of patches can therefore be attributable to both abrupt and gradual changes in metabolism within patches, and to abrupt changes in structure within patches. As we discussed earlier, abrupt structural changes, or disturbances, can extend beyond patch boundaries and affect parts or all of several patches. We have not always tried to separate metabolic or functional alterations from disturbances since the two are often closely linked in complex causal relationships. Stress to metabolism can lead to structural disruption, and structural disturbances can result in metabolic stresses. The examples of patch change and mosaic change we have laid out above show these complex interactions routinely. Organisms, humans, and human institutions can act as metabolic and disturbance agents. Physical disturbances include the construction associated with development, natural disturbances, and social disruptions. Often these are associated with one another or are linked through various interactions. It is crucial to construct a model of the linked events that lead to patch change, rather than try to see the whole history as a single point in time.

We close this section by reminding ourselves of one of the most powerful complexes of human activities, acting in heterogeneous ways, that affects urban patch change. Investment and disinvestment are particularly powerful drivers of patch change in the contemporary global service economy that now dominates capital exchange.[118] The fluxes of material, energy, people, and capital across patch boundaries, through the mediation of the structure of those boundaries or the network of patches specifically designed to facilitate exchange, are important agents of patch and mosaic change. The distribution between economic investment and disinvestment across metropolitan space pushes and pulls the concentration of human population, of human groups, and of human institutions across an urban region. Governmental subsidies in the form of transportation infrastructure, energy exploitation and taxation, the infrastructure to deal with water and other material resource delivery and waste removal, creation of amenities such as parks, and economic incentives for development or redevelopment are major contextual drivers. The disposition of manufacturing, service, consumption, and investment decisions across many nations also affects the form of local urban development and patch condition. Plants, pests, pollution, and other ecosystem components that people see as amenities and disamenities are redistributed along with the economic and development decisions in the metropolis.[119]

The bundle of drivers affecting urban patch change has much to do with real estate in all its forms and implications. Just as President Eisenhower cautioned at the end of World War II about the perverse effects of the military-industrial complex on American society and political life, so too have contemporary observers noted the significance of the real estate industrial complex.[120] Bundled in this are institutional, commercial, and governmental concerns that

- provide extended regional transportation and utility networks;
- acquire land for development;
- negotiate the regulatory shoals of local and regional authorities and government agencies;
- build houses and provide new appliances for them;
- generate new commercial and business centers on the urban fringe and in old suburbs ripe for redevelopment;
- provide and guarantee mortgages for new housing.

Also closely related is the increasing combined role of the shift from a production economy to a consumption economy incorporating marketing theory and data, media representations of lifestyles, and advertising. The real estate industry appears to have taken over the integrative economic role of the military-industrial complex. The development desired by this industry is linked to the consumer economy and its global industrial manufacturing and financial components. It is indeed a complex that embraces features as seemingly disparate as the culture of the automobile and the role of the media in defining lifestyle groups.

Summary

From our summary of key concepts in chapter 2, we concluded that a number of concerns could be captured in an analysis of how different types of drivers of organizational complexity had been treated. We noted that three types of organizational complexity emerged when different levels of hierarchical detail and different scales of influence were considered. One type of contrast was top-down and bottom-up drivers. Some scholars proposed top-down control of social organization while others emphasized patterns emerging from the bottom up due to actions of individual actors and institutions.

A second type of driver concerned the relative effects of collective and individual action. For instance, the classical studies of the Chicago School focused on the integration of new immigrant groups from overseas and the American South and emphasized collective action. Other researchers focused on the choice of individuals and households about where to settle and emphasized the disaggregated nature of decision making in urban pattern formation.

A third type of driver pointed to differences in internal versus external control of structures and processes found within a certain area. Internal dynamics were underscored by those who studied the role of neighborhood social cohesion on the ability of residents of a patch to respond to stresses and opportunities from both within and external to the neighborhood. Other researchers indicated that outside influences and forces may be more powerful than internal dynamics in structuring and organizing the biophysical and social conditions and aggregations within patches. Natural disturbances, federal policies and regulations, and the global reach of corporate decisions are examples of outside influences.

Whether urban systems are seen as static or dynamic is another major type of complexity: temporal complexity. Some researchers point to the persistent structures and legacies of urban systems, noting the role of anchoring institutions, functions, and landmarks in the city. Others, perhaps the majority, focus on the agents and causes of change in metropolitan systems. Given that the period over which urban studies have emerged has been one of rapid and widespread change in cities worldwide, this dynamic emphasis is not surprising. However, different studies have described a very broad range of temporal perspectives, including legacies, lags, and slow and fast rates of change.

Organizational and temporal concerns for understanding the structures and processes of urban social-ecological systems are quite compatible with the spatially explicit approach to patch dynamics laid out in this chapter. First, because patch dynamics recognizes organizational complexity, it can accommodate both top-down and bottom-up causation. Second, individual and collective action also fit within a patch dynamics perspective. Patch dynamics accepts that individual agents, such as households, can affect patch change, and so can collective actions, such as policy making or management entities. Third, external and internal control are both featured in patch dynamics. Flux across a patch mosaic, conditioned by boundaries among patches or by certain specific patch behaviors, is accommodated by patch dynamics. Fluxes of energy, matter, information, and organisms, including people, are commonly seen in patch mosaics. Specific models for the structure of those flows and the interventions of patch boundaries or gradients in those flows are a product of the patch dynamics perspective. Here especially, spatial configuration of patches in a mosaic is a critical attribute for understanding fluxes. Fourth, although the patch dynamics approach includes the term *dynamics* in its label and focuses on temporal complexity, a patch dynamics approach can accept static patterns, legacies, or very slow rates of change as special cases or spatially localized conditions. In other words, different types and rates of dynamism can be incorporated into a patch dynamics approach.

Thus, a patch dynamics approach serves as a useful and well-developed conceptual tool for integrating contemporary perspectives from both the biophysical and social sciences. It addresses causes and effects, patterns and processes in terms of spatial heterogeneity, multiple levels of organization, and different types of change over the long term. These features are essential for advancing our understanding of urban social-ecological systems. Furthermore, we recognize that Baltimore is not the only city relevant to urban ecology. There are several thousand cities in the world with more than 150,000 people, all with legacies, challenges, and opportunities. A patch dynamics approach can be useful to understand each of these urban systems.

From Baltimore to Bangkok

Interdisciplinary Issues and Strategies

Bangkok, City of Angels

Bangkok sprawls on the humid alluvial plain, only one and one-half meters above sea level. The ancient town was a way station on the road to Ayutthaya, the capital of Siam, as Thailand was known until the 1930s. The settlement was a small village, *bang,* populated by farmers caring for their *kok* trees. When Ayutthaya was sacked by the Burmese in 1767, the capital was emptied of population, going from 1 million residents to approximately ten thousand survivors, and reduced to rubble, ruins, and ash.

Rama I eventually took power as monarch and began to reestablish the Thai kingdom. He moved to rebuild Ayutthaya on the location of the Bangkok village. Started in 1782, the new capital grew steadily; brick from the ancient city was transported downriver for reconstruction. The new city was organized around perpetual water and seasonal flooding. The *klongs,* or canals, attuned the historical city to its floodplain environment, organized its rich culture and driving economy, and diverted the seasonal flooding, or at least a bearable portion of it.

By circa 1950 the modern city had reclaimed the original population size of ancient Ayutthaya and boasted nearly one hundred navigable klongs. Industrial exuberance, lack of planning, the cold war and alliance with the United States during the Vietnam War, and conversion to an automobile-based transport system led to decades of canal neglect and road construction that reduced the number of klongs, raised the human population to over 10 million, and forever altered the ecology of the city.

To foreigners, Bangkok can appear to be "a perfect bedlam." To the Thai, it retains its ancient and permanent title Krung Thep, City of Angels. And in both its transformation and shimmering permanence, the City of Angels is a parable for interdisciplinary understanding of urban ecological systems.

Consider the challenges of conserving—even expanding—high-quality ecosystem services within contemporary urban ecological systems. The provision of clean water, clean air, adequate open space, moderation of climate, and other services is both essential and demanding. Bangkok's 10 million residents produce 2.4 million cubic meters of wastewater per day and only 20 percent is treated. The result is frightful: "Tossed into the brew are toxic chemicals, restaurant discharges, paper, cans, dead farm animals—and the occasional human corpse. Bacteria contamination is everywhere from 75 to 400 times above permissible limits."[1]

Belying the assumption that only the poor suffer the consequences is the fate of Thai pop star Apichet Kittkomcharren (aka Big D2B). In July 2003, he accidentally drove his BMW into a klong. Rescued by bystanders, he was expected to recover. Instead, a lethal fungus from the polluted klong led to hemorrhage, repeated brain operations, coma, and death.

At the same time, government projects for controlling flooding, the continued expansion of wastewater infrastructure, and the development of the Bangkok Metropolitan Flood Control center all attempted to mitigate the rising level of ecological stress. Less than a year after pop star Big drove into the fetid canal, the king of Thailand received the Habitat Scroll of Honor Award from the UN for water-related projects. Bangkok remains both a perfect bedlam and Krung Thep.

Overview

In attempting to understand the complexities of urban ecological systems, narrow disciplinary approaches appear myopic, minimalist, and incremental. Under the harshest of light, biology is largely proxy, as it does not confront the driving forces that perpetuate and pertubate

urban ecological systems—in-migration from the hinterlands, industrial expansion, consumerist capitalism, and overreaching technology,
among others. Sociology is partially delusion in its avoidance of base
conditions, ecological processes not conducive to "social meaning," such
as the epidemiologically dangerous klongs, or the constraints on social
systems created by biological ecosystems. Even further, neoclassical economics can be seen as a kind of trafficking, with little attention to the
cultural or moral values that underlie human choices. Proxy, delusion,
and trafficking do not seem useful foundations for a true urban ecology.

Instead, interdisciplinary strategies hold the best chances for understanding and progress, creation of usable knowledge, and effective
application of adaptive management. For patch dynamics, with its focus
on disturbance regimes, the dynamicism of relationships among patches,
and attention to scalar hierarchical interactions, interdisciplinary strategies are essential. The "new paradigm" in ecology that provides the foundation for patch dynamics hints at the interdisciplinary imperative: "A
new ecological paradigm has emerged that recognizes ecological systems
to be open, regulated by events outside of their boundaries, lacking or
prevented from attaining a stable point equilibrium, affected by natural
disturbance and incorporating humans and their effects."[2]

In this chapter, we examine the interdisciplinary issues and strategies relevant to a patch dynamics approach as it is applied to urban
ecological systems. Many of the issues are common to a wide range of
interdisciplinary research topics and fields. Some are specific to patch
dynamics. A few are specific to patch dynamics applied to urban ecological systems. Based upon this assessment, we review the benefits and
burdens of interdisciplinary research as practiced using patch dynamics.
We suggest some practical mechanics or effective practices to encourage
successful programs of research. Our belief is that an interdisciplinary
patch dynamics approach can invigorate studies of urban ecological systems and confront the essential issues of twenty-first century cities.

The Standard Litany of Difficulty

There is a standard litany of difficulty associated with doing interdisciplinary research. First, it is difficult. There is a pressing need for com-

mon language, made even more challenging by the use of metaphor.[3] Terms like *community, competition, evolution,* and others can, and often do, mean very different things within disciplines. Imagine the difficulty of constructing a definitive glossary of ecological terms acceptable to biophysical and social science researchers.

Difficulties extend beyond language and include the challenge of merging fundamentally different theories across different paradigms and epistemologies.[4] Assumptions vary, as do the capacity of researchers to understand the methods and traditions of researchers from other disciplines.[5] Such differences in understanding can, of course, spill over into difficulties of group interaction. Interdisciplinary research teams can display a significant lack of patience, trust, and respect, as well as varying depths of commitment and disagreement over the ownership of ideas and more.[6]

There are also institutional difficulties of organization and logistics. These include the effort required to assemble an interdisciplinary program, the time demands for learning the rudiments of partner disciplines, and the commitment required to develop mutual understanding and willingness to synthesize new ideas, concepts, theories, methods, data, and conclusions.[7] Strong organizational and structural constraints are commonly featured as key difficulties. The doctoral degree system at research universities encourages both specialization and Thorstein Veblen's "trained incapacities." Even the spatial separation of potential collaborators within the same university, college, or office building can act as a barrier to communication.[8] Hierarchical power structures, concentrated authority for decision making, and even "departmental chauvinism"[9] have limited the free trade of ideas and encouraged intellectual protectionism. Daily and Ehrlich note in a rapid series of economic metaphors: "Channels developed to direct flows of capital into university schools and departments; infrastructure and discipline-oriented reward systems were established, and positive feedbacks favoring established disciplines naturally developed, amplifying the career value of a disciplinary focus and deepening the channels controlling resource flows."[10]

A second charge is that interdisciplinary research is "out of the mainstream." Interdisciplinary research is often considered that way because of the proven reliability of the disciplinary sciences,[11] the difficulty of even defining levels of interdisciplinarity,[12] the problems created by interdisciplinary research in the scientific publication review process,[13] and the perceived threat to established disciplinary knowledge development and funding.[14]

The issue of time is a key element in the litany: interdisciplinary research is claimed to take too much of it. Time is needed to learn other disciplines' language and meanings, overcome the potential difficulties of group processes, conduct interdisciplinary analysis of data, and report these results through collaborative writing.[15] The overconsumption of time, or at least its increased consumption that is required to participate in interdisciplinary research, can extend from problem definition and project design all the way to publication.[16] In addition to time consumption, interdisciplinary research can require sophisticated and carefully negotiated *timing*. For example, the challenge of providing the interdisciplinary research team with needed data from one discipline to another at the optimal stage of the research project can be daunting, even if issues of mutual understanding, shared protocols, and other facets of the research enterprise are agreed upon.[17]

The litany includes the third charge that interdisciplinary research is "methodologically challenged." In particular, the lack of existing and robust conceptual frameworks means that theorizing and hypothesis making is often divorced from a clear and articulate interdisciplinary framework—hence the charge of ad hoc and fragmented efforts at advancing theory. Similarly, the lack of a common set of protocols, procedures, and research techniques, which Turner and Carpenter describe as having "no cookbooks," makes methodologically rigorous interdisciplinary work even more difficult.[18] An example is the problem of differential scales. Mismatches of time and space scales arising out of the varying disciplinary traditions and techniques can thwart precision and accuracy, and make integration problematic.[19]

If interdisciplinary research is charged in the litany of difficulty as being methodologically challenged, it follows that the litany includes the claim that interdisciplinary research can be scientifically suspect. Issues range from too much knowledge necessary for requisite interdisciplinary expertise, which Daily and Ehrlich call the "No Renaissance People Principle";[20] its close corollary that interdisciplinarians must therefore be less competent;[21] and the general perceived lack of depth in interdisciplinary studies.[22]

The merging of inductive-qualitative approaches with deductive-quantitative procedures adds suspicion, mostly by the deductive-quantitative practitioners, but it can go both ways. In particular is the challenge that inductive approaches are undervalued in ecology.[23] There is also the cloud of murky evaluation. It is difficult to evaluate the comparative quality of interdisciplinary research, and few efforts or criteria exist for such evaluation.[24] Hence, assessment remains at the level of component disciplines, with overall interdisciplinary programs neither evaluated nor legitimized.

Finally, the litany of difficulty is also personal. Interdisciplinary research can be seen as career threatening. The publish-or-perish demands of professorship combined with the disciplinary command and control of the scientific publication system make for difficult career choices: "Finding appropriate places to publish interdisciplinary research is a more difficult problem. Most journals that publish interdisciplinary work are relatively new and do not (yet) have large readerships or world-class reputations. This makes it hard to reach desired audiences; it also makes it difficult for young interdisciplinary scientists to acquire the publishing credentials required for promotion and tenure. Right now one more over-examination of a trivial issue published in *Ecology, Science, The American Economic View,* or *Current Anthropology* will count more with a department chair than a path-breaking article in *Ecosystems.* Sad, but true."[25]

In addition, issues of tenure evaluation, promotion, and reward-for-work are raised as problematic. Interdisciplinary research has applied value and usefulness, and is often responsive to public concerns. This strength often leads the committed researcher to engage in public education, serve on multiple university and other committees, coteach or teach in departments other than their own, and engage in activities that the academy, and in particular its administrators, have found difficult to consider, credit, or encourage.

Given this long and sober litany of difficulty, why attempt interdisciplinary research and, specifically, why apply its strategies to the patch dynamics of urban ecological systems? To answer these questions, we begin by defining, in working terms, interdisciplinary research.

A Definition of Interdisciplinary Research

There are almost as many definitions of interdisciplinary research as there are interdisciplinary researchers, and they range from vague ("linking different disciplines") to reasonably specific. The National Academy of Science's definition is representative and comprehensive: "Interdisciplinary research (IDR) is a mode of research by teams or individuals that integrates information, data, techniques, tools, perspectives, concepts, and/or theories from two or more disciplines or bodies of specialized knowledge to advance fundamental understanding or to solve problems whose solutions are beyond the scope of a single discipline or area of research practice."[26]

This definition suggests, and we concur, that interdisciplinary research is created when multiple disciplines are integrated during the full range or cycle of the research process. For patch dynamics applied to urban ecological systems, this would first include *problem recognition,* understanding complex urban ecological patterns and processes; and *theory,* a merging of bioecological and socioeconomic theories to explain complex urban ecological patterns and processes. It would also include *methods,* the collection of urban ecological data through the widest variety of scientific methodologies and at scales suitable to patch dynamics; *analysis,* the blending of analytical techniques from different disciplines; and the *application* of results, the transfer of patch dynamics insights to general ecology, urban ecology, other physical, biological, social, and engineering sciences, and policy and management.

Consider the challenges and opportunities of interdisciplinary problem recognition. A substantive list of core research problems can be addressed by interdisciplinary patch dynamics—including multiple scale effects and their emergent properties, interaction of multiple levels of organizations and agents, interrelationships of fast- and slow-acting variables, and more. Interdisciplinary patch dynamics may be particularly useful for the analysis of open complex ecological systems, where inputs and outputs flux in different sizes, speeds, and patterns. By articulating urban ecological system research problems in terms that several disciplines can contribute to through their base of knowledge, problem recognition can better reflect the true complexity of urban ecological systems.

Similar arguments can be made for the other stages of the research process. One of the difficulties described earlier in the litany is that few evaluation criteria exist to identify or decant true interdisciplinary research from the more vague, and common, interdisciplinary "teams," "projects," or "programs." In many of these efforts, interdisciplinary enthusiasm gives way to traditional disciplinary confidence somewhere early in the study design or data collection stages, only to be rediscovered during application of results or requests for additional funding.

We suggest a simple yet formidable test. Interdisciplinary research occurs when at least some of the independent, intervening, and dependent variables in a specific hypothesis being tested are derived from the specialized knowledge of different disciplines. There is no requirement that all three variable sets—independent, intervening, and dependent—be interdisciplinary, only that at least some of the variables in the hypothesis be taken from different disciplines. For an example, we return to Bangkok.

The quality of Bangkok's water supply is both essential for public health and a largely biogeochemical condition. Water quality can be measured in terms of chemical composition (mg chemical per liter), suspended solids (millions of tons per year), and so forth. As a dependent variable in urban ecological system research, water quality can be largely derived from the biophysical sciences, particularly studies of water chemistry and human biological response to disease pathogens (figure 4.1).

Intervening variables that influence Bangkok's water quality are numerous and varied. They include increased human population and per capita waste generation (liters per day per capita), loss of canals (km^3 volume per year), spatial differentiation of population into patches—the poor living near the remaining klongs with limited or no waste treatment—and the resulting concentration of waste. At least some of these variables are from the socioeconomic sciences, such as migration measures from demography.

The independent variables that drive changes in water quality are also several. The geology and geography of Bangkok's natural floodplain

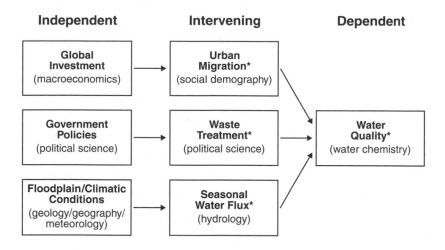

Figure 4.1. An interdisciplinary model of water quality and Bangkok's klongs. Disciplines are shown in parenthesis. Several of the variables reflect patch dynamics characteristics and are identified with an asterisk.

and the meteorologic and climatic processes of monsoons combine to dictate much, but not all, of the water flux within the urban ecological system. Government laissez-faire policies regarding city planning, or the relative lack thereof, lead to limited sewage infrastructure and push human waste into the klongs. Global economic strategies, which lead to economic growth within the Bangkok urban region and attract migration from rural Thailand and elsewhere, drive a significant portion of in-migration and resulting population increase.

Figure 4.1 illustrates the hypothesis and potential disciplines contributing to a basic model of water quality in Bangkok. Under our operating definition, such research would be *interdisciplinary research* and reflect the burdens and benefits of that as practiced using a patch dynamics approach.

The Unique Traits of Urban Ecological Systems and Their Relevance to Patch Dynamics

Given our definition of interdisciplinary research, why then study *urban* ecological systems? What unique traits of urban ecological systems make a patch dynamics approach a useful research paradigm or technique? More fundamentally, what, ecologically, defines a city? Pickett and colleagues define urban ecological systems as "those in which people live at high densities or where the built infrastructure covers a large proportion of the land surface. . . . The boundaries of urban ecosystems are often set by watersheds, airsheds, comuting radii, or convenience."[27]

Cities are, of course, complex systems comprised of people, social institutions, technologies, infrastructures, and natural environments.[28] The city is both an outward form—expressed as spatial pattern—of housing, factories, streets, and parks and an inward pattern of life—expressed as processes—such as cycles of nature, rhythms of work and play, routes of travel, rules of conduct, and so forth. Modern cities are strongly *heterotrophic ecological systems*, that is, highly reliant on external sources of energy and material resources. Collins and colleagues note: "Heterotrophic ecosystems are rare on earth, including some marshes, the deep ocean and streams, but even among such systems cities are extreme."[29]

A brief history may be useful. During the Neolithic stages of urbanization, the emerging cities of the Indus Valley and Fertile Crescent relied heavily on local ecological systems. These cities utilized organic sources of energy and local supplies of drinking water. Cultivated land was within walking distance of the urban center. Human and animal wastes were used as fertilizers in situ. Relatively low concentrations of inorganic refuse, such as glass and metal, were produced. The Neolithic city survived from resource supplies provided by local ecological systems and was limited by their capacity.[30]

A variety of technological and organizational advances released the urban settlement from reliance on local nature. The paved road made transport independent of season. The granary and reservoir allowed storage of food and water. Concentration of administrative and military power, its physical form exemplified by the buttressed wall, allowed the city to conquer other populations and draw from more distant ecological systems. Control of flows became a geopolitical and economic weapon, as when the city of Florence attempted to redirect the Arno River to defeat Pisa, its downriver rival. The project was, astoundingly, designed by the aged Leonardo da Vinci and managed by the young Niccolò Machiavelli.[31]

In the modern city, the actual interdependence between the urban population and its immediate natural areas can be relatively small. The majority of food, water, energy, and other resources can come from locations geographically distant. The city relies on what Catton calls "ghost acreage."[32] New Yorkers draw water from upstate, eat vegetables from California, and drink orange juice from Brazil. One measure of such importation rates is the concept of ecological "footprint."[33]

The larger natural areas of most cities are either limited to providing recreation, such as parks, or acting as a convenient sink for residential and/or industrial wastes, such as riverfronts or Bangkok's klongs. Smaller natural areas are often engulfed by economic processes that limit their usefulness, cycling in and out of public and private ownership and access. An example is Baltimore's abandoned urban lots converting to open space.

The result is an ecological system type particularly appropriate for interdisciplinary patch dynamics. Alberti and colleagues provide a partial inventory of unique urban ecological system traits: "Relative to non-human systems, urban ecosystems have low stability, different dynamics (complex and highly variable on all temporal and spatial scales), more non-native species, different species composition (often simplified, always changed), and unique energetics (antientropic in the extreme). They have rich spatial and temporal heterogeneity—a complex mosaic of biological and physical patches in a matrix of infrastructure, human organizations, and social institutes."[34]

In addition, urban ecological systems have (1) high population densities and resource demands; (2) large-scale habitat modification and widespread habitat fragmentation; (3) novel assemblages of species, particularly in association with the exotics described by above; (4) altered successional patterns and highly managed disturbance regimes; (5) modified and mitigated natural cycles and climatic conditions, for example, the urban heat island and air-conditioning of Bangkok or the artificial watering of Las Vegas; (6) complex social systems with highly variable spatial patterns—"territories" to social scientists, "patchiness" to urban ecologists; and (7) novel combinations of resource fluxes, stresses, disturbances, and responses.

In each case, interdisciplinary patch dynamics approaches have significant potential for the development of concepts linking nature and humans, biophysical and sociocultural systems.[35] The benefits of an interdisciplinary patch dynamics approach can be identified at each stage of the research process—problem recognition, theory, methods and data, analysis, and application.

The Benefits of Interdisciplinary Patch Dynamics

The application of patch dynamics in its interdisciplinary form has significant benefits for the study and management of urban ecological systems. Some of the benefits derive from the paradigm and techniques of patch dynamics as practiced by biological ecologists. Some of the benefits derive from interdisciplinary research as described earlier in this chapter. And some benefits are derived from the synthesis, that is, there may be extra value in the unique combination of patch dynamics and interdisciplinary approaches. We consider each stage of the research process in turn.

PROBLEM RECOGNITION

As the opening example of Bangkok makes clear, the urgency of urban ecology problems is often a function of the *integrity* of urban problems, that is, the interrelationship and tight coupling of social, economic, cultural, biological, and physical variables into an integrated and comprehensive human ecosystem.[36] Few, if any, urban problems are narrow in scope, intellectually provincial, amenable to study by single methods and simple analysis, or solvable by standard solutions.

The integrity and urgency of urban ecological system problems are particularly conducive to interdisciplinary patch dynamics, for patch dynamics well enables the differentiation and complexity of urban systems to be described in spatially explicit forms. Patch dynamics can act as a "paradigmatic bridge" linking the concerns of the biophysical ecologist and the social scientist through variables of spatial differentiation (patchiness), temporal cycles, nested scalar hierarchies of effects, and multiple independent, intervening, and dependent variables.

THEORY

It follows that interdisciplinary patch dynamics has the potential for broad explanatory power as well as robust prediction and insight. Because interdisciplinary patch dynamics employs both biophysical and socioeconomic variables, it can powerfully address research questions not amenable to single-discipline approaches. Prediction of Bangkok's water regime's quality, distribution, use, disposal, and social impacts is an example. Because patch dynamics focuses on spatial differentiation, the density of variation found in urban ecological systems is treated carefully, rather than overlooked or oversimplified in theory, model construction, or hypothesizing.

Hence, useful interdisciplinary models of human ecological systems can be reasonably achieved, with interdisciplinary patch dynamics providing an important approach for revising and refining such models at the level of hypothesis testing. An example is the human ecosystem model (HEM) developed by Machlis and colleagues[37] and further explored by Pickett, Burch, and Grove.[38] Figure 4.2 illustrates the most current version of the model. Within any particular human ecosystem, including urban ones, a set of *critical resources* is required in order to provide the system with necessary supplies. These include *biophysical, socioeconomic,* and *cultural resources.* The flow and use of these critical resources are regulated by the *social system,* the set of general social structures and processes that guides much of human behavior (see box 4.1: "A Brief History of the Human Ecosystem Framework").

The social system is composed of three subsystems—*social institutions,* which are the rules and organizations that generate social order; *social cycles* of temporal patterns; and the *social order,* including territory and rank hierarchy. This social system, combined with key flows, creates the human ecosystem. Human ecological systems are multiscaled, hierarchically nested, and amenable to analysis of first-, second-, and third-order effects.

The human ecosystem model as described, with its mix of structure and process, territory and timing cycles, social institutions and bio-

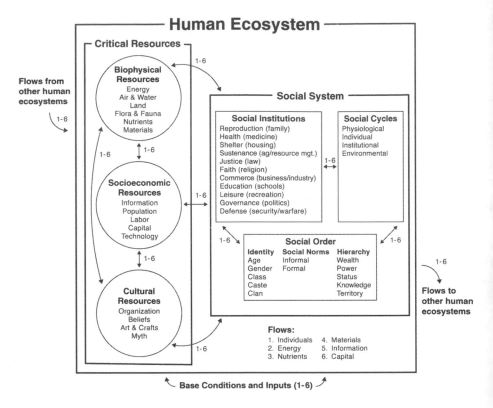

Figure 4.2. The human ecosystem framework: critical resources, social system, and flows. Social identities and hierarchies can play a significant role in the inequitable distribution of critical resources.

physical flows, is an example of conceptual models that can contribute to urban ecosystem research. Importantly, interdisciplinary patch dynamics can "animate" such models—creating interdisciplinary midrange theory and specific hypothesis from the models' proposed relationships.[39]

Patch dynamics, with its focus on nested hierarchy, is particularly beneficial for examining context, the scale above, and mechanisms, the scale below, of urban ecological subsystems. As such it can also effectively address emergent properties, such as ghost acreage dependencies, or infrastructure cohort effects, as well as nonlinearities and spatial disturbances. This ability to address both pattern and process is a feature of both the human ecosystem model and interdisciplinary patch dynamics.

Box 4.1. A Brief History of the Human Ecosystem Framework

The development of the human ecosystem model began with the publication of Bill Burch's *Daydreams and Nightmares: A Sociological Essay on the American Environment* in 1971.[a] *Daydreams and Nightmares* dealt with the environmental issues of the time, but also called for a scholarly approach to those issues that was at once "biologically grounded and socioculturally alert." Reading *Daydreams and Nightmares* for the first time in 1974, Gary Machlis committed to joining Burch at Yale as a doctoral student.

At Yale, the oil crises of the 1970s drove the search for new and interdisciplinary frameworks for studying environmental problems. A class handout of Burch's defined an ecosystem as "the interacting environmental and biotic system that provides the habitat flows that nurture the human species," and had a hand-drawn schematic of the "human ecosystem framework" in generalized form. In 1984, Burch and William DeLuca published a coedited volume (Machlis and other students contributed chapters) with a more elaborated version of the framework.[b] The book included several case studies that applied selected portions of the model.

By that time, Machlis had begun work at the University of Idaho with a new colleague, Jo Ellen Force. Machlis and Force began a series of research projects on national parks, community stability (particularly of resource-dependent communities), biodiversity, and international forestry. All of these projects applied the human ecosystem framework in some form or another. By 1995, Machlis began to attempt a more comprehensive conception of the framework—treating it as a "model to reflect its formal and predictive properties." Burch and Force collaborated in this effort, and in 1997, they collectively published a two-part essay, "The Human Ecosystem as an Organizing Concept" in the journal *Society and Natural Resources*.[c] The work presented a revised and comprehensive model, describing each variable in some detail.

Both Burch at Yale and Machlis and Force at the University of Idaho began to use this model version with their graduate students. Working with Burch at Yale, Morgan Grove and others began to apply the model to an NSF-funded LTER project for Baltimore,

Maryland. Eventually, Grove, working with his new colleagues such as Steward Pickett and Mary Cadenasso, began to experiment with adapting and modifying the model to deal with urban issues of patch dynamics.[d] Others began to apply the model to specific problems—from desert ecosystem monitoring to resource accounting for Asian megacities. Both Burch and Machlis developed model-based training programs for urban resource managers in Asia (Burch in China, Machlis in Thailand), and the current version of the model reflects refinements to the basic model outlined in the 1997 paper.

Notes

a. W. R. Burch Jr., *Daydreams and Nightmares: A Sociological Essay on the American Environment* (New York: Harper and Row, 1971).

b. W. R. Burch Jr. and D. R. DeLuca, *Measuring the Social Impact of Natural Resource Policies* (Albuquerque: New Mexico University Press, 1984).

c. G. E. Machlis, J. E. Force, and W. R. Burch Jr., "The Human Ecosystem, Part I: The Human Ecosystem as an Organizing Concept in Ecosystem Management"; J. E. Force and G. E. Machlis, "The Human Ecosystem, Part II: Social Indicators for Ecosystem Management," *Society and Natural Resources* 10 (1997): 347–67, 369–82.

d. J. M. Grove, J. Morgan, and W. R. Burch Jr., "A Social Ecology Approach and Applications of Urban Ecosystem and Landscape Analyses: A Case Study of Baltimore, Maryland," *Urban Ecosystems* 1, no. 4 (1997): 259–75; S. T. A. Pickett, M. Cadenasso, J. M. Grove, C. H. Nilon, R. Pouyat, W. C. Zipperer, and C. Costanza, "Urban Ecological Systems: Linking Terrestrial, Ecological, Physical, and Socioeconomic Components of Metropolitan Areas," *Annual Review of Ecology and Systematics,* no. 32 (2001): 127–57.

METHODS AND DATA

Interdisciplinary patch dynamics benefits from its capacity to mix research methods and data sets in ways that confront and test theory. The admixture of methods can include biophysical monitoring—either remotely sensed or field sampled; measures of flux—using biological ecology protocols; behavioral studies—particularly, but not exclusively, of *Homo sapiens;* survey research methods; ethnographic studies; and more.

Importantly, patch dynamics can take this mix of methods and data and "integrate for insight," using its focus on spatial heterogeneity and patch units. Water-quality indices can be mapped upon the landscape as well as rent prices, population density, housing age structures, and energy flows. This common display can provide both inductive and deductive opportunities for understanding,[40] and serve to bring methodological order to data sets collected by the different methods of different disciplines. Cartography—the discipline of mapping—is the methodological "glue" that can hold interdisciplinary patch dynamics to a rigorous and robust standard of theory testing. Advances in cartography have meant, and will continue to mean, advances in patch dynamics. The dominant example is the advent of advanced geographic information systems (GIS) techniques, which we will discuss later in this chapter and in chapter 5.

Urban ecologists can find themselves, ironically perhaps, "awash in data,"[41] and patch dynamics can provide "greater understanding of methods and outcomes of different disciplinary components."[42] In addition, the multiple scales and contextual effects derived from *multidisciplinary* data collection empower patch dynamics to deal with interdisciplinary theory, hierarchical scales, and open systems—all important when studying urban ecological systems.

APPLICATION

Interdisciplinary patch dynamics has significant benefit in its application, both to advancing the science of urban and other complex ecological systems and the solving of urban problems through policy, planning, and management informed by urban ecology.

Toward advancing science, interdisciplinary patch dynamics can help break through the boundaries of disciplines. At course scales, patch dynamics can serve as a paradigmatic bridge between the biophysical and socioeconomic sciences. At the finer scale of individual research projects, the "cartographic commons" created by patch dynamics' spatial focus and production of maps can serve to reveal new insights created through interdisciplinary hypothesis testing. New knowledge can be created and used to complement traditional disciplinary work—providing context and mechanism for many disciplinary findings and results. The outcome is a broader understanding of urban ecological system patterns and processes.

Interdisciplinary patch dynamics can also be an important driver of new disciplinary research questions and new synthesis across disciplines. Importantly, scientists engaged in interdisciplinary patch dynamics are likely, though this is admittedly speculation, to develop broader conceptions of urban systems and processes. *Doing* patch dynamics can alter the researchers' worldview in ways beneficial to their science and the science of others.

Patch dynamics also has the significant potential to create "usable knowledge," that is, a particular form of science application useful for policy and management.[43] To be usable knowledge, research results must directly address decision makers' needs at the level of detail and units of analysis appropriate to the decision. Patch dynamics, with its attention to spatial differentiation, is well suited to the creation of usable knowledge for urban managers and citizens.

By broadening its reach to interdisciplinary theory and hypothesis testing, patch dynamics can address complex real-world problems not amenable to traditional disciplinary solutions. It can aid in understanding underlying causes such as our example of Bangkok's water quality. Patch dynamics' spatial explicitness can help create policy options at different levels of organization—allowing policies and their implementation to reflect on-the-ground variation in conditions and increasing the options and effectiveness of urban policy makers. The same "cartographic commons" that enables communication between and among disciplinary scientists can also create a common communication tool for citizens. Patch dynamics has potential benefits as an educational and planning tool that laypersons can understand, apply, and claim as a citizen's tool.

A summation suggests that interdisciplinary patch dynamics is a useful and beneficial paradigm and approach. It has the potential for understanding the complexities of urban ecology as an emerging scientific field and urban ecological systems as critical landscapes around the world. Hence, what strategies of action do we suggest? And equally relevant, what are the "mechanics," that is, practical tasks, associated with effective efforts to *do* interdisciplinary patch dynamics research? Yet again, we examine strategies and mechanisms across the four key phases of research—problem recognition, theory, methods and data, and application.

Strategies and Mechanics for Doing Interdisciplinary Patch Dynamics

The strategies and mechanics for doing interdisciplinary patch dynamics are not unique. Many of these suggestions would apply to other forms of interdisciplinary research. Nor are these suggestions unique to patch dynamics applied to urban ecological systems. Research teams proposing to study other ecological system types might also benefit from many of these strategies and mechanics for their research enterprise.

PROBLEM RECOGNITION

As described earlier, mutual learning across disciplines, the development of common concepts, and an agreed vocabulary are essential foundations. Surprisingly few interdisciplinary research teams explicitly construct their vocabularies. One example is the extended biodiversity gap analysis group convened by Machlis in the 1990s: these researchers' meetings and first reports included a consensus glossary of technical language.[44] A second example is the BES glossary of terms, which is updated on an ongoing basis and accessible in real time through the Internet and as an on-demand, self-published booklet (http://besurbanlexi con.blogspot.com).

Interdisciplinary problem recognition is almost always enriched by asking what has happened in this location or landscape mosaic over time. The historical narrative is a valuable precursor to asking insightful questions about urban ecological systems. Consider the historical evolution of Bangkok's klongs. An analysis of historical change is necessary for understanding dynamic processes and historical contingencies. Research teams will greatly benefit from including urban historians.

Issues of boundaries and levels of organization are often treated as challenges to research at the problem recognition stage. In fact, they may present key opportunities for interdisciplinary problem solving. Patch dynamics approaches, as well as the human ecosystem model described earlier, are largely scale free. A multilevel focus allows for the questioning of multiple processes and properties emergent at different levels, all of which can develop new ways of framing problems that can in turn lead to greater insights. Spatial boundaries and boundary issues are opportunities to reflect on problem definition from multiple perspectives. The commonly perceived differential between administrative and ecological boundaries may actually reflect the emergent properties of human ecological system functioning, where political institutions impact biophysical systems, and landscape geography and geomorphology influence political, economic, and managerial systems.

The mechanics of informal meetings, seminars, and workshops lend themselves to the development of common confidence, trust, and understanding.[45] Exploring place-based history can both energize problem recognition and develop common interest among disciplinary researchers within interdisciplinary teams.[46] Early involvement of graduate students is likely to encourage a "creative willingness" among experienced researchers, as student queries about "the obvious" demand answers that in turn create new insights. Project leaders should never underestimate the value of fine drink and good food in the creation of scientific research teams.

THEORY

Theory building for interdisciplinary patch dynamics is not unlike theory building for other realms of science: there are multiple paths to progress and there is no one right way to do it. Because patch dynamics has a special "eye" for spatial differentiation and interactions across landscape patches, its most predictive power is as a "place-based" science. Its most robust theorizing is likely to be theories of the middle range.

There is, of course, considerable extant theory available to the patch dynamicist. Patch dynamics theory itself has established a growing predictive power.[47] Hierarchy theory[48] and its corollary hierarchical patch dynamics[49] are sources of theoretical insights. Panarchy theory was developed to address multiscale spatial and temporal dynamics of socioecological systems.[50] Its similarity to and insights for interdisciplinary patch dynamics should be embraced.

These theoretical resources, and there are many others, do best at predicting emergent properties and explaining differentiation, both of interest to patch dynamics. The *density* of differentiation expressed in urban ecological systems, that is, the level of patchiness and the intensity of change across space and time, makes these theories good candidates for understanding urban ecological systems.

From these theories and other disciplinary traditions as well, conceptual models can and should be strategic options. As Heemskerk and colleagues note, conceptual modeling can help develop mutual understanding of assumptions behind theories and lead to understanding of interactions—a necessary step toward hypothesis generation.[51] Earlier we described the human ecosystem model as a strong candidate.[52] Grove and Burch have extended the model to apply even more directly to urban ecological systems and the problems of patch dynamics.[53] Whether it is the human ecosystem model or alternatives, the conceptual modeling clearly must be able to accommodate patch dynamics' interest in spatial differentiation and interactions over the landscape.

Because of the spatial focus of patch dynamics, hypotheses derived from patch-relevant theory are likely to be (1) interdisciplinary, (2) expressive of emergent properties, and (3) multiscale. Each has implications for research strategy. In every case, the optimal test for interdisciplinary research is whether a specific hypothesis includes variables from different disciplines as either independent, intervening, or dependent variables.

Patch dynamics applied to urban ecological systems provides ample opportunities for scientific advance, particularly when hypothesis are derived from the theories described above. As Pickett and colleagues note: "Contemporary ecosystems ecology exposes the roles of specific species and interactions within communities, flows between patches and the basis of contemporary processes in historical contingencies. These insights have not been fully exploited in urban ecological studies."[54]

Robust hypotheses derived from interdisciplinary patch dynamics reflect all the characteristics of sound hypothesis construction elsewhere in the sciences: (1) clarity and appropriate precision; (2) the capacity to operationalize, measure, and test; (3) avoidance of truisms, circular reasoning, and other forms of marred logic; and (4) potential for replication. Because patch dynamics is very "place based," the dangers of treating idiosyncratic or localized historical contingencies as more generic patterns or processes should be a constant concern. A useful strategy at the theory stage of research may be careful thought experiments: place the hypothesis in Bangkok, transport it to Baltimore, shift it to Beijing, and if it still makes logico-theoretical sense *as a hypothesis,* then test the hypothesis in one or more real-world urban systems.

The mechanics of interdisciplinary theorizing and hypothesis testing are self-evident but often ignored or undervalued. "Interdisciplinary" research teams sometimes succeed at the problem recognition stage, develop several interdisciplinary grand challenges, and then divide and go their separate ways. Hypotheses are generated individually, often within disciplinary boundaries, and then brought back to the research team for testing. The comfort level of such a strategy is high. However, the mechanics of doing so can result in significant missed opportunities for advancing understanding of complex ecological systems. Hence, team meetings, paired-researcher assignments, explicit hypothesis-testing sessions, and continued informal gatherings all are important to consider. Generous provision of fine drink and food continues to be an important organizational tactic.

METHODS AND DATA

If interdisciplinary divergence during the construction of hypotheses is a challenge to interdisciplinary research, the methods and data-gathering stage is even more vulnerable to refracted and divergent research. Disciplines often have deep ties to a particular research method, and researchers tend to be most comfortable using methods and data that were introduced to them during their disciplinary training. Think of sociology and its common reliance on survey questionnaires or ecology and its love of quadrat-based sampling.

Yet if interdisciplinary patch dynamics is to be successfully applied to urban ecological systems, a new synergy between methods and data collection must be developed. Water-quality data, whether in Bangkok's klongs or Baltimore's inner harbor, can still be collected using the best-available hydrological and water chemistry techniques, but with a strategic purpose of integration using the patch dynamics approach, a human ecosystem model, and interdisciplinary hypotheses.

One useful strategy is *scaled data framing:* the explicit collection and integration of data such that slower and/or larger variables are used to characterize context and smaller and/or faster variables are used to characterize mechanisms. Allen and Hoekstra note: "For an adequate understanding leading to robust prediction, it is necessary to consider at least three levels at once: 1) the level in question, 2) the level below that gives mechanisms; and 3) the level above that gives context, role, or significance."[55]

What scaled data framing does is create opportunities to develop multilevel data sets rather than discard measurements of a particular variable as being "wrong" in scale. For example, data on the granting of sewer permits, such as the number of new permits per month per capita, may be available only at the county, city, or ward level; water consumption for household waste management might be collectible for individual households and aggregated to neighborhood or ward level. In the development of a patch dynamics data set using the scaled data-framing strategy, both of these data sets can be useful: county-level sewer permits providing context for neighborhood wastewater flows and household water consumption providing a mechanism to predict sewerage capacity and limits at ward or county level.

Similar arguments and examples can be made for scaled data framing over time. Variables that operate at faster speeds, such as energy transfers or shifts in market prices, provide explanatory mechanisms for slower time-scaled variables, such as energy retrofitting of older housing stock or early adoption of new technologies. What is essential is an a priori and disciplined plan for data management and a set of agreed core protocols. For interdisciplinary patch dynamics, such a plan should revolve around best-practiced geographic information systems (GIS). Numerous textbooks and instruction guides exist for the development of GIS systems for research.[56] Most large cities have GIS operating systems, as do research programs in urban ecology. Newer systems and hardware can accommodate the large and multiple data sets implied by scaled data framing. Remotely sensed data, census, zoning and city planning data, and primary data collected on specific variables are all candidates for a patch dynamics approach. Rather than treat GIS systems as electronic mylar, only making easier the display of McHarg's mylar layers of thematic data,[57] advanced GIS tools are available to analyze emergent spatial properties, dependencies, and relationships among data sets.

From a logistical or mechanics point of view, patch dynamics research requires a heavier investment in data management than many other forms of social-ecological research. The investment must be front-loaded, that is, the design of data management systems and protocols should precede data collection and be revised as experience suggests or requires. The investment should be in adequate hardware (there is no such thing as too much memory), software and, most important—wetware: human smarts. The data manager, or data management staff, should be skilled, experienced, and an integral part of the research team—not a "downstream" employee asked to "make some data files" or "handle the data" after research planning and data collection are done.

Like early investment in data management, significant up-front investment in high-quality cartography is a sound strategy for interdisciplinary patch dynamics. Like the data manager, the cartographer should be a part of the research team from the start and attention to the cartographic display of data considered an essential element throughout the research project. In addition, care should be taken to distinguish between basic GIS output and the creation of insightful maps. Much of GIS output can be a fog of poor cartographic design.[58] For interdisciplinary patch dynamics, maps are the common ground of contributing scientific disciplines.

ANALYSIS

Analysis, like other stages of the research process, requires special attention if it is to be effective for interdisciplinary patch dynamics. Partly as a function of interdisciplinary theory, models, and hypotheses, and partly as a function of mixed data sets and the scaled data framing described earlier, analysis within patch dynamics can be challenging. At the same time, innovative analytic tools are available to the patch dynamicist. The richness and time scale of much urban ecology data make these tools highly effective.

An example, described earlier, is the use of GIS-based mapping to display and organize urban ecology data across spatial units. Simple overlays of population and water quality for Bangkok can be powerful in revealing potential relationships. More sophisticated GIS-based analytical tools can also provide powerful insights. Spatial and statistical analysis of distances, adjacencies, edge effects, boundary values, and more are available. Combined, such analyses can describe the spatial context of urban patterns and processes, creating "location syndromes" that can be used to create both an archeology or natural history of settlement and practical tools for change detection.

Strategies for using those tools, and there are many others than those described here, hinge on integration. Redman and colleagues note that such a multiscale approach requires that "data be collected with complementary protocols in order to measure action-and-response relationships as well as feedbacks among social and ecological processes."[59] Action-and-response analysis will require some form of longitudinal data, hence the time-scaled data framing described earlier, as well as historical description for context and background, if patch dynamics is to reveal spatial processes. Time and periodicity become critically important variables. New technologies for spatial time-series analysis or the conversion of spatial data, such as adjacencies or boundary values, into time-series data sets are potentially important for patch dynamics. New spatial visualization techniques that display change over time across landscapes are crucial as well.

An important strategy for interdisciplinary patch dynamics is to overcome the all-consuming attraction of intensive case studies and begin the equally challenging, and perhaps more insightful, effort of extensive population studies. Cross-site comparison studies with matching foci can help researchers discover underlying processes. The matching foci can and should be derived from the patch dynamics approach and human ecosystem models of some kind. The comparisons can, like singular case studies, use scaled data framing to provide information on higher-scaled context and lower-scaled mechanisms. Importantly, such comparisons can allow the patch dynamicist to evaluate not only the generalizability of action-and-response relationships, but the potential influences of context and mechanisms. Does the contextual affect X in case A appear in case B? Are different contextual effects associated with the same or similar target-scale conditions or processes? These are the typical research questions made answerable by such strategies. The development of extensive-intensive frameworks are essential for scaled data-framing strategies.

The mechanics of such analyses are surprisingly traditional. The steps of strong inference, a priori thresholds for accepting hypotheses, careful testing of the null, and explicit acceptance or rejection of hypotheses are all valuable. Research teams should maintain a diligent watch for reifying concepts, accepting spurious relationships, committing the so-called ecological fallacy, which may wrongly assume that mechanisms at one scale are operative at another, data "fishing" for confirmatory results, and other standard missteps. It may be useful to separate the responsibilities for data management from analysis, or at least make acceptance/rejection of specific hypotheses a carefully distinguished and rigorously held event. Patch dynamics, with its opportunity to discover new and exciting emergent properties, requires—if not a falsification standard—a warning that researchers should not be too infatuated with their hypotheses.

APPLICATION TO RESEARCH

The strategies and mechanics for doing interdisciplinary patch dynamics extend to the application stage of research. The results of interdisciplinary patch dynamics research projects have bearing and application for science, for social-ecological studies in general, for urban ecology specifically, and for decision making.

For general ecology, interdisciplinary patch dynamics is likely to reveal numerous patterns—particularly discontinuities in emergent properties. That is, testable hypotheses using the patch dynamics approach may identify nonlinear relationships between landscape patches that emerge at certain densities, flux levels, or scales—and that may recede or be replaced at still other thresholds. Hence, patch dynamics has application for "fine-tuning" general ecological principles, particularly at the landscape level, as well as adding to our understanding of the dynamicism of complex urban ecological systems.

In addition, patch dynamics' focus on organizational complexity, coupled with the methodological strategy of scaled data framing, positions patch dynamics research to reveal important insights as to scale effects within urban ecological systems. Ironically, the "scale-free" nature of patch dynamics allows analysis to systematically focus on processes and patterns that emerge between scales once they are specified. How does a mechanism or process at one scale affect system characteristics at a higher scale? What is the process, or processes, that empowers contextual effects to influence system characteristics at a lower scale? Patch dynamics can help answer these questions, with useful application to social-ecological theories.

Interdisciplinary patch dynamics has additional strategic applications, particularly as a paradigmatic bridge between the biophysical and socioeconomic sciences. The construction of interdisciplinary conceptual frameworks, such as the human ecosystem model, and interdisciplinary hypotheses enable the development of new insights into the relationships between biophysical and socioeconomic systems. Rather than generating bland generalizations regarding "the environment," patch dynamics can be applied to the steady development of a rigorous form of contemporary social ecology, which Machlis and colleagues have described as a "new life science."[60]

The results of patch dynamics research in urban ecological systems has had, and will have, direct application to urban ecology science and decision making. The patchiness and complexity examined by this research strategy are reflective of the real-world complexity and differentiation of urban systems. For example, the klongs of Bangkok and the wastelands of row house demolition in Baltimore create, or at minimum are influenced by, the density of variation within these great urban systems. For the researcher interested in cities, patch dynamics has direct application for problem recognition, theory development, hypothesis testing, methods and data collection, and analysis. For the researcher interested in process and change across the urban landscape, patch dynamics is an invaluable paradigm, strategy, and research tool.

The mechanics of these applications require some ingenuity, creativity, and intellectual confidence. Publication of results from interdisciplinary patch dynamics research is more difficult than other publication challenges—key journals may shy away from interdisciplinary studies, the peer review process may take longer, evaluation standards may be unclear or unavailable and vary by discipline, and there is no single outlet or publication mode that is paramount. Hence, senior principal investigators may need to take the lead in publication, bringing junior investigators and graduate students in as full collaborative partners. Articles reporting the results of patch dynamics research will need to be exemplars of conciseness, clarity, and precision. In such articles, assumptions should be rare and definitions common. In addition, considerable care should be invested in the maps, figures, and charts. Cartographic principles of spatial data visualization should be closely followed, and the same exemplary characteristics of clarity and precision should be adhered to, with the added visual requirements of grace and persuasion.

In addition to the traditional journal article, even if it contains nontraditional interdisciplinary findings, the mechanics of patch dynamics approaches may suggest other forms of scientific communication. Studies of urban ecological systems, with their richness of data and density of interested readership, may be especially appropriate for the monograph format, particularly where the research has dealt with both the patchiness of space and change over time. The opportunities afforded by electronic publication, dedicated Web sites, and other new forms of scientific communication are worthy of consideration. Web sites, with their potential for hyperlinks among topics, data sets, and units of analysis, are both a rough analog of the patch dynamics approach and a powerful tool for applying patch dynamics research. Linked to high-quality, cartographically accurate maps, such Web sites can become electronic laboratories for patch dynamics research and communication.

APPLICATION TO POLICY AND MANAGEMENT

Interdisciplinary patch dynamics has specific value in its application to policy and management. As described earlier, it can create useable knowledge for decision makers, resource managers, and citizens. In part, its value for practice emerges from its focus on spatial variation and interactions across the urban mosaic and over time. Patch dynamics can reveal important boundaries, social-ecological patches, and differences among these patches. It can help evaluate impacts of policy and management options across a varying urban mosaic—revealing how a single policy or management strategy may succeed in one location, fail in another, and have unintentional consequences in both. Its spatial explicitness may create customized policy options for a patch or group of similar patches. Its ability to illustrate complexity mirrors the reality of most social-ecological systems, particularly urban systems.

Interdisciplinary patch dynamics is also valuable for practice because it integrates variables that decision makers, resource managers, and citizens are concerned about. To the Thais of Krung Thep, both neighborhood population change and klong water quality are important issues. Interdisciplinary patch dynamics can provide important evidence of relationships and be useful in the struggles over policy and management choices. By linking social and biophysical conditions with science, patch dynamics mirrors linkages that exist in the real world of urban life and can help identify underlying causes, address real-world problems, and ultimately help make urban life better.[61]

The mechanics of making patch dynamics applicable to policy and management are not unique, with one possible exception. Like other forms of knowledge transfer, the research question and theory must be described in clear terms, avoiding the disciplinary code that often poses for scientific sophistication. Methods must be presented as steps toward results rather than scientific exercises valuable in their own right. Data should be presented with an eye for clarity and summation rather than complexity and obfuscation. A large literature on the visual display of information is available.[62] Patch dynamicists presenting their results to broader audiences should not only read these guides but follow them.

The possible exception to the common list of reminders regarding public use of science has to do with patch dynamics' focus on variation across an urban patch mosaic. As we have mentioned elsewhere, this spatial explicitness creates an unusual reliance on maps—base maps, thematic map layers, GIS outputs, map displays of patch mosaics and change over time, and so forth. Hence, effective applied patch dynamics will partially be dependent on effective public cartography.

Public cartography is demanding, for it requires creativity and adherence to cartographic principles, sophisticated mapmaking, and a commonsense understanding of public use. How many public-planning maps have been produced in stunning colors, only to be photocopied for the public as indecipherable, fuzzy black-and-white images? Again, a large "how-to" literature exists.[63]

Curiosity and *Kyosei*

Selected strategies and mechanics for doing interdisciplinary patch dynamics have been suggested in this chapter. Undoubtedly there are other approaches and techniques useful to the task. Yet beyond the strategy, mechanics, and institutional structures conducive to interdisciplinary patch dynamics, two emotive values seem imperative.

The first is *curiosity*—a drive to know as much as possible about what is relevant. Patch dynamics applied to urban systems requires an intense intellectual curiosity because its focus on flux over time and space demands an unraveling of relationships that are often hidden, counterintuitive, and subject to nonlinear effects. The echo of the 1930s-era Home Owners' Loan Corporation maps in the racial structure of many cities today is an example. Only a steady curiosity can hope to tease out substantive insights from patch dynamics. The surface is all too often a kind of banal geography—simple mylar on simpler base map. *Interdisciplinary* patch dynamics raises the requirement for curiosity even higher, for now the researcher must strive to relate variables and processes from one discipline to those of another. The shift in mapping causal variables related to industrial productivity to understanding the spatial patterns of consumption is an example of a multidisciplinary insight. While the litany of interdisciplinary difficulties can be partially overcome by sound strategy and smart mechanics, it is curiosity that can drive the patch dynamicist or research team to create truly interdisciplinary research, and hence make useful discoveries.

The second emotive value is *kyosei,* the Japanese concept of "working together for the common good." Kyosei is the corporate philosophy of the Japanese electronics giant Canon, Inc., and has been applied to both the company's business practices and its philanthropy, which includes environmental programs of international scope. Kyosei requires contribution (not to be confused with blind conformity) to a common cause and is an essential element of effective team building. In the case of patch dynamics research, with its reliance on interdisciplinary teams of scientists, graduate students, and staff, team building is essential for long-term success. The project director and the data manager, GIS specialist and statistician, ecologist and social scientist must all be able to practice kyosei. Interdisciplinary patch dynamics is predominantly a team- or group-oriented form of social-ecological research. Commitment to a common cause and the delivery of individual expertise and insight to the group effort are both necessary and rewarding, as kyosei describes.

Combining curiosity and kyosei with the strategies and mechanics of patch dynamics can be both challenging and exhilarating—a potent scientific tool for examining difficult questions. The result can be an interdisciplinary patch dynamics that confronts the issues of the twenty-first century urban ecological systems—the "perfect bedlam" of Bangkok, and not just Bangkok.

From Bangkok to Las Vegas

Las Vegas sprawls on the flatland of the harsh and arid Mojave Desert. Its annual rainfall is four inches. The original frontier town was a way station on the route from Salt Lake City to Los Angeles. In 1829, artesian springs were discovered and the site was named Las Vegas: "the meadows." Gold strikes in the area in 1860 created Las Vegas as a mining town for provisions and supplies, and the boom-and-bust pattern of American gold mining was played out in traditional cycles of economic hyperdevelopment and decline.

In 1928, the U.S. Congress passed the Boulder Canyon Act, funding what was then the world's largest dam, on the Colorado River. Construction of Boulder Dam brought thousands of workers, millions of dollars, and large-scale water infrastructure to Las Vegas. In the American West, water mixed with money creates energy, and energy was required by the U.S. military buildup in the western part of the country between the two world wars. The Las Vegas Army Air Corps Gunnery School was established to take advantage of desert climate flight conditions, and the Basic Magnesium Plant was built to take advantage of the abundant energy supply.

Gambling was legalized in 1931, and the "swamp cooler," a technology for air-conditioning, was introduced. Gambling attracted tourists, as did the short residency for uncontested divorce, and air-conditioning powered by Boulder Dam–produced electricity helped make visiting Las Vegas pleasurable. Bugsy Siegel opened the Flamingo in 1946, combining mob funding and control, Hollywood fantasies and celebrities, theme resort planning, and the provision of vices.[64] Other casinos followed, and Las Vegas became a major tourist destination.

With the decline of mob control in the 1970s, the casinos became corporate, and the creation of "planned communities" made the real estate industrial complex of speculation, housing development, and population growth the new "engines of growth" for Las Vegas. These planned communities often were built with bond-financed infrastructures, a modicum of services, and little "intercommunity planning."

The population of Las Vegas soared. The city and its surrounding county grew 483 percent from 1960 to 1990.[65] The modern tourist industry—a postmodern mix of gambling, which is now called "gaming," family theme parks, conventions, and the sex trade—has driven desert accommodations to astounding levels. As Kunstler notes, Vegas has become a growth "metajoke": "The hotels on the four corners—*Excalibur; New York, New York; MGM Grand;* and the *Tropicana*—contained all together more hotel rooms than the entire city of San Francisco."[66]

The ecosystem demands of Las Vegas reflect the hypergrowth of economic development and absurdist infrastructure. There is low annual rainfall even for a desert environment—for instance, Tucson, Arizona, in the Sonoran Desert has three times the rainfall of Las Vegas. The residents of Las Vegas average 325 gallons per day water consumption, a higher per capita amount of consumption than any other city in the world.[67] Groundwater overdrafts are creating subsidence of infrastructure foundations; the high mineral content of water supplies combined with Las Vegas's sewage and pesticide/fertilizer runoffs result in poor and declining water quality. Ironically, the arroyos of Las Vegas can se-

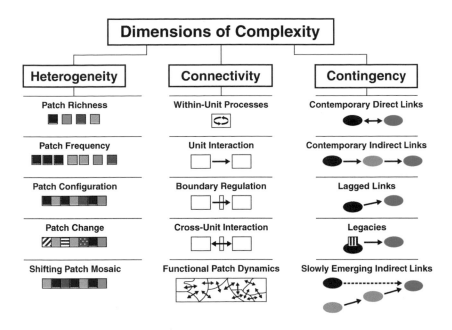

Plate 1. Framework for complexity of social-ecological systems. The three dimensions of complexity are spatial heterogeneity, organizational connectivity, and temporal contingency. Components of the framework are arrayed along each axis, increasing in complexity from top to bottom. A more complex understanding of spatial heterogeneity is achieved as quantification moves from patch richness, frequency, and configuration to patch change and the shift in the patch mosaic. Complexity in organizational connectivity increases from within-unit processes to the interaction of units and the regulation of that interaction to functional patch dynamics. Historical contingency increases in complexity from contemporary direct effects through lags and legacies to slowly emerging indirect effects. While not shown in the figure, organizational connectivity can be assessed within and between levels of organization.

Plate 2. Comparison of land cover classifications derived from high-resolution National Agricultural Imagery Program (NAIP) imagery and mid-resolution Landsat TM imagery of the same area. (a) High-resolution imagery for an area in New York City; (b) classifies those portions of the area with tree canopy cover, using the NAIP imagery; (c) classifies the same area using the Landsat TM data (National Landcover Database). Comparing (b) and (c) shows that Landsat TM data are insufficient for detecting fine-scale vegetation in the more heterogeneous parts of the study area.

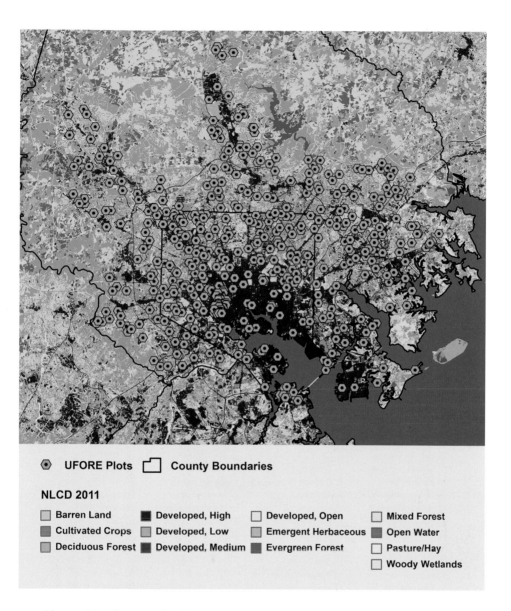

UFORE Plots ⬡ **County Boundaries**

NLCD 2011

Barren Land	Developed, High	Developed, Open	Mixed Forest
Cultivated Crops	Developed, Low	Emergent Herbaceous	Open Water
Deciduous Forest	Developed, Medium	Evergreen Forest	Pasture/Hay
			Woody Wetlands

Plate 3. Distribution of Baltimore urban forest effects model (UFORE) vegetation field plots. UFORE plots are stratified and randomly distributed based on twelve land use categories (n = 400: 200 Baltimore City, 200 Baltimore County).

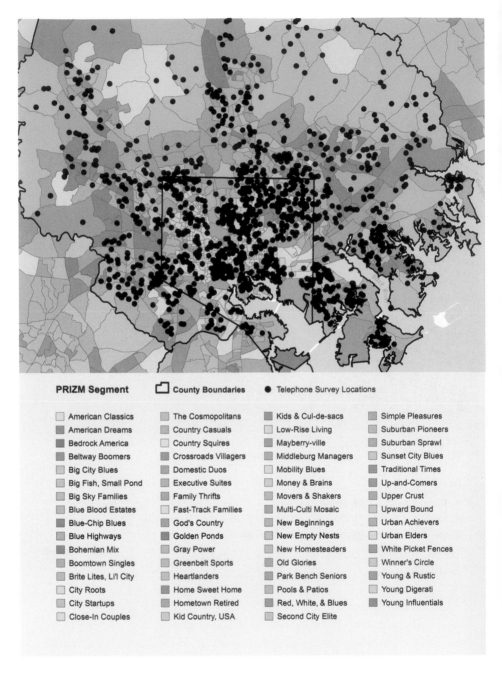

PRIZM Segment ☐ County Boundaries ● Telephone Survey Locations

American Classics	The Cosmopolitans	Kids & Cul-de-sacs	Simple Pleasures
American Dreams	Country Casuals	Low-Rise Living	Suburban Pioneers
Bedrock America	Country Squires	Mayberry-ville	Suburban Sprawl
Beltway Boomers	Crossroads Villagers	Middleburg Managers	Sunset City Blues
Big City Blues	Domestic Duos	Mobility Blues	Traditional Times
Big Fish, Small Pond	Executive Suites	Money & Brains	Up-and-Comers
Big Sky Families	Family Thrifts	Movers & Shakers	Upper Crust
Blue Blood Estates	Fast-Track Families	Multi-Culti Mosaic	Upward Bound
Blue-Chip Blues	God's Country	New Beginnings	Urban Achievers
Blue Highways	Golden Ponds	New Empty Nests	Urban Elders
Bohemian Mix	Gray Power	New Homesteaders	White Picket Fences
Boomtown Singles	Greenbelt Sports	Old Glories	Winner's Circle
Brite Lites, Li'l City	Heartlanders	Park Bench Seniors	Young & Rustic
City Roots	Home Sweet Home	Pools & Patios	Young Digerati
City Startups	Hometown Retired	Red, White, & Blues	Young Influentials
Close-In Couples	Kid Country, USA	Second City Elite	

Plate 4. Distribution of BES household telephone surveys. The BES household telephone survey is stratified and randomly distributed based on a classification including sixty-six lifestyle groups (n = 3,000).

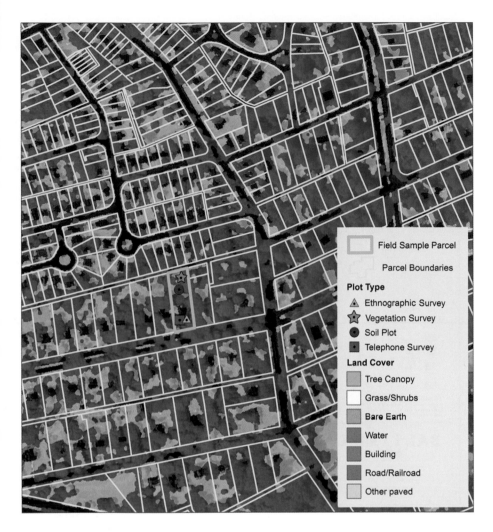

Plate 5. Linking pixels, plots, and parcels. Pixels (land cover) and plots (telephone, ethnographic, and vegetation surveys, and soil plots) can be colocated at the parcel scale.

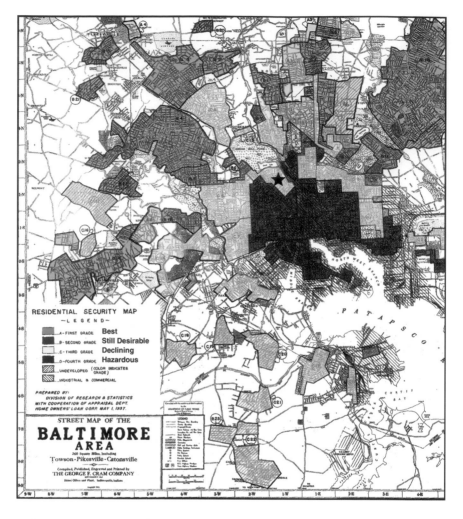

Plate 6. Home Owners' Loan Corporation map for Baltimore city, 1937. The inset description reads: "Security Grading: Declining. Location: The portion of the Ward lying south of Druid Hill Park bounded on the East by Mt. Royal Terrace; South, North Avenue; West, Reistertown Road. Description: An old residential section seriously threatened with negro encroachments. A small section along Reistertown Road consists of fairly modern two story brick rows. Mixed—some negroes, some owners of long standing still occupying old residences—converted apartments containing white collar class-skilled mechanics, etc., Population 1930 (whole ward) 38,596, 10.5% negro, 8.7% foreign born. Population increase since 1920 (whole ward) 14.7%. Favorable Features: Druid Hill Park and good transportation. Detrimental Features: Obsolescence and negro encroachment."

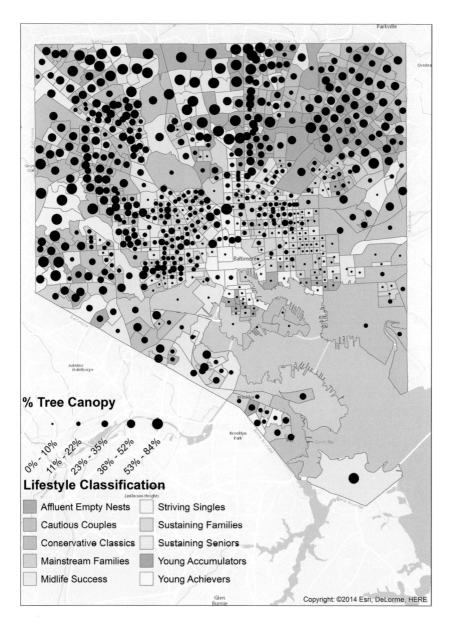

% Tree Canopy

0% - 10% 11% - 22% 23% - 35% 36% - 52% 53% - 84%

Lifestyle Classification

Affluent Empty Nests	Striving Singles
Cautious Couples	Sustaining Families
Conservative Classics	Sustaining Seniors
Mainstream Families	Young Accumulators
Midlife Success	Young Achievers

Copyright:©2014 Esri, DeLorme, HERE

Plate 7. Urban tree canopy cover and PRIZM lifestyle market categories. Neighborhood patches in Baltimore can be classified using PRIZM lifestyle market categories. The size of the circle indicates the amount of residential canopy cover in each neighborhood. Neighborhoods may have similar levels of population density, and households may have similar levels of income and education but are at different life stages. Differences in the amount of urban tree canopy cover per neighborhood may be significantly associated with household life stage.

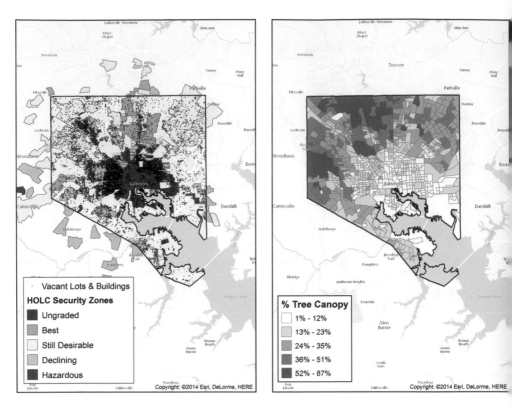

Plate 8. Legacies of redlining: Comparing the HOLC map of security zones (a) with a map of urban tree canopy cover (b) shows that neighborhoods classified as "hazardous" or "declining" in 1937 still had the lowest rates of canopy cover in 2007 and the highest concentration of vacant lots and buildings in 2012.

verely flood like the klongs of Bangkok—even an inch of rain can cause flooding due to soil type and poor drainage planning.[68]

With one thousand new residents arriving each week,[69] and water supplies constrained by the Southern Nevada Water Project and other supply streams, Las Vegas may reach its absolute limit within the decade. Decadal droughts and climate change may hasten the crisis, for which the human systems of Las Vegas may be uniquely ill prepared. Kunstler notes: "In evolutionary biology, at the threshold of extinction organisms often attain gigantic size and a narrow specialty of operation that leaves them very little room to adapt when their environment changes even slightly. This is the predicament of Las Vegas."[70]

From the "perfect bedlam" of Bangkok to the "metajoke" of Las Vegas, urban ecological systems reflect the challenges of the twenty-first century settlement of *Homo sapiens*. To manage these challenges may require a new kind of ecology and, perhaps, a new kind of ecologist. Interdisciplinary strategies hold the best chance for understanding and progress, the creation of useable knowledge, and effective application of adaptive management (table 4.1). Interdisciplinary patch dynamics may be a substantive tool of use and purpose in these efforts.

Table 4.1. Benefits and recommendations for interdisciplinary patch dynamics

Variable	Benefits	Recommendations
Problem recognition	Historical narrative necessary for understanding dynamic processes and historical contingencies (called place-based histories) Multiscale focus, ability to identify emergent processes	Benefit from use of historians Informal meetings, early involvement of graduate students Examine boundary and scale issues to develop new ways of framing problems
Theory	Special "eye" for spatial differentiation Theories developed useful for predicting emergent properties and differentiation Patch dynamic theories are likely interdisciplinary, expressive of emergent properties, and multiscale Need to develop joint hypotheses	Explore patch dynamics, hierarchy, and panarchy theories Develop conceptual models Patch dynamics being "place based" means that historical contingencies should be constant concern Use thought experiments: place the hypothesis in several locations to check for logico-theoretical sense Team meetings, paired research assignments, explicit hypotheses sessions, and continued informal gatherings with fine drink and victuals
Data and methods	Methods should have "strategic purpose" to fit the patch dynamics, human ecosystem model, and interdisciplinary hypotheses	Synergy between methods and data collection must be developed Use scaled data framing by context and mechanism and time

Table 4.1. *continued*

Variable	Benefits	Recommendations
	Requires heavy investment in data management Spatial representations (maps) are the visual "common ground" for contributing scientific disciplines	A priori and disciplined plan for data management, and a set of agreed core protocols Use best-practice GIS Design of data management systems and protocols should precede data collection Data managers and cartographer should be integral part of research team
Analysis	GIS-based mapping for display and organization of interdisciplinary data across spatial units used to reveal relationships Spatial and statistical analytical tools useful for identifying patterns and processes	Need to use complementary protocols among disciplines to measure "action and response relationships as well as feedbacks" Need longitudinal data and historical description to understand dynamic processes Need cross-site comparisons to discover underlying processes
Application	Results of interdisciplinary patch dynamics has bearing on science and practice Ability to identify scale effects, emergent properties, nonlinearities, and dynamic processes Ability to rigorously identify links between human and ecological systems	Principal investigators may need to take lead in publications, bringing in junior investigators and graduate students as full collaborative partners Articles need to be concise, clear, and precise with lots of definitions and care given to visual displays, figures, and charts

continued

Table 4.1. *continued*

Variable	Benefits	Recommendations
	Publication may be more difficult and take longer	This type of data has particular fit to other forms of publication; Web sites with hyperlinks to data sets, topics, and maps
	Value for practice emerges from its spatial variation	
	This paradigm can reveal boundaries of different social and ecological units and differences between them	Specific application to policy and management by developing useable knowledge
	It allows evaluation and local targeting of policy	To be useful to decision makers, the knowledge transfer needs to have the research question described in clear terms, avoiding jargon; methods presented as steps toward results; and data presented with clarity
	Integrated variables that decision makers, managers, and citizens are concerned about	
	Addresses real-world problems and identifies underlying causes, helping to make life better	Data on visual display of information should be consulted
		Particular caution needed for how to display maps as the spatial representation is the key "bridge" between disciplines when using interdisciplinary patch dynamics

Pixels, Plots, and Parcels

Data Issues and Strategies

The Need for New Empirical Strategies for a Patch Dynamics Approach to Urban Ecology

T he transition to an ecology of cities using a patch dynamics approach is a conceptual advance in urban ecology.[1] This conceptual advance requires novel empirical strategies to address its four underlying propositions: (1) analogs to mosaics; (2) spatial, organizational, and temporal complexity; (3) an integrative pursuit; and (4) linking science and practice. In this chapter, we use a building metaphor and the image of a Greek temple facade to describe our empirical strategy. In the first section we describe some of the critical building blocks: pixels, plots, and parcels. These building blocks are crucial to our second section, the data platform, which provides the foundation to our building. The third section describes the supporting columns that rest on the foundation and support the roof. These columns are four ways of knowing: long-term monitoring, experiments, comparative analyses, and modeling. Finally, we have the research themes that make up the roof. These research themes are constructed from midrange theories from the biophysical and social sciences.

Building Blocks: Pixels, Plots, and Parcels

Remote sensing pixels and field plots are two of the most familiar and traditional approaches to collecting ecological data. These two approaches have been important types of data collection for making the urban-rural comparisons associated with an ecology *in* cities. The use of parcels has emerged as an important unit of analysis for an ecology *of* cities for both research and decision making. In this section, we discuss the strengths and weaknesses of these building blocks in terms of our four propositions.

PIXELS

Remote sensing is the science of obtaining information about an object or area through the analysis of data acquired by a device that is not in direct contact with the object or area.[2] Sensors can be passive or active. Remotely sensed data are made up of pixels, which are the smallest physical unit in a raster or gridded image. Pixels can be characterized in terms of their spatial, spectral, radiometric, and temporal resolutions. Two familiar types of remotely sensed data sensor devices are Landsat thematic mapper (TM) and light detection and ranging (LiDAR). Landsat TM is an example of a passive-sensor multispectral device that can be used to classify the land cover of an area. LiDAR is an example of an active-sensor laser device that can be used to measure surface topography and the heights of objects on that surface, such as trees and buildings.

Remote sensing can be a powerful approach for collecting data about urban ecological systems for several reasons. First, remotely sensed data can be used to create a census of an entire urban ecological system. Remotely sensed data can be used to classify an urban ecological system into mosaics of different patches. Based on data of interest or on research questions, there may be many different types of mosaics in an urban area. If remotely sensed data are collected over time, changes in the patch mosaic can be measured.

Analogs Versus Mosaics

Urban ecological systems are highly heterogeneous and this heterogeneity is manifest at a fine spatial resolution. Until recently, only coarse- and

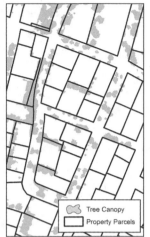

Tree Canopy
Property Parcels

NLCD % Tree Canopy
100%   1%

Figure 5.1. Comparison of land cover classifications derived from high-resolution National Agricultural Imagery Program (NAIP) imagery and mid-resolution Landsat TM imagery of the same area. (a) High-resolution imagery for an area in New York City; (b) classifies those portions of the area with tree canopy cover, using the NAIP imagery; (c) classifies the same area using the Landsat TM data (National Landcover Database). Comparing (b) and (c) shows that Landsat TM data are insufficient for detecting fine-scale vegetation in the more heterogeneous parts of the study area. (See also Plate 2.)

midresolution remotely sensed data have been available. For instance, regional vegetation cover data have typically been derived from midresolution Landsat TM satellite imagery, where the resolution is 30 meters and each pixel is therefore 900 m². Although midresolution imagery has been sufficient for mapping the green analogs that have been the focus of an ecology in cities, these data are insufficient to accurately discern phenomena such as vegetation cover among other elements of urban form across the entire mosaic (figure 5.1 and plate 2).

Patch delineation and characterization. Data produced from high-resolution remote sensing can be used to delineate and characterize an urban area as a patch mosaic. There are two basic approaches to this process of delineation and characterization of patch mosaics. The first

approach is to use "given geographies" such as preexisting administrative boundaries, which include county, municipal, and subdivision
boundaries, or U.S. Census boundaries such as tract and block group
boundaries.

An important issue associated with the use of given geography
boundaries is called the modifiable area unit problem (MAUP). The
modifiable area unit problem is a potential source of error associated
with spatial data using aggregated sources.[3] When the attributes of spatially heterogeneous phenomena such as the distribution of households
are aggregated and treated as homogenous within specified areas, the
summary statistics for those geographies can be influenced more by the
boundaries used than by the underlying spatial patterns of the original data. As we noted previously, administrative and census data can be
summarized in a number of different ways and for different purposes.
The fact that there are numerous administrative and census units of aggregation and analysis illustrates that social geographies are modifiable.

The modifiable nature of spatially aggregated social data can cause
analytical problems. Block groups may be similar in size but yield misleading comparisons, depending upon the homogeneity of the social
phenomena that are included. For instance, boundaries might be drawn
to distinguish between three given areas of detached, single-family
homes, with one area containing mostly young couples and small children, another area predominantly retired couples, and a third made up
almost entirely of young couples and small children but also including
a recently built, high-density, multistory apartment complex for senior assisted living. In this example, a comparison of median family age
among these three areas would yield very different results, even though
they may be similar in geographic size and predominant housing type,
because of the large population living in the high-rise for seniors in the
third area.

The MAUP also presents a challenge when researchers attempt
to combine ecological data with given geographies and spatially aggregated social data. For example, the entire area of block group X might
be classified as residential land use, while block group Y might include
both residential land use and a forested park classified as open-space
land use. In a comparison of these two scenarios, the two block groups

might have similar overall household characteristics, but the relationship between household characteristics and land cover would yield very different results because block group X contained only residential areas with high levels of grass cover and low levels of canopy cover, while block group Y contained a mix of residential and forested land use and, for the whole area, had much higher levels of canopy cover. If the comparison between block groups X and Y does not account for the presence of the forested area in block group Y, then block group Y will incorrectly appear to have much more canopy cover per household than block group X.

There are several strategies to minimize these two types of the MAUP. The first is to conduct the analyses based upon the smallest unit available. This will usually produce relatively more homogenous aggregations. For instance, block groups may be more socially homogeneous than census tracts. However, this does not necessarily address the problem of ecological heterogeneity of the given social geographies. In this case, the use of dasymetric analyses are useful when given social geographies must be used with ecological data. Dasymetric maps are a type of map where the boundaries for data analysis are constrained by supplemental information. For instance, census block group data can be combined with land cover data by constraining the land cover data to only the area associated with the residential land use within the census block group. In this case, the residential land use data are the supplemental information. If parcel-level land use data are available, the resolution of the dasymetric analysis can be improved even further.[4]

An alternative to the use of given geographies is a second approach in which the urban patch mosaic is delineated and characterized by using the original, unaggregated data and their associated geographies. For instance, spatial clustering techniques can be applied to land cover data or household data and their associated parcels to create "derived geographies" of homogeneous areas.[5] However, the creation of derived geographies may not always be possible because such analysis may be too computationally intensive or household data may be unavailable due to privacy issues. Also, derived geographies may not always be desirable because they are not meaningful or useful for decision making. In these cases, given geographies will need to be used and the strategies described above may be employed to minimize the MAUP.

Mosaic Complexity and Pixels

Remote sensing data are often a complete census of the landscape. Thus, remote sensing data are effective for delineating and classifying an urban area into a set of patches. The first three components of spatial complexity can be quantified with these data: patch richness, frequency, and configuration. When the delineation and classification is repeated, both patch change and change in the mosaic over time can be measured.

Remotely sensed data can be aggregated to different levels of social or ecological organization. Process variables can be quantified to measure within-patch dynamics, such as the normalized-difference-vegetation-index (NDVI) to quantify vegetation productivity. In most cases, however, remote sensing data are not effective for directly measuring the range of organizational complexity components, from within unit processes to the functional interactions for the patch mosaic within and between levels. However, cross-unit interactions within and among levels may be hypothesized and the processes inferred indirectly based upon changes in the patch mosaic over time. For instance, between two time periods (T_0 and T_1), patch type A may change to patch type B (A→B); or when A is a member of a higher-level patch 1, patch type A may change to patch type B (A→B), but when A is a member of higher-level patch 2, patch type A may change to patch type C (A→C). Remote sensing can be used to indirectly test these hypotheses.

Remote sensing data cannot be used to directly measure temporal complexity. Similar to the case for organizational complexity, time-series data are needed and temporal complexity can only be inferred by predictions and quantification of changes in patch patterns over time.

Integration and Pixels

Remotely sensed data are useful for social, ecological, and interdisciplinary patch analyses. As discussed in chapter 3, remotely sensed data can be used to delineate and classify both structural elements of urban areas such as land use, land cover, and new classifications such as HERCULES, and process phenomenon such as land use change or vegetation productivity.

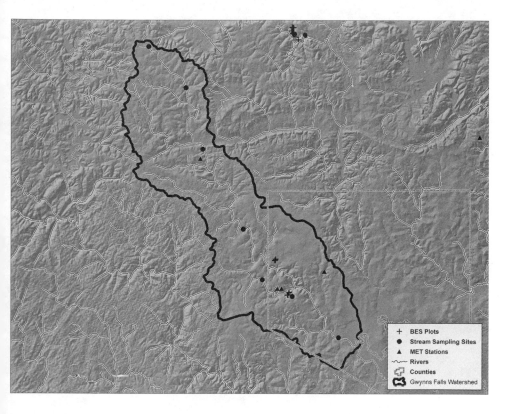

Figure 5.2. BES field-sampling types and locations in the Gwynns Falls water-shed. BES plots for long-term vegetation sampling, stream-sampling sites, and meteorological stations (MET) are distributed along a gradient from urban to suburban to rural. Field-sampling sites are also located in Baisman's Run, a native reference site northeast of the Gwynns Falls watershed.

PLOTS AND OTHER TYPES OF DIRECT MEASUREMENTS

An ecology in cities approach often uses plot-based methods developed in nonurban areas and applies them to their urban counterparts. For instance, study plots have been implemented in urban parks as analogs of rural forests and in vacant lots as analogs of post-agricultural fields or prairies. Similarly, hydrologic gauging stations have been established in urban streams in the same way they are used in wild and rural areas (figure 5.2). Although the main focus of these comparisons has been to study and monitor differences in population and community dynamics and ecosystem processes, these comparisons have also demonstrated that the methods and measurements developed for nonurban areas can be applied to urban ones. Examples of typical measurements include vegetation abundance, density, and species composition; vegetation growth rates and condition; leaf litter decomposition rates; and soil and hydrologic biogeochemical properties and processes. These nonurban sites are not only a source of methods, they can also serve as "native reference sites" for understanding the long-term changes in the urban patch mosaic.

In addition to plot-based methods, there are other types of direct field-based measurements from the biophysical and social sciences. In community ecology, there is a variety of observational and collection surveys for sampling plants, mammals, fish, and birds. Likewise, in the social sciences there are observational and interview survey approaches. The main point is that there are diverse and well-developed approaches from the biophysical and social sciences to directly measure biophysical and social structures, processes, behaviors, attitudes, preferences, and so on.

Analogs Versus Mosaics

The transition from an ecology in cities to an ecology of cities requires a shift from comparisons between urban-rural analogs to comparisons among different types of patches within an urban patch mosaic. When we make this shift, we confront several issues, including sampling strategies; sample size; the so-called ecological and atomistic fallacies; linking databases using spatial hooks; and costs, permissions, and privacy.

Sampling strategies: gradients and categories. The first issue is associated with developing a field-based sampling plan for the entire urban patch mosaic. Several sampling strategies have emerged: (1) gradients; (2) random, spatially independent grids; and (3) stratified, random sampling. Sampling strategies to collect field data may use gradients of difference along an ecological, social, or combination of variables to determine where to locate field plots. Some examples of gradients include topography, distance from urban core, population density, socioeconomic status, or ethnicity. These gradients may be direct and measurable along linear

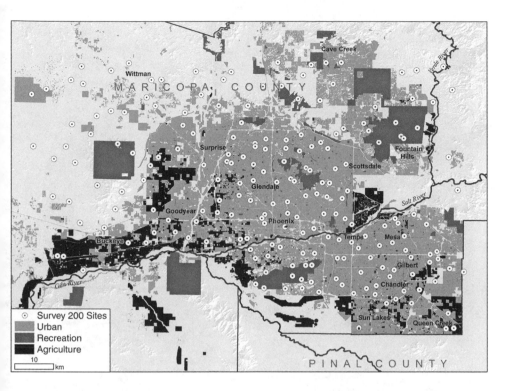

Figure 5.3. Central Arizona–Phoenix LTER field-sampling plan. Field-sampling plots are located based on a grid matrix to distribute plots randomly and spatially independently (n = ~200).

transects or they may be indirect, and therefore not quantifiable using a literal transect approach. Field-based data can be distributed randomly and spatially independently as points using a grid matrix (figure 5.3). Finally, plots can be randomly distributed based upon an a priori stratification of specific patch categories, such as soil type, land use (figure 5.4 and plate 3), or lifestyle group (figure 5.5 and plate 4).

A special case of a field-sampling strategy is when data are collected to measure anticipated changes in the patch mosaic (BACI: before-after-control-impact). This involves sampling before, during, and after a change in a patch or sets of patches. Examples of predicted change include climate change, economic recovery, and demographic shifts. Cases of planned change include new environmental regulations, stormwater projects,

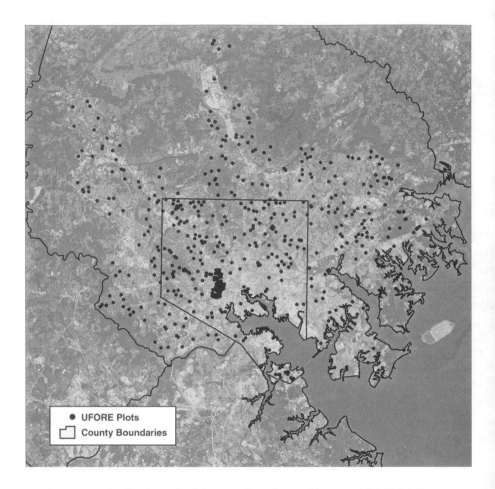

Figure 5.4. Distribution of Baltimore urban forest effects model (UFORE) vegetation field plots. UFORE plots are stratified and randomly distributed based on twelve land use categories (n = 400; 200 Baltimore City, 200 Baltimore County). (See also Plate 3.)

and community redevelopment projects (figure 5.6). In these cases, it is important to collect identical data from reference sites—similar unaffected areas—so that comparisons can be made to determine whether changes associated with the BACI were unique to that patch or observed in similar patches in the rest of the mosaic.

Number of samples needed. A second issue is the adequacy of the number and distribution of plots necessary to sample across the urban

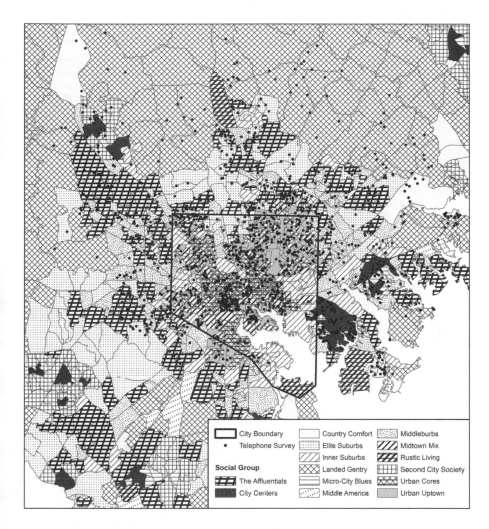

Figure 5.5. Distribution of BES household telephone surveys. The BES household telephone survey is stratified and randomly distributed based on a classification including sixty-six lifestyle groups (n = 3,000). (See also Plate 4.)

mosaic. The use of field-based strategies depends upon collecting data from a sufficient number of plots or field observations in order to achieve the statistical degrees of freedom required for the number of variables or categories included in the statistical model. This issue has been less problematic in the past because researchers have used relatively coarse indices

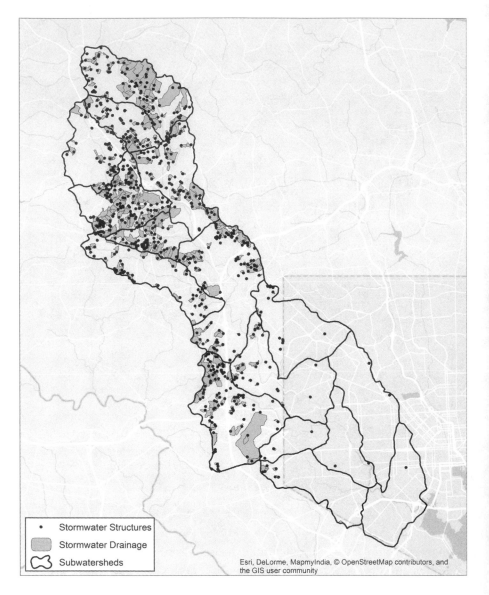

Figure 5.6. Example of planned change: stormwater structures built by Baltimore County Department of Environmental Protection and Sustainability in the Gwynns Falls watershed.

such as population density, socioeconomic status, ethnicity, impervious surface, or vegetation cover as the basis for their sampling design.

When we shift to an ecology of cities, the number of required observations might be quite large. For instance, the combination of social and ecological data may result in a large number of patch categories.[6] In this case, a substantial number of field observations may be necessary or the number of categories may have to be strategically limited. The number of field observations can also increase quickly if it is necessary to account for confounding land use histories and contexts associated with each plot or field observation. For example, there are seven land use categories in figure 5.3, twelve categories in figure 5.4, and sixty-six categories in figure 5.5. In the Baltimore Ecosystem Study, we have conducted a periodic telephone survey of sixty-six lifestyle market categories over the past fifteen years. Approximately three thousand completed telephone surveys are necessary per time period for the Baltimore metropolitan region in order for us to make comparisons among different lifestyle patches.

Ecological and atomistic fallacies: levels of organization, aggregated data, and inferences. The so-called ecological fallacy and the atomistic fallacy refer to inferences made from one level of aggregation to another, particularly when those levels are based upon area. In sociology, the smallest unit of analysis is the individual; this increases to higher levels of organization such as groups, communities, regions, and societies. Neighborhoods are an example of a spatially based social aggregate. Ecological fallacies may occur when two variables are observed at one level and assumed to have a relationship at a lower level. For instance, we might observe relatively high levels of income and high rates of suicide in certain neighborhoods. We would be wrong to assume, using these data, that high-income individuals are more likely to commit suicide. Atomistic fallacies are the reverse, when two variables at one level are inferred to be related at a higher level. The atomistic fallacy is also sometimes called the individualistic fallacy.

Linking databases using spatial hooks. Field-based data require spatial hooks in order to link databases together. There are two ways to create these hooks: spatial coordinates such as latitude-longitude, and unique property addresses. Spatial coordinates are necessary when a specific location is important for repeated measurements, colocating different types of data collection, or linking to remotely sensed data. Addresses are often necessary to connect with a variety of administrative data, particularly social data collected by other organizations. In the case of telephone surveys, for instance, the telephone list for a survey can be acquired to include both latitude-longitude and address, while field observations and interviews can be recorded with both an address and GPS location when surveys are conducted. All of these data can be linked to and leverage census geographies. These geographies include demographic and socioeconomic data from the census and can be joined with other sources of data, such as different types of commercial marketing data. For example, marketing data about household expenditures on lawn care supplies and services can be used as proxy estimates of residential land management practices.

Cost, permissions, privacy. The use of plots is constrained by several practical issues. First, there are the costs of data collection, and when laboratory analyses are required, processing and analyses of samples can be cost prohibitive. Additionally, data quality assurance can be costly. Second, physical access to both public and nonpublic properties for field sampling can be difficult to obtain, requiring permission of landowners, tenants, or managers. When ownership or tenancy changes or landowners change their minds, access to field sites can be lost and cause inconsistencies in long-term data sets. Finally, the privacy of individuals and households might need to be protected. To keep data anonymous, well-developed methods exist for accessing, sharing, and aggregating data containing personal identifying information (PII).

Mosaic Complexity and Plots

Field-based data collection is typically not effective for describing the spatial complexity of patch mosaics because it is not a census, 100 percent sample, of an area. It is conceivable that field data could be collected on a sufficiently dense spatial pattern that spatial patterns could be extrapolated. Examples can be found in belowground mapping for contaminated groundwater, for instance, but these approaches are not frequently used on a widespread basis in urban ecology.

Field observations are effective strategies for directly measuring processes associated with the full range of organizational complexity, from within patch processes to boundary interactions, and functional interactions for a patch mosaic within and between scales.

Time-series, field-based data are also effective for directly measuring each type of temporal complexity. These data can be used to measure direct and indirect contemporary relationships between phenomenon. Field data can also be used to purposefully sample and measure slow and fast rates of change, thresholds, and legacy effects.

Integration and Plots

Numerous methods exist in the social and biophysical sciences for collecting field-based data. Social and biophysical data collections can be co-located (figure 5.7 and plate 5), facilitating the integration of data from diverse disciplines.

PARCELS, A CRITICAL UNIT OF ANALYSIS

Parcels are the basic unit of urban land ownership. Although land can be owned by all types of public, private, and community actors, the fact remains that all land and water is delineated into parcel boundaries and has an assigned ownership. Neither ownership nor boundaries are immutable and can change over time. The empirical ability to digitally examine and integrate social and ecological characteristics for both the parcel unit and across a regional extent is relatively new. The widespread adoption of geographic information systems (GIS) by federal, state, and local governments has greatly increased the availability of high-resolution geospatial data. Cadastral data are particularly valuable. These include information such as the boundaries and ownership of land parcels and the location of infrastructure such as streets, storm drains, and retention ponds. Cadastral information that has been maintained by local governments in hardcopy format is increasingly available digitally. Parcel data can include attributes such as building type, age, and other building characteristics such as the number of bedrooms and

Figure 5.7. Linking pixels, plots, and parcels. Pixels (land cover) and plots (telephone, ethnographic, and vegetation surveys, and soil plots) can be co-located at the parcel scale. (See also Plate 5.)

bathrooms, condition, the transacted value in the most recent sale of the property, owner, land use, and zoning.[7] Cadastral data can be combined with high-resolution land cover data to distinguish vegetation extent, structure, and productivity between private property and public rights-of-way, including along streets.

Analogs Versus Mosaics

Parcel data are effective data for characterizing the entire patch mosaic because they are a complete census of an entire urban area and all ownership types. Since most of the land in urban areas is not the "urban-rural" analogs of an ecology in cities, the use of parcels is critical for the shift to an ecology of cities.

Mosaic Complexity and Parcels

Parcel data, on their own, are similar to remotely sensed data in terms of their ability to address different types of mosaic complexity. Parcels are effective for quantifying spatial complexity and limited in their utility to measure organizational and temporal complexity. Parcels have spatial location and spatial dimensions: perimeter, area, slope, height, shape, adjacency, and orientation (front/back). Parcels can be employed to minimize the risk of the modifiable area unit problem because they can be used to derive geographies or can be aggregated, using dasymetric techniques, with given units of analysis such as neighborhoods, watersheds, and municipalities.[8] Unlike pixels, however, parcels are also a fundamental patch unit and level of organization. Subparcel analysis is also possible, for example, to investigate differences between biophysical and social features of front and backyards in residential areas.[9] Parcels and their owners have social and ecological histories, and their geographies and attributes can be documented and described over time through a variety of sources (figure 5.8).[10]

Integration and Parcels

Parcels are a basic unit of decision making. Since parcels have two spatial hooks, latitude-longitude and address, they can be linked to remotely sensed and field-based data by geographic location and to a variety of administrative and commercial data by address (figure 5.7). These spatial hooks and diverse data sources permit parcels to be characterized with a variety of social and ecological phenomena such as household and firm locational choices; consumption behaviors; and land management practices associated with land cover, vegetation productivity, and biodiversity. These data can be further combined with a variety of archival data that are address based, including real estate

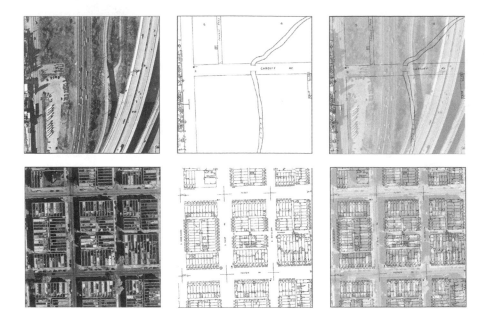

Figure 5.8. Changes in parcel boundaries over time in Baltimore. The first column shows conditions in 2005, combining a remotely sensed image and parcel boundaries. The middle column shows parcel and stream boundaries in 1915. The third column shows the overlay of the two time periods. The top row shows significant change over time, with the construction of a highway and displacement of a stream, while the lower row shows little change in a downtown neighborhood of Baltimore.

transactions, business directories, legal and health records, biographies and diaries, photographs, and neighborhood association minutes.[11] This emphasis on historical data suggests the importance of partnerships with urban historians and organizations that are responsible for the curation of historical data such as state and municipal archives and historical societies.

Data and Links to Decision Making

Data sources to characterize urban social-ecological systems are not limited to those produced by scientists. Indeed, recent growth in the developing fields of "Big Data" and "Smart Cities" highlights the opportunity to combine the exploding growth of different types and sources of data to produce new understandings, policies, plans, and management.

At a local scale, there is a growing trend among city governments to develop GIS-based systems that monitor a wide range of indicators in nearly real time. For instance, a number of U.S. cities have developed programs that provide accurate and timely intelligence that can be used to develop effective strategies and tactics, rapidly deploy resources, and facilitate monitoring and assessments. A pioneering example is the CitiStat program developed by the City of Baltimore (www.baltimorecity.gov/news/citistat/). Cities have begun to use their CitiStat approach in combination with their 311 telephone portals. The 311 system functions in three ways: citizens reporting problems to the city, citizens requesting information about city services, and as a mutual learning system that builds upon the first two functions. The novel idea behind the 311 service is that this information exchange is genuinely two-way. In a sense, the city's 311 system functions as an immense distributed extension of the city's perceptual systems, harnessing millions of local "eyes on the street" to detect emerging problems or report unmet needs.[12]

The development and use of 311 systems suggests two essential principles for how cities can increase their ability to learn about themselves. First, technologies like 311 amplify the voices of local amateurs and "unofficial" experts and, in doing so, they make it easier for "official" authorities to learn from them. The second principle is the need for cross-disciplinary flows of ideas that can challenge the disciplinary stovepipes of knowledge, data, interests, and advocacy associated with many government agencies, NGOs, and the training of professionals. This second principle is increasingly realized by the diversity and interdisciplinary nature of sensing and interpretation facilitated by the Web, the combination of social networks and locational data, and new forms of amateur cartography built upon services like Google Earth and Yahoo! Maps. Local perceptions, behaviors, and knowledge that had so often remained merely in the minds of neighborhood residents can now be translated into digital maps and shared with the rest of the world. These new tools have begun an immense change in the exchange and interpretation of data because data no longer need to be created by distant professionals. These data can be used to map blocks that are not safe after dark, playgrounds that need to be renovated, community gardens with available plots, or local restaurants that allow dogs. Locals can map location of trees, leaking sewers, and stream bank erosion. These tools enable residents to map their history as well—where things were or what things were like—creating and sharing long-term local knowledge.[13]

The scale of these observations can extend from a neighborhood to the entire planet as these local data and knowledges become networked. Formal examples of these types of systems include public health officials, who increasingly have global networks of health providers and government officials reporting outbreaks to centralized databases, where they are automatically mapped and published online. A service called GeoSentinel tracks infectious diseases among global travelers and the popular ProMED-mail e-mail list provides daily updates on all known disease outbreaks around the world.[14] Although these types of systems are intended to be early-warning systems on specific topics, they are likely to become interdisciplinary as the interdependence of challenges and solutions is recognized, facilitating comparisons and learning among scientists and decision makers.

The huge volume, diversity, and novelty associated with these examples can create a hypnosis of the daily now. Because of this, the need to understand the dynamics of change can be forgotten. Public agencies, nonprofits, businesses, and community groups often do not perceive their data to be part of a long-term data set, nor do they have the resources to archive their data. It is also not guaranteed that some of these organizations will persist over the long term. Thus, there is a need to acquire, document, and archive the ephemeral daily now of these diverse streams of data so that we can understand the medium- and long-term change in urban ecological systems. This is a challenge that has not yet been solved for urban ecological research and decision making.

From Pixels, Plots, and Parcels to the Empirical Foundation for a Patch Dynamics Approach: An Extensive-Intensive Data Framework

In Baltimore we have developed a parcel-relevant approach that combines both plot-based and pixel-based data in an extensive-intensive sampling framework (figure 5.9). Pixels are a type of extensive data, plots are a type of intensive data, and parcels are a level of analysis. This framework fulfills key requirements of our patch dynamics approach.

This framework can (1) be applied to the entire mosaic; (2) quantify the full range of spatial, organizational, and temporal complexity; (3) include social and biophysical data; and (4) incorporate diverse sources of data, particularly decision makers' data and their units of decision making.

We define "extensive sampling" to be sampling where the subject matter or geographical coverage is diffuse or widespread and sampling is typically designed to monitor change over large areas. In contrast, "intensive sampling" typically implies: (1) sampling in a particular area with a dense array of sampling points, (2) sampling where information on a restricted range of topics is sought by probing them deeply with an intricate schedule of questions, or (3) sampling involving mixed-method approaches that combine quantitative and qualitative data. Administrative and commercial data are examples of data that may be both extensive and intensive. For instance, property, health, energy and water use, and product consumption data are direct measures and detailed characterizations of all households within an urban patch mosaic.

This framework can be used in a number of ways. An extensive-intensive sampling framework provides the ability to link pattern and process, create scaled data frameworks, and address the full range of spatial, organizational, and temporal complexity (figures 5.9 and 5.10). In general, extensive sampling may be more useful for measuring pattern and inferring process, while intensive sampling may be more appropriate over time for the direct measurement and quantification of process and mechanism, particularly the motivations of social actors. A joint extensive-intensive data framework provides complementary sampling opportunities. Extensive sampling provides a basis for developing strategies for more intensive sampling, including the formulation of stratified sampling plans across space and time. Intensive sampling can be used to validate extensive data because the same phenomenon can be measured both extensively and intensively. For instance, vegetation productivity can be measured using both remote sensing and field-based measurements. Intensive sampling can be used to generate more detailed, process-based and mechanistic models. Subsequently, extensive sampling provides the basis for generalizing process-based models across space and time.

Our research in Baltimore on long-term trends in environmental justice illustrates how extensive and intensive data can be combined to

| Scale | Extensive | | Intensive | |
	Social	Ecological	Social	Ecological
State	*Gross State Product* *Public Expenditures* **Organizational Networks** **Institutions**	*Land Cover* *High-resolution imagery, LiDAR* **Species Productivity/ Condition, Hyperspectral**	**Institutional Practices and Networks** **Political Culture** **Science Policy**	*Forest Inventories* *Primary Productivity* *Species Diversity* *Climate* *Drought Indices*
County	*Socio-demographic* *Economic* *Population* **Organizational Networks** **Institutions**	*Land Cover* *Hydrology* **Species Productivity and Condition**	*Socio-demographic* *Economic* *Population* *Land ownership/zoning* **Structure and Function of Organizations and Institutions**	*Disturbance Event Maps: Floods, Fire, Risk/ Hazard*
Block Group	*Socio-demographic* *Economic* *Population* *PRIZM Marketing Data* **Community Groups, NGOs**	*Hydrology* **Land Cover**	**Landscape Practices by Neighborhoods** **Homeowner Associations (HOA)** **Perspectives, Attitudes, and Behavior by Groups** **Environmental Risks/ Pollution** **Archival/Historical Data**	**Biogeochemical** **Species Diversity** **Species Interactions** **Climate**
Parcel	*City Directories* *Sanborn Atlases* *Assessment Rolls* *Birth Records* *Death Records*	**Land Cover** **Biogeochemical** **Species Diversity** **Species Interactions** **Climate**	*Water/Energy Use per Capita* *Consumption* **Landscape Practices** **Perspectives, Attitudes, and Behavior**	**Biogeochemical** **Species Diversity** **Species Interactions** **Temperature** **Humidity** **Wind**

Already available through federal, state, municipal, university, or commercial entities.

Need to collect using remote sensing (extensive) and field-based measurements (intensive) such as plots, gauges, and surveys.

Figure 5.9. Examples of socioecological data types organized by scale and intensity of analysis. Data types in italics are typically available from other sources. Data types in bold are typically collected by urban ecological research programs.

Scale

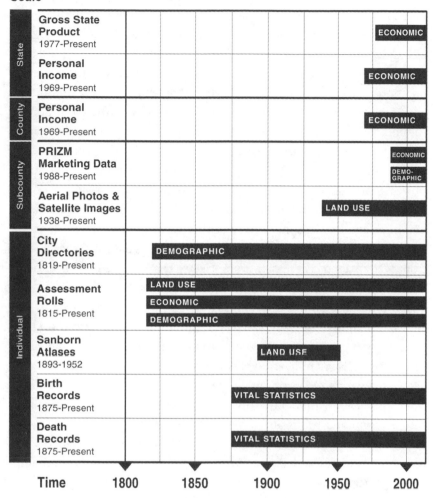

| | | | 1800 | 1850 | 1900 | 1950 | 2000 |

State

Gross State Product 1977-Present — ECONOMIC

Personal Income 1969-Present — ECONOMIC

County

Personal Income 1969-Present — ECONOMIC

Subcounty

PRIZM Marketing Data 1988-Present — ECONOMIC, DEMO-GRAPHIC

Aerial Photos & Satellite Images 1938-Present — LAND USE

Individual

City Directories 1819-Present — DEMOGRAPHIC

Assessment Rolls 1815-Present — LAND USE, ECONOMIC, DEMOGRAPHIC

Sanborn Atlases 1893-1952 — LAND USE

Birth Records 1875-Present — VITAL STATISTICS

Death Records 1875-Present — VITAL STATISTICS

Time   1800   1850   1900   1950   2000

Types of Records:
- Demographic
- Economic
- Land Use
- Vital Statistics/Public Health

Figure 5.10 Example of non-census data organized by scale and time for the city of Baltimore from 1800 to 2000.

examine patterns and processes that structure the urban patch mosaic over the long term. In 2010, the law journal *Environmental Law* published the article "Cities as Emergent Systems: Race as a Rule in Organized Complexity" by Charles Lord and Keaton Norquist.[15] What Lord and Norquist set out to understand and report in their article was a central question that has long troubled the environmental justice community: which comes first, the environmental disamenities or the community? In other words, do environmental hazards exist and then disadvantaged communities move nearby because of the lower housing costs? Or are environmental hazards placed near communities that lack the political power to prevent the locating of the environmental hazards?

Lord and Norquist assembled a database of long-term extensive and intensive data to conclusively answer these questions. For their research in Baltimore, extensive data included census data at the tract level from 1940 to 2000. These data were used to characterize neighborhoods by race and income. Lord and Norquist reviewed Baltimore's nuisance and zoning laws from the mid-1910s to the present. Intensive data included individual zoning variance applications. Lord and Norquist identified every application for a zoning variance since zoning was established in the 1930s. Each application was coded for whether the variance was associated with an environmental hazard or not. For variance applications associated with an environmental hazard (n = ~1,000), the court case decision and testimony were examined to determine whether the variance was approved or declined and to scrutinize the detailed legal reasoning behind the decision. Also, the parcel address associated with every application was mapped and coded as either approved or declined.

Lord and Norquist were able to definitively establish that there was a racial bias in zoning decisions, but that racial bias decreased over time (figure 5.11), coinciding with the period over which the city became predominantly African American and reforms were instituted to the zoning variance approval process.

Lord and Norquist were also able to establish that the actions of the Federal government's Home Owners' Loan Corporation (HOLC) created a legacy of disinvestment and decline in specific neighborhoods in the city. Those areas that were redlined in the 1930s were and remain predominantly African American communities (figure 5.12 and plate

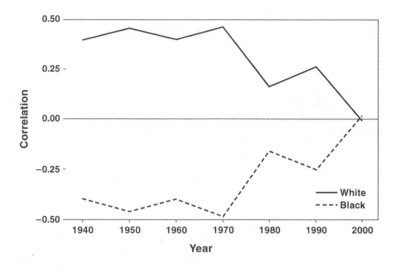

Figure 5.11. Correlation between race and distance to disamenities in the city of Baltimore from 1940 to 2000.

6). Documents that accompanied these maps, produced by the HOLC, reveal that in addition to housing age and condition, other factors such as household race, immigration status, and occupation were important in determining the level of "risk" for lending in these communities. Additional historical research on restrictive covenants and minutes from neighborhood improvement associations show that racial discrimination continued long after the HOLC maps were produced.

Four Supports for Knowing: Monitoring, Comparisons, Experiments, and Modeling

Research in Baltimore is organized around the idea that long-term social-ecological research can be viewed as a table with four legs: (1) long-term monitoring, (2) comparative analyses, (3) experiments, and (4) modeling. This strategy is modified from an analysis by Carpenter (figure 5.13).[16] The table metaphor suggests that the largest goal of the scientific enterprise is understanding or theory, represented by the table top. For complete understanding of a topic, such as urban ecological systems in the long term, all

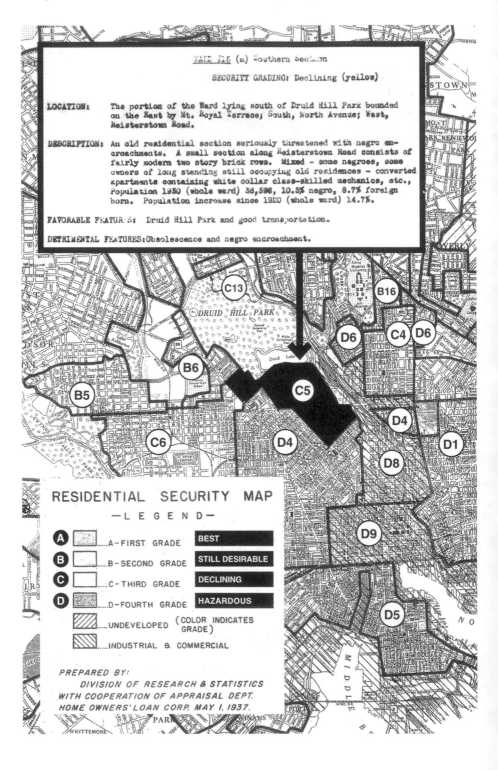

AREA D15 (a) Southern Section

SECURITY GRADING: Declining (yellow)

LOCATION: The portion of the Ward lying south of Druid Hill Park bounded
             on the East by Mt. Royal Terrace; South, North Avenue; West,
             Reisterstown Road.

DESCRIPTION: An old residential section seriously threatened with negro en-
             croachments. A small section along Reisterstown Road consists of
             fairly modern two story brick rows. Mixed - some negroes, some
             owners of long standing still occupying old residences - converted
             apartments containing white collar class-skilled mechanics, etc.,
             Population 1930 (whole ward) 38,596, 10.5% negro, 8.7% foreign
             born. Population increase since 1920 (whole ward) 14.7%.

FAVORABLE FEATURES: Druid Hill Park and good transportation.

DETRIMENTAL FEATURES: Obsolescence and negro encroachment.

RESIDENTIAL SECURITY MAP
— L E G E N D —

A A - FIRST GRADE   BEST
B B - SECOND GRADE   STILL DESIRABLE
C C - THIRD GRADE   DECLINING
D D - FOURTH GRADE   HAZARDOUS

UNDEVELOPED (COLOR INDICATES GRADE)

INDUSTRIAL & COMMERCIAL

PREPARED BY:
   DIVISION OF RESEARCH & STATISTICS
WITH COOPERATION OF APPRAISAL DEPT.
HOME OWNERS' LOAN CORP. MAY 1, 1937.

four activities are important. To the extent that one or more of the activities are absent or poorly developed, understanding will be incomplete.

Long-term monitoring. In BES, long-term monitoring includes a variety of social and biophysical data that are organized within our scalable data framework, including both extensive and intensive data. Long-term monitoring is intended to continue for decades into the future. Consistency of method, overlapping of methods when it is necessary to change instruments or approaches, regularity of sampling, and continual quality assurance and quality control are features of successful long-term monitoring.[17] The collection of long-term data includes those from historical sources, such as archives and published records. Paleoecological approaches also extend long-term data into the past.

Comparative analyses. Comparative analyses occur between social and ecological geographies, political and management units, and periods of time within the BES research area. Comparative analyses can also be made with other urban research projects.

Experiments. Traditional manipulative experiments are difficult to carry out in urban watersheds due to concerns about environmental justice and regulatory constraints on human subjects research.[18] However, spatial variation in the nature and extent of land cover, that is, the urban-rural gradient, provides numerous opportunities for experimental variation of factors controlling biophysical and social parameters. In addi-

---

Figure 5.12. Home Owners' Loan Corporation map for Baltimore city, 1937. The inset description reads: "Security Grading: Declining. Location: The portion of the Ward lying south of Druid Hill Park bounded on the East by Mt. Royal Terrace; South, North Avenue; West, Reistertown Road. Description: An old residential section seriously threatened with negro encroachments. A small section along Reistertown Road consists of fairly modern two story brick rows. Mixed–some negroes, some owners of long standing still occupying old residences–converted apartments containing white collar class-skilled mechanics, etc., Population 1930 (whole ward) 38,596, 10.5% negro, 8.7% foreign born. Population increase since 1920 (whole ward) 14.7%. Favorable Features: Druid Hill Park and good transportation. Detrimental Features: Obsolescence and negro encroachment." (See also Plate 6.)

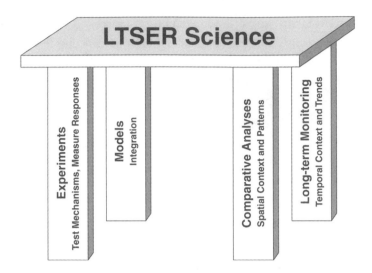

Figure 5.13. Long-term social-ecological research (LTSER) platforms are similar to a table with four legs, each of which is essential to the integrity of the whole. The four legs are long-term monitoring, comparative analyses, experimentation, and modeling.

tion, planned changes such as efforts to improve sanitary sewer infrastructure, stream restoration projects, implementation of Baltimore's urban tree canopy goal, and conversion of abandoned lots to community managed open space are all examples of potential experimental opportunities. The planned changes can be treated as "natural" experiments or BACI studies. These management efforts provide strong opportunities for integration of biophysical and social sciences and for education and outreach.

Modeling. A long-term goal of social and biogeophysical modeling activities in BES is to establish an "end-to-end system" of models and observational instruments to gather and synthesize information on social and biogeophysical components of the human ecosystem represented in the human ecosystem framework. This synthesis includes a number of interacting components: (1) individual and institutional behaviors, (2) the urban landscape and infrastructure, (3) ecosystem services and other push/pull factors, and (4) climate. The combination of these components is used to understand flux and storage of water, carbon, nutrients, and latent heat in terrestrial and aquatic systems. We use a suite of biogeophysical models to simulate water, carbon, and nitrogen cycle processes and a set of econometric and structural models to simulate locational choices and patterns of land development and change at multiple levels of organization across the region. Coupling of these models is intended to provide predictive understanding of the feedbacks among environmental quality, ecosystem services, locational choice, and land development and redevelopment. Working with decision makers, we employ specific policy scenarios aimed at enhancing sustainability in the Baltimore region related to water quality and carbon sequestration to motivate its coupled modeling and synthesis activities. These models can be used with decision makers to test future scenarios based upon current conditions, future trends, and possible policy interventions.

Improving the structural integrity of the table. Although these are not shown in figure 5.13, it is useful to imagine that there are side and cross-member supports that improve the structural integrity of the table. The reason for imagining these structural connections is that the connections among long-term monitoring, experiments, comparative analyses, and modeling can be used to strategically enhance the overall effectiveness of urban ecological research and decision making. For instance, long-term monitoring data may provide baseline and reference data for experiments. The findings from experiments may indicate the need for new types of long-term data. Comparative analyses require long-term monitoring and suggest how the patch mosaics perform under different social and ecological conditions. Modeling activities are crucial for formalizing our existing knowledge of how a patch mosaic functions under different conditions as well as identifying gaps in our observational systems and current theory. For example, models might be used to identify new input data needs, which require changes to long-term monitoring, or for new process parameters, which require experiments to better understand the relationships among components of the system.

Putting It All Together: Data Framework, Supports for Knowing, Midrange Theories

The visual representation of our data strategies, fully assembled, is the facade of a classical Greek temple composed of three primary elements (figure 5.14). The first element is the foundation of the temple, or our multilevel

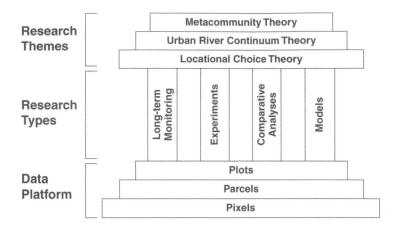

Figure 5.14. The LTSER data temple, with specific BES research themes included.

data framework, which provides the base for all our activities in Baltimore. This base is made up of pixels, parcels, and plots, which are organized using our extensive-intensive approach (figures 5.9 and 5.10). The second element of our temple is the four columns, or research types (figure 5.13), which we originally introduced with Carpenter's table. These research types are supported by the data framework and, in turn, support the roof of the temple, representing research themes. Each research type uses our patch dynamics approach and pursues different types and levels of complexity appropriate to the research theme. Also, each of these supports can be connected with each other in order to strategically enhance the overall effectiveness of the urban ecological research program. In figure 5.14, the roof of the temple is made up of our current BES research themes. Each theme is (1) developed from mid-range theory, (2) can be detailed using the human ecosystem framework, and (3) is located in Pasteur's quadrant of use-inspired basic research.

Conclusion

This chapter has described recent advances and future directions in empirical strategies for an ecology of cities and patch dynamics approach. These empirical strategies are relevant to both researchers and decision makers. From a research perspective, scientists need to consider the empirical changes required in the transition from an ecology in to an ecology of cities. In the case of both research and decision making, there will be increasing needs for analytical capacities: data, computation, tools, and expertise. From a practical perspective, cities increasingly need the ability to assess, monitor, and evaluate their ability to achieve benchmarks set by their sustainability and resiliency goals.[19]

The ability of cities to achieve their goals will depend upon their capacity for conducting assessments, generating scenarios, and informing decision making. These tasks require that cities establish information-gathering, analysis, management, and communication capacities— that is, informatics. It is also crucial that such sustainability-based informatics platforms be transparent, contribute to developing trust among decision makers, stakeholders, and constituents, and build support for action. Sustainability-based informatics will require physical, biological, and social data at relevant temporal, spatial, and decision-making scales, the computational capacity to store, document, and analyze these data, the statistical tools for such analysis, and the contributions of data and analysis from diverse sources. Much of this increased capacity will occur through partnerships among practitioners and researchers, and subsequent training of students. At a local scale, there is a growing trend among governments and NGOs at local and state levels to develop GIS-based systems that monitor a wide range of indicators in nearly real time. It is important not to treat GIS as an end in itself but rather as a tool for informatics in service of conceptual and practical research questions. It is likely that improved informatics for sustainability will require more frequent interactions and even collaborations among practitioners and researchers, simultaneously improving our knowledge about the ecology of cities and enhancing the tools and capacities to manage urban ecological systems. Ultimately, these partnerships are likely to become embedded in recently established offices of sustainability in government, universities, and businesses as they attempt to address interdependent problems with interdependent solutions.

Cholera in London and Urban Tree Canopy in Baltimore

Linking Science and Decision Making

Through Patch Dynamics

A patch dynamics approach is useful for decision making in urban systems in several important ways. Many of the issues that decision makers address include the entire urban mosaic or areas that are influenced by the patch mosaic context. Issues are often complex and involve social and biophysical drivers and outcomes. Extensive and intensive data are needed as well as different ways of knowing.

In this chapter, we present two examples to illustrate the utility of a patch dynamics approach for decision making: London's cholera epidemic of 1854 and Baltimore's urban tree canopy goal and sustainability plan. We have also chosen these two examples because they exemplify two important inflexion points in how we conceive of cities: the Sanitary City that emerged in the late 1800s and the Sustainable City idea that emerged in the late 1900s. The cholera epidemic of 1854 in the Soho district of London was an important event that led to advances in public investments, public administration, and science, which were important to the emergence of the Sanitary City. Baltimore's urban tree canopy goal and sustainability plan is representative of the changes necessary for the Sustainable City: managing the entire urban mosaic, polycentric forms of governance, and interdisciplinary science. In order to clearly connect our examples to a patch dynamics approach, each illustration is described in terms of the story, the ways of knowing, the data framework used, and the advances in practice and science.

The Advent of the Sanitary City: London's Cholera Epidemic

The story of London's cholera epidemic of 1854 and the Broad Street pump has become relatively well known outside of epidemiology because of Edward Tufte's use of it and John Snow's map in *Visual Explanations* and Steven Johnson's engrossing account in *The Ghost Map*.[1] The following illustration is based primarily on Johnson's narrative.

There are many facets to the story that unfolded between September 1 and September 8, 1854, in the Golden Square neighborhood of Soho. The story's most essential elements are the neighborhood's living conditions, the rise of cholera, a race to stop the epidemic, the removal of a pump handle, and a historic turning point in science and practice that transformed urban living.

Nearly seven hundred people would die before the epidemic was over. Most of those who perished lived on or near Broad Street. It was not the first outbreak of cholera in a city, or even the first in London. Yet the responses to the epidemic led to changes in the public administration of water supply and sanitation, changes in public health data, and advances in scientific fields of study, theories, and data analysis. The responses also led to a triumph over prejudice.

In 1854, London contained 2.5 million people within a thirty-mile area. In its most dense areas, London had a population of 432 people per acre. In comparison, present-day Manhattan has a population density of about 100 people per acre. In 1854, Londoners depended upon water supplies from either private companies or community wells. Many of the government roles that we now associate with the contemporary city did not exist then: safe water supply, sanitary disposal of human waste and refuse, and public health regulations. The Broad Street pump in the

Golden Square neighborhood was well known as a source of cool and clean water.

The epidemic started slowly on Monday, August 28, and did not begin to subside until September 8. The epidemic was dramatic because of its intensity and impact. Most victims died within twelve hours; some lasted only two. By Saturday, September 2, full carts carried the dead down the street. As many as one hundred people died in a single day.

There were two primary theories in 1854 for explaining cholera outbreaks: miasma and contagion. Miasma theory was based on the idea that diseases were transmitted by poisoned air from unsanitary places. The alternative theory, the concept of contagion, was that diseases were transferred from one person to another, but few thought cholera was transmitted by water. The miasmists' theory was reinforced by prejudice against cities and the poor. Many miasmists were revolted by the foul air of inner-city areas. The miasmists also believed that moral rectitude was a predictor of whether persons fell ill. Thus the poor, associated with uncleanliness and drunkenness, were more susceptible because of their supposed moral failings. The morality component of the miasmists' theory had the useful benefit of explaining inconvenient evidence that might cast doubt on their theory. For example, if the disease killed some members of a household but others survived, then the explanation was that those who died were somehow less morally upright. Not only were the victims dead, they were also slandered with innuendo to explain and justify their demise.

The two main protagonists of our story are John Snow and Henry Whitehead. Snow, forty-two, was a surgeon and apothecary who was consumed with the practice of medicine and the intellectual challenge of science. Snow lived ten blocks from Broad Street. He subscribed to the contagion theory based on his observations of how the disease attacked the human body. If the miasmists were right and the disease was associated with foul air, then cholera should affect the human respiratory system. But this was not the case. Snow observed that cholera affected the human digestive system, specifically the small intestine. Snow believed, therefore, that cholera was associated with what people ingested, not what they inhaled. To understand cholera and the epidemic, Snow believed that there must be some predictive patterns in what the cholera victims ate or drank. To test his theory, Snow wanted to observe that pattern at the city scale.

Henry Whitehead, twenty-eight, lived one block from Broad Street. He was an assistant curate at St. Luke's Church and passionate in his ministry. Whitehead did not have his own theory of cholera, but he did have his own local observations. He had been visiting members of his congregation in Golden Square and adjacent neighborhoods. What he heard were variations of the miasmist theory. The poor were dying in Golden Square because of their moral failings or constitutional weaknesses. But Whitehead knew his parishioners in Golden Square. They were dying, but they were no more immoral or weak than the residents in nearby neighborhoods.

Snow and Whitehead would eventually join forces, contributing materials to a report on the epidemic on behalf of the St. James Vestry. Before any report could be written, however, the mystery of the epidemic had to be solved. Snow thought the source of the sickness came from water, not from bad air. Neither Snow nor Whitehead believed that these people were dying because of their moral condition. This affected the explanations they sought.

LONG-TERM MONITORING

Several data sets were essential for Snow to move beyond his street-level, direct observations and enable him to observe patterns at the city scale. These data included maps of drinking water sources in the city, including the Broad Street pump and others nearby. He also had the city's maps of drainage patterns. Crucial to his investigation, Snow had the *Weekly Returns of Birth and Deaths* from London's registrar general, William Farr.

Farr's *Weekly Returns of Birth and Deaths* was one of the first examples of observational systems for surveying broad patterns of disease in a city. The report was based on information conveyed to Farr by local physicians and surgeons. Farr asked these sources to record deaths and report the cause of death when possible. These reports recorded not only deaths and disease but also the deceased's age, sex, occupation, and parish district.

Farr subscribed to the miasmist theory of cholera and believed that elevation was the best environmental predictor of the disease. After an earlier cholera outbreak in London, in 1849, he began summarizing cholera deaths by elevation. Farr's results showed that the higher elevations were the healthier places to be. But Farr, aware of Snow's waterborne contagion theory of cholera, had added a new variable: sources of drinking water. This openness to alternative explanations and the data that might evaluate them was a remarkable commitment to a scientific approach on the part of Farr.

As the epidemic erupted, Farr provided Snow with initial calculations for the week of August 28. When Snow mapped these data, it was clear that reports of cholera deaths in London were concentrated in the Golden Square neighborhood. Between Thursday, August 31, and Saturday, September 2, eighty-three deaths had been reported in Soho. Snow asked Farr for the entire list, including addresses. Snow suspected the Broad Street pump was the source of the epidemic, but he was going to need to map the drinking patterns of the epidemic's victims.

While Snow was mapping the patterns of cholera deaths and their water habits in the Soho district, Whitehead was attending to those who were in cholera's grip. Whitehead noted that in one affluent home in Soho, all twelve residents died. In contrast, in one of the most unsanitary homes in the district he visited, no one was ill. These observations caused Whitehead to further doubt the miasmist theory.

COMPARATIVE ANALYSIS

Snow realized that his pattern data would not be enough to conclude that the Broad Street pump was the source of the epidemic and *not* foul airs or moral failings. To do this, Snow needed two sets of cases (table 6.1: B and C). Although Snow already knew that he had victims who lived in Golden Square and drank the water from the Broad Street pump (A), these victims could have died from either the water or the foul airs of the neighborhood. To partially discredit the miasmist theory, Snow needed to find Golden Square residents who had survived the foul air and had not drunk water from the Broad Street pump (B). To confirm his waterborne theory and further test the miasmist theory, he needed

Table 6.1. Comparative analysis to test the miasmist theory

Location	Broad Street water consumption	
	Yes	No
Local (Golden Square)	A	B
Nonlocal	C	—

cases in which victims had drunk the water from Broad Street and had not lived in the foul air of the Golden Square neighborhood (C).

Using Farr's list of cholera deaths by address, Snow created a mental map of where the victims had lived. Using this, Snow had a sampling plan and set off to learn about the ten nonlocal victims (C) and their water-drinking habits. Two of the nonresident victims were a tailor and his son. The son had gone out in the middle of a hot night to fetch water from the Broad Street pump. Three other victims were children. Their parents reported that the children attended school near the Broad Street pump and would drink from the pump before and after school. Relatives of three other victims told Snow that the victims preferred the water of the Broad Street pump even though there was another source that was closer. Finally, Snow interviewed the Ely brothers to learn about the deaths of their mother and cousin. The brothers told Snow that their mother preferred the water from the Broad Street pump and they regularly had this water brought to her. Further, their cousin had been visiting their mother and had consumed some of the water delivered from the Broad Street pump. Snow had accounted for all ten of the nonlocal victims—and they all had drunk water from the Broad Street pump.

Snow also used his mental map of cholera victims to identify local areas in the Golden Square neighborhood where there were few deaths (B). Two cases stood out: the laborers of the Lion Brewery and the St. James Workhouse. The Lion Brewery at 50 Broad Street had seventy workers but not one death had been reported for that address. Snow visited the brewery and interviewed the owners, Edward and John Huggins. The Hugginses were perplexed that none of their employees had been stricken with the disease. Snow asked about the source of their drinking water. The Hugginses reported they had their own sources of water: a private pipeline and well. Snow visited the St. James Workhouse at 50 Poland Street, home to 535 people. Snow interviewed the workhouse directors who also reported that their establishment had a private pipeline of drinking water; residents had no reason to get water from the Broad Street pump even though it was less than fifty yards from their door.

Within twenty-four hours of receiving the list from Farr, Snow had interviewed surviving family members and neighbors of more than seventy of the eighty victims. Based on his mental map, Snow had built a comparative case against the Broad Street pump. Of the ten persons who lived distant from the pump, all could be connected to drinking water from the pump (C). In substantial cases of local residents who had not fallen ill (B), they had private sources of water. Further, of the local persons who had died (A), sixty-one of the seventy-three could be conclusively tied to the Broad Street pump.

EXPERIMENT

Three events occurred during the epidemic that can be conceived of as experiments. First was the contamination of the Broad Street well. The Broad Street well was known for its clear and cool water and it certainly appeared so when Snow inspected it on Sunday, September 3. Although the reason for the change was unknown, by the time Snow drew water samples from the well the next day, the water was cloudy and he saw small white particles. Snow was not able to conclude anything from his inspection of the water, except to note that the water quality had changed.

The second experiment occurred on Tuesday, September 5. The board of health had become sufficiently alarmed by the epidemic that it ordered the streets to be washed with chloride of lime to purge the neighborhood of its miasmatic foul airs. The epidemic continued to spread.

The third experiment was installed on Friday, September 8. The night before, the board of governors of St. James Parish had held an emergency meeting to assess the continuing spread of the epidemic and consider alternative options to end it. Snow attended the meeting and claimed that he knew the cause of the epidemic. He described the high number of deaths associated with residents who lived near the well, the absence of deaths among those who lived nearby but had different sources of drinking water, and the fatalities among those who were not local but had drunk the water. Snow concluded that the evidence clearly indicated that the well was the source of the epidemic and that the pump handle needed to be removed so that water could no longer be taken.

The board of governors was reluctant. The well had a reputation for cool, clean water. The governors were also fully aware of the stench of the neighborhood. Yet they were running out of options. The governors voted and the pump handle was removed the next morning, one week after the epidemic had exploded throughout the neighborhood. The epidemic subsided, though historians have since argued that although the pump handle was removed for the right reasons, it had no effect because the original source of contamination had ended and the well water was no longer a risk.

MODELING

What about the original source of the contamination? Snow had no mechanistic model for how the well had become contaminated. The government would initiate several investigations to determine the cause of the epidemic. The paving board would inspect the well for any direct openings for contamination. It found none, and the government's investigations would offer no conclusive evidence for the cause of the epidemic.

Dissatisfied with the government's response, the Vestry of St. James decided in November 1854 to form its own investigation of the cholera epidemic. Snow and Whitehead were asked to work together on the team. It was at this time that Snow created a revised version of his now famous map showing the street layout of the Golden Square neighborhood, the location of the Broad Street pump and nearby pumps, the residence of the cholera victims, and the likely "consumption" boundaries of residents for each pump (figure 6.1).[2] It was at this time too that Whitehead established the mechanistic explanation for the outbreak.

In the vestry report, Whitehead recounted his observations, which ran counter to the miasmist theory. He described many cases of well-kept homes whose residents had died and filthy homes whose inhabitants

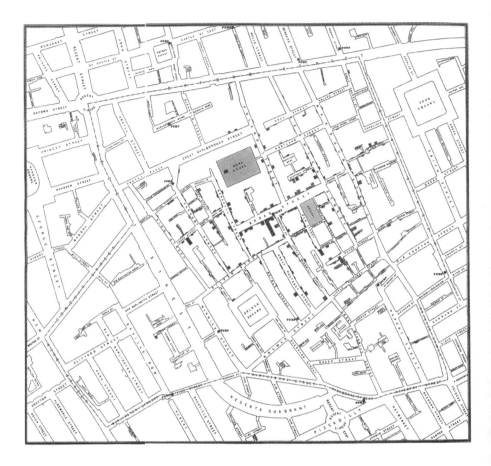

Figure 6.1. Snow's map of the Golden Square neighborhood, the Broad Street pump and nearby pumps, and the location of victims of the epidemic. The height of the stacked lines indicates the number of persons who died at the address. Snow did not make this map, which was part of his report, until after the pump handle had been removed and the epidemic had subsided.

survived. Snow calculated the data in terms of upper and lower floors (wealthy households occupied upper floors and poorer households lower floors in the same apartment) to show that cholera had struck residents regardless of class. The picture that emerged was clearly a case against the Broad Street pump. Yet the well was known for its high-quality water. Further, the paving board had found no obvious openings for contamination.

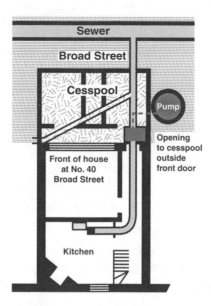

Figure 6.2. 40 Broad Street and the home of the Lewis family. A leak from the deteriorated cesspool in the front of the house connected to the Broad Street pump was the source of the cholera contamination.

Whitehead realized that if Snow was right, there had to be an initial case of cholera whose "evacuations" had somehow been introduced into the Broad Street well. Whitehead reexamined the list of deaths for any cases that had occurred during the initial outbreak among those who had lived close to the well. In the list, Whitehead found "Baby Lewis," 40 Broad Street, who had become ill on August 28. Whitehead went to the home of Baby Lewis, where Mrs. Lewis was still living. Whitehead asked Mrs. Lewis how she had rinsed her baby's dirty diapers and disposed of the washing water. Mrs. Lewis replied that she dumped most of the buckets of dirty water down a drain in the backyard. However, she had also dumped some of the buckets into a cesspool in the basement of the front yard. When Whitehead reported what he learned to the Vestry Committee, the committee hired a surveyor to inspect the cesspool and any possible connections to the well. The surveyor found that although the cesspool was constructed to connect to the sewer, the cesspool was deteriorating and leaking into the Broad Street well (figure 6.2).[3]

LINKING SCIENCE AND DECISION MAKING

The responses to the cholera epidemic in 1854 led to changes that are fundamental to the transition to the Sanitary City: public administration of water supply and waste disposal, regulation of living and work conditions, and changes in public health data. The short-term and immediate change in practices was the removal of the Broad Street pump handle. Over the long term, London would engage in massive public works projects to provide safe drinking water and effective sanitation systems for the city's residents. These public works projects would be a model for similar projects in cities throughout the industrializing world. These projects would also reconceptualize the proper role of government in ways that endure to this day. Government could and should directly "engage in protecting the health and well-being of its citizens, particularly the poorest among them; . . . a centralized bureaucracy of experts can solve societal problems that free markets either exacerbate or ignore; . . . public-issues often require massive state investment in infrastructure or prevention."[4] Industrial cities, as a grand experiment of global scope, would become safe places to live.

The cholera epidemic also led to changes in science. The London Epidemiological Society had been formed in 1850. The 1854 cholera epidemic drew attention to the growing need for epidemiological data and statistics that could be linked to the changing role of government. Snow would invent a new form of mapping and spatial analysis, now called a type of Voroni polygons, that combined the extensive data that Snow had received from Farr and water consumption boundaries that came from Snow's local knowledge of residents' likely paths to fetch water. Such local knowledge might be considered an example of the concept of "urban villages" presented in chapter 3. The epidemic and its resolution cast the miasmist theory further in doubt. Germ theory would eventually emerge, miasmist theory would be discredited, and the cholera bacterium (*Vibrio cholerae*) would be isolated and identified.

SUMMARY

The cholera epidemic of 1854 was part of an important transition in industrial urbanization from an unsanitary, laissez-faire model of governance to a more sanitary, progressive model of governance. The story of the cholera epidemic, the Golden Square neighborhood, and Snow and Whitehead was also an implicit illustration of how a patch dynamics approach to urban ecological systems can be used. Snow and Whitehead raced to combine extensive data about the water supply and sanitary systems and Farr's weekly death and disease reports with their own local knowledge and direct observations and interviews of residents in the Soho district. Addresses provided a spatial hook. They combined social and biophysical data. The water supply boundaries associated with community wells and private sources were one type of patch. Within-patch and between-patch interactions were investigated as well as levels of organization from the human digestive system to the city's water systems. Snow and Whitehead built their understanding of the system through long-term monitoring, comparative analysis, experiments, and mechanistic models. They combined science and practice and advanced both domains within Pasteur's quadrant.

The Emerging Sustainable City: Baltimore City's Urban Tree Canopy Goal and Sustainability Plan

The linkages between science and decision making can be dynamic and iterative (figure 6.3). In this story, we describe the interactions between science and decision making and how the cycles of these interactions led to advances in both domains (table 6.2). We describe this story over seven cycles of feedbacks. During this time, Baltimore became one of the first cities in the United States to establish an urban tree canopy goal, in contrast to the many Million Tree campaigns that have been announced. Over those feedback cycles, the city's tree program, Tree-Baltimore, would be linked to other sustainability goals and broaden its connections to diverse stakeholders and other city programs.

THE STORY, PART I: ESTABLISHING AN URBAN TREE CANOPY GOAL

Cycle 0: Riparian denitrification and riparian tree buffers. The Baltimore region is characterized by ecologically functional watersheds and stream

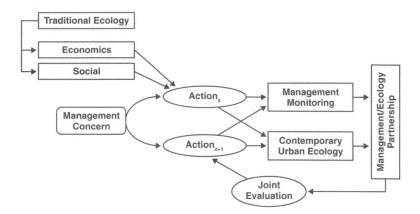

Figure 6.3. Dynamic links between science and decision making: an abstracted cycle of interactions among scientists and decision makers.

valleys that have contributed to Baltimore's economic and cultural history. An early test of our Baltimore urban research project was to apply and demonstrate the utility of forested watershed studies from the Coweeta, H. J. Andrews, and Hubbard Brook Experimental Forests[5] to an urban watershed system. All are LTER projects in the United States. One of the initial questions that BES asked, using a watershed approach, was "Do riparian patches, thought to be an important sink for N in many nonurban watersheds, provide a similar function in urban and suburban watersheds?"

Somewhat surprisingly, BES analyses found that rather than sinks, riparian patches had the potential to be sources of nitrogen in urban and suburban watersheds. This finding could be explained by observing changes in hydrologic connectivity among riparian and upland patches in urban watersheds. This change in organizational connectivity was caused by the incision of stream channels and reduction in infiltration in upland patches due to stormwater infrastructure, which led to lower groundwater tables in riparian patches. These changes in patch connectivity produce what is called "hydrologic drought," which creates aerobic conditions in urban riparian soils and decreases denitrification, an anaerobic microbial process that converts reactive nitrogen into nitrogen gases and removes it from the terrestrial system.[6]

Table 6.2. Dynamic cycles and feedbacks of science and decision making

	Cycle	Science: Theory and/or methods	Decision making: Management concern
Part I: UTC goal	0	Riparian denitrification	Riparian tree buffers
	1	Urban hydrologic drought	Urban tree canopy (UTC) policy
	2	High-resolution land cover mapping	UTC goal
	3	Ecology of prestige	All lands, all people: the new forest landowner
	4	Political economy of place	Environmental equity and justice
Part II: UTC goal and sustainability plan	5	UTC prioritization tools	Multiple sustainability goals
	6	Civic governance Diffusion of knowledge	Stewardship networks
	7	Adoption of innovation	UTC prioritization and markets

Cycle 1: Urban hydrologic drought and urban tree canopy policy. Based upon BES findings about urban riparian patch function, the Chesapeake Bay Program reassessed its goals for forest restoration of riparian patches in urban areas.[7] Given that riparian patches in deeply incised urban channels were not likely to be functionally important for nitrate reduction in urban watersheds, the program focused instead on establishing broader urban tree canopy (UTC) goals for entire urban mosaics with the idea that increases in canopy cover across the city would have important hydrologic and nutrient cycling benefits to the bay.[8] This change was associated with research showing that urban trees reduce stormwater runoff by interception, evaporation, and transpiration, and thus slow or reduce the flow of stormwater.

Cycle 2: High-resolution land cover mapping methods and UTC goal.
The City of Baltimore decided to participate in the Chesapeake Bay Program's urban tree canopy initiative that was stimulated by the BES findings. Before the city could establish a goal, however, it needed to quantify the amount of existing and possible canopy cover for the entire city patch mosaic. For this analysis, the city defined possible canopy cover as those patches that did not have existing tree canopy cover and were not roads, buildings, or water. Furthermore, the city needed to know how much of existing tree canopy patches was in public ownership, particularly in parks and public rights-of-way such as street trees. These questions required detailed, parcel-level analysis. The midresolution, remotely sensed data of an ecology in cities approach were insufficient for this analysis.

Through BES, we developed new methods for combining high-resolution, remotely sensed imagery and LiDAR data in order to produce highly accurate and visually representative data at the parcel level (figure 5.1). Visually representative and parcel-level analyses were two important requirements that decision makers had for the development of these methods. The data product needed to be visually representative at a parcel level in order to convince decision makers and the general public that the data were realistic and therefore legitimate because the data corresponded to how they thought of and perceived their environment. A tree should look like a tree, not a pixel. Summarizing the data in terms of parcels was important because it is the basic unit of decision making and management. The city needed to know how much of the existing and possible urban tree canopy was under its management and how much was associated with other types of ownership or management.

The results from these new land cover mapping methods indicated that the existing canopy cover for the city was 20 percent. The presence of canopy cover varied from 1 percent to 85 percent across different neighborhood patches. Given the combination of existing and possible canopy cover by neighborhood, some neighborhoods could ultimately have a canopy cover as high as 97 percent or as low as 29 percent. In terms of ownership patches, public ownership—street trees and parks—contained only 20 percent of the existing canopy patches and 14 percent of the possible canopy patches; while private ownership contained 80 percent of the existing and 85 percent of the possible canopy cover. Thus, the city's urban tree canopy goal would be severely limited if it depended only upon conserving existing trees and planting new trees on public lands.

With this information, the city knew the extent of existing and possible canopy cover and its distribution by ownership type and by neighborhood. Yet the city did not know what the canopy goal should be. Recent watershed research in the region had indicated watershed health declined significantly when existing canopy cover fell below 43 percent. Given that the city's existing canopy cover was 20 percent, and in consideration of how to "sell" its canopy goal, the city set a target of nearly doubling its canopy cover, from 20 percent to 40 percent.

Cycle 3: An ecology of prestige and an "all lands, all people" approach. Given the limited role of public lands to achieve the city's UTC goal, the city recognized that it needed to adopt an "all lands, all people" approach that addressed the entire patch mosaic. The importance of residential patches to the city's UTC goal required a better understanding of the social factors that predicted variations in the distribution of existing and possible urban tree canopy on residential patches among different neighborhoods. Our analysis employed a variety of extensive data from the U.S. Census at the block group level. These data included total population, income, education, family size, life stage, and race and ethnicity. Using dasymetric mapping techniques, land cover data were constrained to the residential land use of each block group and included in the analysis. The results from this research suggested a phenomenon that we call an ecology of prestige.[9]

An ecology of prestige is based upon the essential idea that housing styles, yard characteristics, tree and shrub plantings, and green grass can be considered social-ecological symbols, reflecting the type of neighborhoods in which people live.[10] These social-ecological symbols can be interpreted as the outward manifestation of each neighborhood's placement in a social hierarchy of group identity and social status in the urban patch mosaic. As such, trees and other yard-care behaviors can be understood as something that is socially valuable, namely, an individual's publicly visible contributions to upholding neighborhood prestige.[11]

Three important findings emerged from our research on neighborhood patches and an ecology of prestige in Baltimore. The first finding was that lifestyle factors such as family size, life stage, and ethnicity appear to be stronger predictors of private residential land management than population density or socioeconomic status. The second finding, which builds on the first, is that the relationship between lifestyle indicators and residential landscape structure and practices provides evidence for the idea that there are ecological indicators of different neighborhood-based and geographically coherent markets associated with different groups' needs, sense of social status, and group identity (figure 6.4 and plate 7). These two findings suggested the need for novel marketing campaigns that differentiated between and promoted UTC efforts to different types of neighborhoods in Baltimore. The third finding was that these relationships were temporally complex. Temporal lags existed between changes in neighborhood characteristics and canopy cover. Neighborhood lifestyle characteristics in the 1960s were the best predictors of existing canopy cover in the 2000s. This finding caused us to reevaluate our research on long-term trends in environmental justice in relation to the city's tree canopy goal.

Cycle 4: Political economy of place and environmental equity and justice. An important component of our research in Baltimore is called a political economy of place. Essentially, we seek to understand what social and economic factors cause neighborhood patches to improve, others to remain relatively stable, and others to decline. Precipitated by Lord and Norquist's work on environmental equity and justice described earlier,[12] we found that seventy years later, the current distribution of existing canopy cover and vacant lots and buildings was still closely associated with the Home Owners' Loan Corporation neighborhood patch classification in 1937 (figure 6.5 and plate 8). In other words, the actions taken by the HOLC institutionalized a racially based pattern and legacy of disinvestment characterized by poor housing quality and limited neighborhood amenities such as street trees and parks, which can still be observed today. This finding and Lord and Norquist's legal research suggested the potential need for a remedial environmental justice component to how the city prioritized the implementation of its urban tree canopy goal.

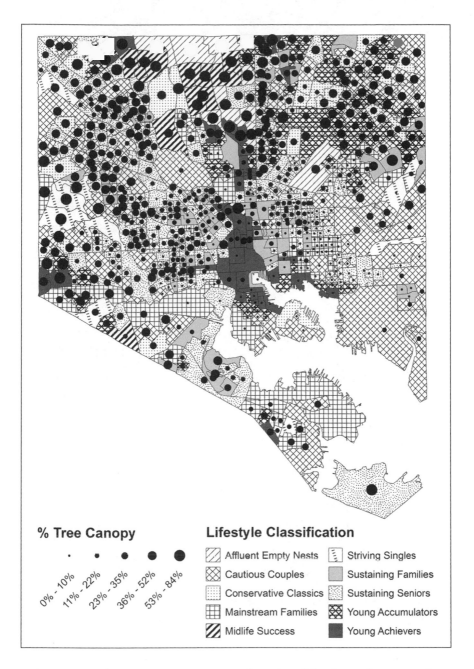

% Tree Canopy

· • ● ● ●

0% - 10%   11% - 22%   23% - 35%   36% - 52%   53% - 84%

Lifestyle Classification

Affluent Empty Nests
Cautious Couples
Conservative Classics
Mainstream Families
Midlife Success

Striving Singles
Sustaining Families
Sustaining Seniors
Young Accumulators
Young Achievers

Figure 6.4. Urban tree canopy cover and PRIZM lifestyle market categories. Neighborhood patches in Baltimore can be classified using PRIZM lifestyle market categories. The size of the circle indicates the amount of residential canopy cover in each neighborhood. Neighborhoods may have similar levels of population density, and households may have similar levels of income and education but are at different life stages. Differences in the amount of urban tree canopy cover per neighborhood may be significantly associated with household life stage. (See also Plate 7.)

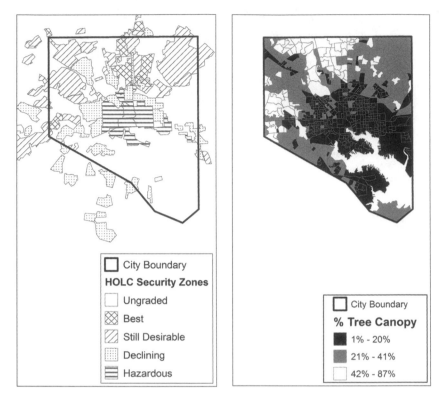

Figure 6.5. Legacies of redlining: Comparing the HOLC map of security zones (a) with a map of urban tree canopy cover (b) shows that neighborhoods classified as "hazardous" or "declining" in 1937 still had the lowest rates of canopy cover in 2007. (See also Plate 8.)

THE STORY, PART II: UTC AND SUSTAINABILITY PLAN

Baltimore's UTC goal was set before the city developed its sustainability plan. Yet, the city's sustainability plan, accompanied by an overall shift in focus on urban sustainability approaches and practices, has significantly influenced how the city's UTC goal will be achieved.[13] First, there has been a shift in terms of governance and involvement of multiple sectors and stakeholders toward more involvement and collaboration within and among public, private, NGO, and community stakeholders. In the case of city agencies, for instance, there is increased collaboration on projects among agencies to achieve multiple sustainability goals. In other words, rather than a one-to-one-to-one approach (agency-project–sustainability goal), there is a growing transition toward a many-to-one-to-many approach. Second, there is growing recognition that there are complementary and alternative approaches to "gray" engineering solutions that include both "green" bioengineering solutions and behavioral changes. Finally, it is increasingly clear that the entire urban patch mosaic and the connectivity among patches needs to be considered in designing structural solutions and behavioral changes of all types in order to achieve the city's sustainability goals. Thus, the science and tools for the implementation of the city's UTC goal are shaped by these shifts in urban sustainability.

Cycle 5: UTC prioritization tool and multiple sustainability goals. The city's UTC goal is a significant environmental component in the city's sustainability plan. Baltimore City's Department of Recreation and Parks is the city agency primarily responsible for the implementation of the UTC goal. However, the UTC goal has also been connected to other sustainability goals and other agencies.[14] Some of these sustainability goals include education and awareness, cleanliness, greening, pollution prevention, and transportation (www.baltimorcsustainability. org/). A survey of city agencies found that nine other city agencies had programs that were directly or indirectly associated with the city's urban tree canopy. Thus, new methods were needed to facilitate collaboration among public agencies as well as groups from other sectors, including NGOs, private interests, and community groups.

Working with these local partners, BES scientists and students developed new UTC methods. The purpose of these new methods was to prioritize where to plant trees based upon diverse sustainability goals and to promote collaboration among stakeholders associated with these goals. Essential requirements were that the methods could incorporate social and biophysical data from diverse sources, organize these data at socially meaningful units of spatial analyses—neighborhood and parcel patches—for the entire city spatial mosaic, and understand the organizational complexity of stakeholders in terms of similarities and differences among stakeholders by sector type and level of organization.

We employed a stakeholder process of interviews, discussions, and written surveys with twenty-five public agencies and organizations. Some of the results of this process are shown in figure 6.6, which shows

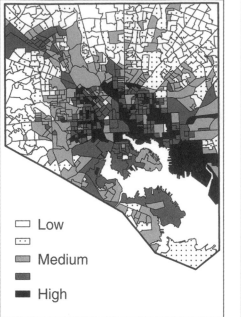 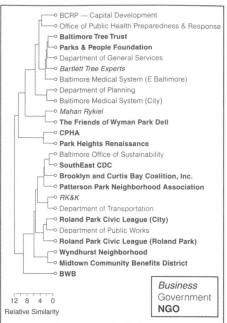

Figure 6.6. Urban tree canopy (UTC) prioritization and similarity of organizations based on prioritization goals. The summary map (a) shows UTC prioritization for Baltimore at the neighborhood scale based on a stakeholder process (n = 25 organizations). The tree diagram (b) shows which stakeholder groups are similar in what they consider the most important factors for prioritizing where to plant trees. Groups closer to each other are more similar.

a summary map of prioritization for the city based on neighborhood patches. The three most popular criteria for where to increase UTC were water quality (impervious surfaces), public health and safety (urban heat island), and the presence of community stewardship groups.[15] The accompanying diagram illustrates the affinity of government agencies, businesses, NGOs, and community groups in the similarities of their preferences for different prioritization criteria. Interestingly, participants' preferences did not correspond to their sector type. For instance, the priorities of the city's Department of Public Works were more similar to some local NGOs than to the city's Department of Public Health.

Cycle 6: Civic governance, diffusion of knowledge, and stewardship networks. The results from the stakeholder process coupled with implementation of the city's UTC goal in priority areas indicated the need to better understand the organizational complexity of the city's stewardship networks. BES researchers employed midrange theories of civic governance in order to understand how governance structures and processes in the city have changed as the city shifts its focus to urban sustainability approaches and practices. We noted earlier that we anticipated a shift toward more coordination and collaboration among sectors and levels of organization. To test this idea, we surveyed all known stewardship organizations in Baltimore (n = 390) and collected spatially explicit time-series data to observe these types of changes in organizational complexity across the city mosaic at the neighborhood level (figure 6.7).[16]

These data are useful for decision making in several ways. First, the presence and density of stewardship groups had already been identified as an important criterion for prioritizing where to plant trees (figure 6.7b). Second, the similarities or complementarities among organizations in terms of their interests (figure 6.6b) can be used to build coalitions for working in neighborhoods that have been identified as high priorities (figure 6.6a). Finally, the organizational diagram (figure 6.7a) can be used to identify which groups are influential in terms of sharing information and other resources and which organizations are marginal. This information can be used to diffuse knowledge through existing networks and modify the network to be more inclusive.

Cycle 7: Adoption of innovation and UTC prioritization and markets. As the TreeBaltimore program has planted trees, it has needed to evaluate how successfully the program has reached its goal in terms of priority areas (cycle 5) and types of markets (cycle 3). To address this need, we have begun a new cycle of research using midrange theories of "adoption of innovations" to evaluate the social and ecological factors that may affect whether homeowners adopt sustainability practices such as tree plantings, rain barrels, and rain gardens. This research also serves as a form of business analysis for the TreeBaltimore program.

We have combined the UTC prioritization classification (cycle 5) with administrative data for tree plantings from the fall of 2013 (figure

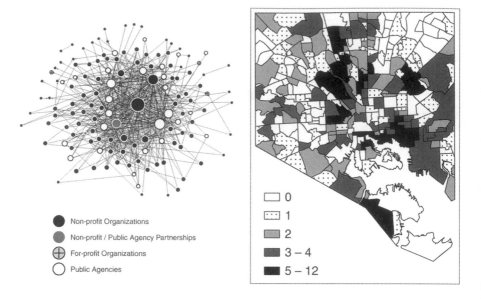

Figure 6.7. The environmental stewardship network for the city of Baltimore and neighborhoods where organizations work. In the network diagram (a) of environmental stewardship organizations in Baltimore in 2011 (n = 390 organizations), larger circles mean the organization has more connections with other organizations. At right (b), the number of environmental stewardship groups per neighborhood is illustrated. Groups that work at the citywide level are not included in the density mapping.

6.8). Figure 6.8a shows the spatial distribution of "free giveaway" tree plantings in terms of the UTC prioritization. The results indicate that the fewest number of plantings occurs in high-priority areas. Further, the city's Forestry Division and an NGO, the Baltimore Tree Trust, are the only two organizations that work exclusively in this high-priority patch type. Only the Parks & People Foundation, another NGO, works in all priority patch types.

When these tree programs and other stormwater "free giveaway" programs are examined by market type (cycle 3), the results show that two market types, *upscale avenues* and *high society,* have the highest rates of adoption *and* the highest rates of existing canopy cover (figure 6.9). Clearly, the idea of trees resonates with these two groups. However, the

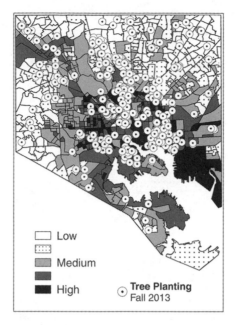

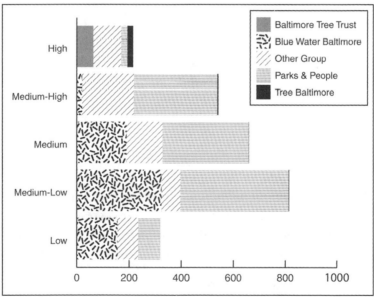

Figure 6.8. Mapping tree plantings by UTC priorities and the organizations that planted the trees. (a) Tree plantings in the fall of 2013 by UTC prioritization category at the neighborhood level. (b) Number of trees planted by organization for each UTC prioritization category.

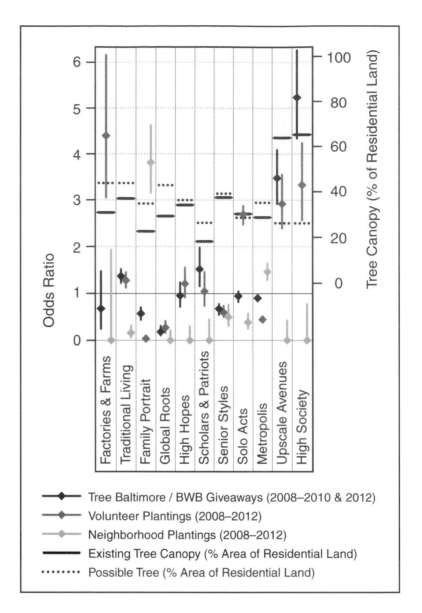

Figure 6.9. Odds ratio for urban greening programs in Baltimore using ESRI's (Environmental Systems Research Institute) tapestry market classification. Expected rate of adoption is equal to a value of 1, based on household populations for each market type in the city. Two neighborhood types—upscale avenues and high society—have both the highest levels of existing canopy cover and the highest rates of adoption of "free giveaway" programs.

adoption rates of other types of neighborhoods are lower than would be expected. Based upon adoption of innovation theory, TreeBaltimore and BES have begun interviews and alternative program strategies to explore how varying the types of messages, messengers, and social-ecological patch contexts might affect whether different types of neighborhood patches adopt these sustainability practices.

THE DATA FRAMEWORK AND WAYS OF KNOWING

The data framework and ways of knowing for the UTC science and decision-making cycles have employed a combination of extensive and intensive data (figure 6.10) and long-term monitoring, comparative analysis, BACI experiments, and models. Extensive social and biophysical data have been used to characterize the urban mosaic of neighborhood patches in terms of UTC markets and priorities. As those patches change, we will be able to observe changes in patch richness, frequency, and configuration. We have used intensive surveys to describe organizational connectivity within and among levels in terms of functional flows of information, staff, and funds and their connections to neighborhood patches. Time-series data have been employed to observe lags and legacies that affect the types and rates of change in different neighborhood patches.

The tree-planting programs can be treated as "natural experiments." City agencies and NGOs have provided their tree-planting administrative data. When these data are mapped to addresses and connected to neighborhood patch classifications, we have "natural experiments" to evaluate which messages and messengers are most effective with different neighborhoods. Follow-up experiments are possible by modifying the messages and messengers for different types of neighborhoods and monitoring the changes in the effectiveness of tree programs. Ultimately, the goal of these natural experiments is to improve the performance of these programs in different neighborhood patch types.

Currently, there are a number of mechanistic, biophysical models that link urban tree canopy extent, location, structure, and species with ecosystem processes and sustainability goals. For instance, these models can relate changes in urban tree canopy to changes in urban heat island and stormwater quantity and quality. From the social sciences, there

Scale	Extensive		Intensive	
	Social	Ecological	Social	Ecological
State				
County	StewMap Social Network Mapping		Key Informant Interviews	
Block Group	Public Health Indicators Demographics Geodemographic Segmentations Historic Districts	Public Transit Open Space Water Flood Plains	Key Informant Interviews	
Parcel	Administrative Records (Coupons/Rebates/ Giveaways) Building Age Assessed Value Crime Critical Places Historic Monuments	**High-resolution Imagery** **7 Class Land Cover** **LiDAR** **Tall Trees** Building Footprints Wooded Areas Road Polygons	Tree-planting Records	

Already available through federal, state, municipal, university, or commercial entities.

Need to collect using remote sensing (extensive) and field-based measurements (intensive) such as plots, gauges, and surveys.

Figure 6.10. Extensive-intensive data framework for Baltimore's UTC goal (cycles 1–7).

are emerging conceptual models of stewardship networks, diffusion of knowledge, and adoption of land management practices.

SUMMARY

Our story of Baltimore's urban tree canopy goal and sustainability plan began with understanding how changes in the organizational complexity of riparian and upland patches affected denitrification in urban watersheds. Since then, we have progressed through seven cycles of advancing science and decision making in terms of social and biophysical midrange theories and methods, and the ability to assess, prioritize, collaborate, and evaluate the city's tree canopy in the context of its sustainability goals.

These advances are not limited to the City of Baltimore. In less than ten years, more than sixty-five UTC assessments have been completed, covering more than nine thousand square miles and 850 communities, and including 30 million people: from small towns to large counties in the United States and Canada. The State of Maryland has legislated that the UTC approach to land cover assessment be used to quantify changes in land cover every five years for the entire state: from its most wild areas to urban regions. In the case of New York City, the Department of Parks and Recreation has used its UTC assessment and prioritization analysis to set a goal and prioritize its tree-planting capital budget: ~$40 million per year for ten years, $400 million total. An important outcome in general is that UTC assessments and prioritization analyses have facilitated the shift toward an "all lands, all people approach" for urban areas, integration of social and ecological knowledge and data, and multiagency and stakeholder collaboration to achieve urban sustainability goals.

Conclusion

We have used two examples to illustrate the utility of a patch dynamics approach to advance both understanding and management of urban ecological systems. We conclude with a few observations. First, a patch dynamics approach involves understanding spatial, organizational, and temporal complexity. It is important to match the appropriate levels of complexity to the research or practical question. More complexity is not always necessary or better; but a little bit more is often useful. Second, we have not offered a cookbook guide to applying a patch dynamics approach for linking urban ecology and decision making. The framing we have provided of propositions, a patch dynamics approach, and data strategies is more akin to a compass and gyroscope to guide the way forward. The way forward is a struggle, with frustrations and rewards, curiosity and kyosei, but the struggle is important because the science of urban ecological systems is relevant and integral to enhancing the sustainability and resilience of our dominant form of human settlement: the city.

Metacities and an Urban Land Ethic

The city is preeminently a place of difference and of differentiation. Early theorists who wished to explain how the city was different from earlier kinds of settlements often pointed to the origin of its different inhabitants from different villages, clans, or tribes, or noted the variety of skills that could exist among the diverse inhabitants assembled as a result of the surpluses that cities have always commanded.

The existence of difference and the process of differentiation have intrigued scholars in many disciplines and urbanists of many stripes. The flags under which these scholars of difference and practitioners of differentiation march are numerous: anthropologists and sociologists may speak of spatial variation, biophysical scientists speak of heterogeneity when they are dressed up and patchiness when they are dressed down, geographers may speak of locale, and of course real estate professionals speak—in triplicate for emphasis—of "location, location, location." Even the formal structure of urban areas has accumulated a general lexicon of difference: districts, wards, parishes, blocks, ghettos, barrios, and neighborhoods, for example. The authors of this book themselves represent different perspectives, training, and experience concerning urban systems. Among us, many specialties can be identified: geography, sociology, rural development, community forestry, landscape ecology, plant ecology, disturbance ecology, conservation, geographic information science, and biogeochemistry, among others. Perhaps it takes differences to best understand and deal with difference.

Difference goes well beyond the abstract. Particular places have their own monikers that are steeped in the connotations and content of difference—the Mainline in Philadelphia, Smoketown in Louisville, Venice in Los Angeles, Pigtown in Baltimore, Greenwich Village in New York City, Southie in Boston. All of these labels and more bear the richness of real and particular difference. Spatial difference speaks powerfully of the varied content of specific places within urban areas, and of the spatial contexts of these particular locations. Notably, difference and the perception of difference change through time. Smoketown once stood for a neighborhood of German brick makers but became a code for an upwardly mobile African American neighborhood after the Civil War. Now it is a label that lives in the memories and conversations of a few old families.

Such difference, differentiation, and change have been the substance of this book. We have been attuned to the heart of the urban situation that has characterized cities from the ancient Near East to the exploding megacities of Asia and Africa. But it is not simply difference for the sake of describing difference. Rather, the concern embraces what difference accomplishes and what it entails. Difference in urban places is potent and kinetic. Difference, even within the so-called creative class, and the serendipitous frissons of innovation that result from informal contact across boundaries of experience, age, training, and motivation, is said to fuel much of what cities seem best able to produce. Difference, when the way is clearly open, is a spur to upward mobility. Difference fuels the specialized markets of mom-and-pop businesses or garage entrepreneurs, and difference lends much of the interest to urban life—the Lebanese grocery, the old-world deli, the quiet Olmsted park, and the always-crowded neighborhood basketball court, its empty rim bearing the frayed tatters of a long-gone net.

So at the core of the urban phenomenon is differential and its interaction. We do not say that all difference is *anchored* in space, although it often is. Rather, difference, even of the most abstract sorts, like status and wealth, always has some spatial *expression*. The elderly black man stepping aside in deference to a white person of any age and sex on a Jim Crow sidewalk in the American South of the early twentieth century is a temporary spatial expression of social status—though a regrettable and sad instance. Also implied in this spatial example is the reality that in some other locations in that same Jim Crow city, the elderly black man's status would have had a very different expression, as even grown men and women might have respectfully acknowledged an elder community leader.

If spatial variation is a general way to express differentiation, then how things and influences move through urban areas is important. Variation can be represented as spatial mosaics—often in maps. Mosaics thus become the field of description and action, parsed by discrete or fuzzy boundaries, or by broad gradients of change. The elements of variation might be denoted as patches, and some patch arrays might be usefully thought of as networks. In such a spatial array, what becomes significant is which patches are adjacent to each other, and how things and influences move through the mosaic. Some movements may be by "conduction" or contact, such that only things from adjacent patches will appear in or influence a neighboring patch. In such cases, the nature of the boundaries between patches—whether they are strong or porous —is important. Social perception can be as potent a boundary as a physical wall. Alternatively, networks of infrastructure or long-distance flows, such as by wind, bring influences from far away. Social and financial influences are particularly susceptible to long-distance flux. So understanding the structure of mosaics, graded fields, boundary structure, and spatial networks is important to understanding the fundamental nature of urban systems as systems of spatial variation. Patch dynamics is the concept that we have used throughout this book to frame and support understanding the existence and function of spatial variation within urban systems.

Space

We have used the term *space* as though it were not freighted with implications and assumptions. Many physical scientists might interpret space as an empty medium, described by Cartesian x, y, and z dimensions. It is the ideal vacuum in which classical physics takes place. Of course, contemporary physics recognizes space to have shape and to be translatable theoretically into time, and indeed to be filled with dark matter.

Contemporary social sciences also recognize the fullness of space. Henri Lefebvre said that a view of space as an empty medium, devoid of social meaning, was a trick of central authority. Space was presented as empty and merely cadastral in order to be sold and ruled by elites. His 1968 masterwork, *The Production of Space,* explains how central authorities strip space of social meaning in order to impose their own values and processes on it and the people who would use and occupy that space.[1] Space as an abstraction is commoditized and centrally controlled. It is also the subject of spatial planning, a top-down regulatory strategy that operates on big blocks of territory, often portrayed as quite uniform, and that has often applied ideal theories, such as modernism, as its planning logic. Spatial planning has in some cases resulted in quite extreme obliteration of local functional urban variation, as noted by Jane Jacobs's still cogent critique.[2] The top-down appropriation of space erases many of the kinds of difference that this book has embraced and rejoiced in. Lefebvre does an excellent job of explaining the social violence resulting from this tactic, but he falls short in acknowledging the biophysical violence this appropriation wreaks. If space is a social construction, as he says, we conclude that it is equally an ecological construction. This insight has been increasingly recognized by urbanists, landscape architects, and urban designers since the 1980s.[3]

The significance of these insights is that empty or abstract space does not really exist in the city of difference. Variation has a multitude of dimensions, each of which suggests its own kind of meaning and value for the elements of urban mosaics, which leads to a consideration of place.

Place

Place is lived space. The values and meanings attached to urban spatial variants convert them each to perceived and lived places. The term *place* here is perhaps best thought of in the context of "sense of place," an expression of customary and vernacular knowledge and experience by people and communities of the spaces they live in, move through, and otherwise use. The concept of sense of place recalls the idea of urban villages identified in chapter 3. They are places that emerge from space layered with values, meaning, rules of behavior, and feelings of attachment. They merit names such as these Baltimore locales: Hampden (pronounced without the "p"), Sandtown, Roland Park, Butchers' Hill, Madison East End, and so on for a total of 276 recognized neighborhood designations in Baltimore City alone. They are places where resident strangers recognize each other and where, at their best, neighborhoods provide the raw material for the incredible energy of cities as cradles of innovation and novelty.

Urban villages can also be crucibles for resilience. Resilience is not a simple bouncing back to some preordained state, for in fact such a state does not exist for any city. Urban systems are increasingly recognized as virtually constantly changing systems. Demography, density, economy, infrastructure, building stocks, transportation routes and technologies, all change at various rates and in different locations. Rather than resist change, the contemporary concept of resilience acknowledges that cities and their components must adapt to changing opportunities, constraints, resources, and threats.[4] Engineering resilience, in the sense of building a system that is elastic in the face of expected stress, or political resilience, in the sense of promising that things will be as they were before some crisis, both have their place. However, they are not the way toward adaptive change. Engineered systems aim to remain in a narrow stated range of tolerance: a bridge must bear certain loads and withstand calculated crosswinds. Politicians wish to protect their tenure by keeping potential voters within their pre-crisis comfort zones. But cities and their constituent urban neighborhoods must adapt to social, economic, and environmental changes of many types that occur at many rates. An urban system, or indeed a neighborhood, that supports institutions that can adjust to change, that builds human and social capital with the skills to meet change effectively, that diversifies economic activities to allow choices in the future, or that marshals information in ways that allow citizens to benefit from changing conditions, is engaging in resilient behavior.

Social construction of space can be authoritarian or democratic. The revolutionary impulse of the 1960s led to an appreciation that all citizens could be involved in the creation of place within the urban realm.[5] Kevin Lynch's documentation of the personal mental maps of residents of Boston,[6] the growth of environmental justice both as activism and as scholarship, and the growth of neighborhood-based revitalization are all roots and symbols of the growing democratization of urban patch construction. The shift from centralized spatial planning to more localized urban design is a professional shift that occurred over this same time frame. Sense of place honors people's perceptions and the local knowledge possessed by individuals, social groups, and institutions, even those who are usually disenfranchised.

Although place is a personally and socially focused set of perceptions and values, it has aspects that can be measured. Chapter 5 has summarized a variety of strategies for measuring socially and ecologically meaningful patchiness. Both spatially extensive and spatially intensive data strategies exist. Importantly, the remotely sensed strategies of planning and regional assessment, and the fine-scaled, plot-based measurements of biophysical patterns and processes usefully meet at the level of property parcels in urban areas. Parcels or their aggregates are the units of management in human settlements. Their boundaries in some form often appear in even objective land cover classifications.

Landscape, as an expression of place, can be seen as a medium for joint action in urban systems. Joan Iverson Nassauer has emphasized that landscape in urban systems can be a powerful medium for interaction and action.[7] Landscape, in the sense of the view outside, is the principal window on a sense of place. It is a view that can be shared, discussed, and envisioned by a community or diverse group of stakeholders. A landscape perspective can lead to effective and accepted designs in urban places that take the social and other dimensions of urban systems into account.

Complexity is an important aspect of place. Various chapters in this book have addressed three dimensions of complexity: spatial, organizational, and temporal.[8] The spatial aspects of complexity address much more than abstract space. Consequently, the hierarchical aspects of patch complexity, ranging from simple difference and frequency of different parch types to the configuration of a patch mosaic and the functional connections within the mosaic, all apply to *place*. It is the content of the patches, which are in the social realm and represented by the things we have described above as defining place, that can be the subject of this axis of complexity. It is content that is place, not abstract space, that is imbued with complexity.

The organizational dimension of complexity likewise embodies features of lived place. These features are crucial elements of the human ecosystem model. How are people organized? What purposes do they organize for? How are formal and informal institutions structured and linked? A nested hierarchy of organization begins with individuals, extends through households, through various informal and formal organizations, and may conclude with formal government and governance arrangements.

Finally, there is temporal complexity. This dimension emphasizes that not all important interactions in a heterogeneous, patchy mosaic may be instantaneous or contemporary. Temporal complexity increases as historical influences play into contemporary relationships, as lagged interactions become important, and as structural legacies of past conditions are seen to have contemporary influence. The spatial nature of such temporal effects is often quite strong, as seen, for example, in the management of urban tree canopy.

As important as the dimension of "place" is above and beyond abstract, controlled urban space, accounts of place often ignore its biophysical environmental aspects. This lapse goes back to the founding of the idea of social construction of space. This is a literature that resides predominantly in philosophical and social realms. The ecological aspects of place have often been neglected. To remedy this neglect, the ecosystem concept comes into play.

Ecosystem

The ecosystem is defined as a bounded *volume* of the Earth containing biota, the physical environment, and the interactions between these components.[9] Although the term *space* is often used in the definition rather than *volume,* we hasten to add that such use does not imply the Lefevbrian authoritarian abstract. Rather, ecosystems are defined by their content, and hence are more akin to the social conception of "place." Ecosystems in biology represent the structure and fluxes of particular places. And we have seen that the ecosystem concept in the contemporary world, including or perhaps especially urban areas, always includes humans and their institutions, artifacts, actions, and effects. Hence, the ecosystem in general terms and human ecosystems as specific instances of this generalized concept are places that have socially constructed meaning as well as what may to some social scientists and to people in general seem to be dry biological and biogeochemical content.

The richness of the social content of ecosystems is well represented by the human ecosystem model. Some incarnations of the model emphasize the social sphere while pointing to crucial biophysical components that support and interact with the social system. Other representations flesh out additional detail in the biophysical components of human ecosystems as a framework and highlight the important work that sphere does. In this respect, the human ecosystem model points to some of the same aspects of relevance that the idea of ecosystem services is meant to embody.[10] Human ecosystems, whether all their occupants or dependents realize it or not, provide the essential services to support life, resources for livelihood, biotic and biogeochemical regulation of the environment, and the artifacts and phenomena that embody cultural and spiritual value. It is not a stretch at all to say that human well-being rests on the foundation of the human ecosystem, and that many of the economic and social crises that fill the headlines emerge from the bad use people make of their human ecosystem home.

The ecosystem is a preeminently integrative concept. Such integration has been the desire since the origin of urban human ecology in Chicago, although we have seen how that early attempt fell short. An important alternative integrative tool is the POET model, in which the nature of social change in specific places was a function of the human population, its organization, the environment, and technology.[11] Perhaps in ecosystem terms, we could see these as a designation of the big components of a human ecosystem. The point is that integration and interactions of components are key to understanding how urban systems are put together and how they change. Feedbacks are the mechanisms, and both human and biophysical features are the components.

We expect that almost any ecosystem model constructed to represent a place at the human scale of perception or action will be spatially heterogeneous. Hence, patch dynamics as a methodological window becomes an essential tool for understanding and working with human ecosystems. Sometimes researchers set the boundaries of ecosystems so as to emphasize the homogeneity within them, as when a patch is modeled as an ecosystem or a uniformly forested watershed is instrumented to assess the processes within it. But even when homogeneity is a goal, often there is some real heterogeneity within the patch that must be understood. The uniform forest cover may shift through dominance by different species from the lowest to the highest elevations in the watershed, or small areas subject to previous human activities or natural disturbances may be silently present within what appears to be a uniform forest from a distance. It is best never to assume that an ecosystem delimited for some research or explanatory purpose is uniform until it has been examined in depth. Our experience suggests that the first best assumption about human ecosystems, and even of the patches recognized within them, is that they are internally heterogeneous. In addition, the heterogeneity within ecosystems is associated with the modifiable areal unit problem. How heterogeneity is bounded in large units on the ground will determine how we understand these patches.

Not all features of human ecosystems are benign. Biophysical hazards as well as social constraints exist. Among the biophysical hazards are such events as natural disturbances, along with topographic and climatic risk factors. Wildfires, floods, tsunamis, earthquakes, tornadoes, hurricanes, ice storms, and blizzards are familiar natural agents of physical disruption of system structure. Of course, in human ecosystems, vulnerability is a hybrid condition that marries hazardous events with socially derived structures, infrastructures, and management strategies in a location.[12] Poverty, poorly constructed infrastructure, and lack of information are often part of the social narrative of "natural" catastrophes. Furthermore, the ability of an urban system or one of its components or districts to respond to disturbance varies with the human, social, and financial capitals that can be mobilized in response. Here again, the concept of system resilience is relevant.

Human ecosystems, because they exhibit dimensions of spatial (place), organizational, and temporal complexity, require adaptive decision making. As indicated in chapter 6, decision makers' issues present the opportunity to define problems and approaches democratically with a comprehensive roster of stakeholders. Selection of socially acceptable interventions, partnerships among private and public actors, and joint assessment of the efficacy and equitability of outcomes characterize adaptive approaches. Engagements with community-based sustainability planning processes and contributions of a patch dynamics approach to measuring milestones toward meeting sustainability goals are important features of human ecosystem practices. Because interventions by designers, planners, and managers in social-ecological systems are necessarily place specific, a patch dynamics perspective is an important ingredient for decision making. All such interventions can helpfully be recognized as manipulation or generation of ecosystem components and the consequent changes in interactions among system components. Ultimately, management is a human ecosystem phenomenon.

One of the themes of this book has been the contrast and complementarity of ecology in the city versus ecology of the city. Of course, by city, we mean the entirety of the urban mosaic, including old core cities, new interstate interchange developments, suburbs of various ages, and varieties of exurbs and urban fringe settlements. The world's emerging urban megaregions[13] are even characterized by the embedding of rural and wild lands and by a proliferating urban-wildland interface.[14]

Traditionally, ecology in such complex urban contexts has focused on analogs of the wild and managed habitats that ecologists have long studied. Such work has been termed ecology *in* the city, and has sought out vacant lots as analogs of post-agricultural fields, wooded parklands as analogs of forests, and wetlands and riparian zones tucked away beyond the pale of development for their own interest. This work has been important for enhancing the quality of human life in cities, for conserving and restoring biodiversity in urbanized areas, and for informing urban planning and design. But an ecology *in* cities takes the vast majority of the urban environment as background and context rather than as an active part of the system of interest. In contrast to such a focus on "green" or clearly biologically dominated patches as separate ecosystems within the urban matrix, is the conceptualization of the entire urban mosaic as an ecosystem in itself. This broader conception is an ecology *of* the city. It employs the ecosystem concept as inclusive of human components and artifacts along with cultural and social meaning, in addition to the biotic and physical components that have engaged ecologists outside of cities for more than half a century. In this sense, the ecosystem conception is the third layer of connotation in urban areas. The first is seemingly abstract space, the second is the lived, perceived, and humanly valued sense of place, and the third is the ecosystem as a human, functioning feedback complex. Ecosystem fills out the richness of space and place.

The Future: Patch Dynamics and the Metacity

We combine the patch dynamics approach, which has been the familiar theme of this book, with a new idea, that of the metacity, to orient us toward the future. Below, we define the metacity concept and link it with patch dynamics. While the intent of both the patch dynamics concept and the more recent metacity concept can be both deeply technical and applied, something of their power is indicated by the poetic intelligence of Italo Calvino in his imagined account of Marco Polo's reports of the urban glories of Kublai Kahn's empire.[15] The multiple perspectives of urban form and function recounted by Marco Polo to the kahn are in fact different manifestations of only one city, Polo's beloved native city of Venice. And these perspectives focus as much on the future as on the past, pointing to the great dynamism of the urban realm: *"Journeys to relive your past?" was the Khan's question at this point, a question which could also have been formulated: "Journeys to recover your future?"*[16]

Patch dynamics is our theoretical lens to account for the great heterogeneity within and among urban areas and for supporting models of change through time. We have explored patch dynamics from several perspectives as a contribution to understanding the city of the present, much like the multiple images of Venice reported by Marco Polo. But ultimately these various models can be put together to provide a more comprehensive understanding of an urban region than any single model, map, or history. Our patch dynamics approach recognizes spatial heterogeneity in both the social and biophysical phenomena of urban ecosystems. Importantly, the term *urban ecosystem* embraces the spatial mosaics and heterogeneity of place recounted in the previous sections of this chapter. Even the term *urban landscape* is intended to include the complex heterogeneity of entire urban settlements or urban regions, not to be a label for only the green patches within cities and suburbs, or the green tendrils in exurbs.

Patch dynamics has been shown to be a methodology that can be shared between the social and the biophysical sciences, one that helps both kinds of specialty measure heterogeneity but, more important, can help them jointly pose questions and establish shared research agendas. Patch dynamics as method and viewpoint adds understanding to the spatial, organizational, and temporal dimensions of complexity of cities, suburbs, exurbs, and indeed entire urban megaregions. *Only this is known for sure: a given number of objects is shifted within a given space, at times submerged by a quantity of new objects, at times worn out and not replaced; the rule is to shuffle them each time, and try to reassemble them.*[17]

Patch dynamics alerts us to the fact that large urban systems comprise smaller, changing, and interacting components. The dynamics of the component parts are the mechanisms by which the larger system within which they are nested either changes or remains similar in the aggregate through time. Such dynamics can be referred to as metadynamics. They are dynamics of the unit *above* the collection of contained elements. Because of the patchy nature of urban settlements, and the variety of dynamics and spatial configurations of those patches, a "metacity" view of urban structure and dynamics emerges. *Contemplating these essential landscapes, Kublai reflected on the invisible order that sustains cities, on the rules that decreed how they might rise, take shape, and prosper, adapting themselves to the seasons, and then how they sadden and fall in ruins.*[18]

A metacity can be considered to consist of a variety of mosaic landscapes, each of which reflects particular perspectives on urban structure and functioning. For example, there may be landscapes of process such as demography, social norms, resource use, economic investment, biophysical regulation of environmental extremes, and the control of biological diversity, among others. Each of these landscapes has its own spatial pattern of drivers and outcomes, and these landscapes can interact to produce hybrid outcomes as well. Together, a complex array of patches and shifting mosaics constitutes a spatially extensive, patchy, and mutable metacity. This conception is applicable at any scale relevant to the consideration of urban systems, from small neighborhoods to the largest urban megaregions.[19]

But perhaps patch dynamics is most important, in this era of rapid globalized urbanization, as a tool to help envision and bring about desirable urban futures. Guided—we hope—by civic and democratic sustainability planning, patch dynamics reminds us that urban areas are patchy at all spatial scales. Patches have the potential to interact both through adjacency and teleconnections,[20] and the entire mosaic of patches at a given spatial scale is subject to change as patch identity, patch size and shape, and the nature of the boundaries between patches all shift. How these changes occur, what drives them, and what adaptive capacities of the patches and the mosaic are established or degraded during such change are the stuff of resilience. *The catalog of forms is endless: until every shape has found its city, new cities will continue to be born. When the forms exhaust their variety and come apart, the end of cities begins. In the last pages of the atlas there is an outpouring of networks without beginning or end, cities in the shape of Los Angeles, in the shape of Kyōto-Ōsaka, without shape.*[21] However, rather than give up in the face of the novel urban forms now emerging in Bangkok or Las Vegas, which we have discussed in chapter 4, or in Calvino's Los Angeles and the Kyoto-Osaka megaregion, or in cities as diverse as Kampala, Uganda in East Africa, or the São Paulo–Rio de Janeiro agglomeration in Brazil, understanding the different kinds, scales, and changes in heterogeneity offers a way forward.

Because there is no climax state for cities, no final industrial or developed Valhalla, the best we can hope for is the adjustment to internally and externally driven changes and shocks. Climate change, shifts in livelihood, changes in the fashions and identities of lifestyle, migration of persons and groups, spatial shifts in global investment and disinvestment, the decay and degradation of building stocks and infrastructure, and the periodic catastrophes of earthquake, storm, and flood are among the many shocks to the familiar and sometimes socially desired status quo. How urban systems marshal, create, distribute, or degrade the various kinds of capital that allow adjustment to such internal and external shocks determines whether any given urban system or patch within a system will meet the challenge of change. Patch dynamics is the arena and the interactive template for resilience.[22] *[Kahn:] "And I hear, from your voice, the invisible reasons which make cities live, through which perhaps, once dead, they will come to life again."*[23]

The metacity, with its various landscapes or spatial mosaics defined by the fluxes of material, energy, information, and people; and by the spatial distribution of people's individual and collective decision making; and by the joint outcomes of fluxes and decisions, is a model that both allows the poetry of Calvino and the rigor of urban structure, metabolism, and complexity to be accounted for. Calvino's vision reminds us of the many layers of description and the myriad perceptions that must contribute to a spatial and dynamic view of cities and extensive urban regions. There is one further bridge between the human and the natural that we must point to in the emerging global network of metacities. *As for the character of Andiria's inhabitants, two virtues are worth mentioning: self-confidence and prudence. Convinced that every innovation in the city influences the sky's pattern, before taking any decision they calculate the risks and advantages for themselves and for all worlds.*[24]

Urban Land Ethics

The environmental ethics of urban systems is the final ingredient in the recipe for desirable futures. In the realm of the biophysical, with its attention to conservation and to ecological restoration, the concern with desirable and just futures can be labeled the land ethic. This powerful idea, introduced by Aldo Leopold in 1949, was novel at the time for its suggestion that it was possible to take an ethical stance toward the use and management of land.[25] This is in contrast to a utilitarian view of the land and the categorization of its animal inhabitants as beneficial versus harmful. Leopold conceived of people, wildlife, plants, soils, and water to be members of a single land community. He thought that the central question of the land ethic was how to live on a piece of land without spoiling it. The land ethic has been central to the development of the field of environmental ethics, and it has helped guide new generations of scholars and practitioners in exploring and applying the deep philosophical implications of Leopold's seminal ideas.[26] The land ethic remains one of the most familiar entry points for biologists into the complex and evolving field of ethics.

LEOPOLD'S LAND ETHIC AND URBAN LANDS

The land ethic of Leopold at first glance appears to have little connection with urban lands. Leopold's ethic emerged from his personal experience in the management of wildlife populations in the American West, and later with the restoration of a degraded farm in Wisconsin. In our reading of Leopold's essays,[27] we have found the urban realm to be absent. His own concern, and that of later applications, was and is with ranches and farms, forests and mountain landscapes; with how to view predatory "varmints," wildland conservation; and with how to manage natural resources. Leopold's ethical stance can be viewed as moving beyond the utilitarian ideology of the Progressive Era during which he himself was trained. He emphasized that people should be part of a community of the land: that humans were obliged to figure out how to live with the other creatures—and, by extension—the other processes that were a feature of any landscape.

It might be argued that Leopold's use of "land" stood in for the ecosystem concept which, although it had been introduced in 1935, was not yet a common idea in scientific or management discourse. Leopold also lived at a time when a majority of Americans still inhabited small cities, rural towns, or farms. Consequently, many of his lay readers, students in forestry and wildlife management, and professional colleagues would have had personal experience with farming, woodlot management, and controlling predatory or crop-damaging wildlife. Urban systems would likely have been relatively rare or newly adopted homes in their personal experience, and essentially irrelevant to their professional concerns. Even many urban residents at the time had recent family histories of, or close existing ties with, farms and rural livelihoods.

We argue, however, that in spite of Leopold's personal distance from the urban—though he ultimately became a professor at the University of Wisconsin in the city of Madison—the ethical door he opened also leads into the city. A scientific argument for this stance emerges from the parallel we draw between Leopold's idea of "the land" and the current view of the ecosystem. It is an easy conceptual step from being a member of the land community to being a part of a human ecosystem. If many human ecosystems are now also urban or parts of urban megaregions, so, then, must the ethical concerns of that membership in that ecosystem community be retained. Urban systems are landscapes, ecosystems—or, more simply—land in the sense of the grounded and connected biological-social community that was Leopold's concern. Why not consider what a land ethic means for cities? Why not embrace environmental justice and environmental citizenship along with the familiar urban concerns with social justice as an outcome and as a process? Indeed, the increasingly common desire for sustainability in urban systems requires equal consideration of biophysical environmental integrity, economic viability, and social equity. Because sustainability is a normative, socially negotiated goal, it must have ethical content, and ethical dimensions exist in all three realms of sustainability— environment, economy, and society—as well as in their interactions.

AN URBAN LAND ETHIC AND PATCH DYNAMICS

Patch dynamics recognizes urban ecosystems as spatially heterogeneous or patchy. Thus, contrasts based on discrete boundaries or gradual changes in structure and process across urban regions are fundamental features of urban life. Patch dynamics also applies to urban areas as integrated ecosystems, embracing the physical, biological, social, and built components. The spatial heterogeneity in each of these major categories of ecosystem structure is relevant to its function and to its interaction with each of the other components. The patch mosaics that are the raw material for patch dynamics are mutable through time. Individual patches change in composition and internal structure, change in the kind or intensity of processes supported, and change in their degree of connectivity to adjacent and distant patches. All of these kinds of changes characterize the dynamic aspect of a patch mosaic. Time and space are equal concerns of patch dynamics, as are local and distal connections. In other words, patch dynamics is about differentials in structure, process, connection, and change.

An ethical treatment of any landscape must acknowledge the pervasive spatial structure and the differentiation of processes that exist within that landscape mosaic. This requires knowing what role each patch type plays in the dynamism and functioning of a mosaic. Patch dynamics thus suggests an ethics of biophysical completeness. And because urban patch dynamics also has social dimensions, so must an urban land ethic take into account social inclusion—the equity of social and economic opportunity, and the role that social segregation plays in access of persons and groups to power, resources, status, and other social features.

Because patch dynamics focuses on all kinds of urban patches, the ethical relevance of all patches is clear. Social and economic inequities have environmental implications that can feed back quite strongly on human well-being. Whether environmental equity can be said to exist or not depends on how environmental hazards, benefits, social status, and power align across space. Furthermore, inclusion, exclusion, inequity, and equity all have spatial distributions, and these are often not static through time. Rather, there are numerous legacies of past injustices that echo today; our example has been the current locations of high vacancy and abandonment that echo the mortgage redlining practices of the early decades of the twentieth century.

AN URBAN LAND ETHIC AND ECOLOGY *OF* CITIES?

Under the banner of ecology *in* the city, an urban land ethic would focus on the effects of human and institutional ideologies, plans, decisions, and activities on particular "green" patches within the urban fabric. At different times and places, such ecotopes, or ecologically important locations within cities, might receive ethical assessment in their roles as sacred groves, cemeteries, pleasure grounds, parks, nature reserves, symbols of historical or cultural significance, or private property. A utilitarian ethic of the ecosystem services that emerged from patches dominated by biotic elements has been articulated.[28] However, focusing on specific patches seen as biological elements within the built environment conceives of them as isolated ecosystems and suggests their preservation and management as distinct locations. The broader ethical stance within the paradigm of ecology in the city might be stated in a requirement that ecotopes must be included in the city either for human well-being, as cultural amenities, or because of the intrinsic value of wildlife, for example.

An example of the contrast between ecology *in* the city versus ecology *of* the city shows both the value of biophysical inclusiveness and the need for an ethical dimension of that inclusiveness. Under the ecology *in* paradigm, one of the kinds of patches regarded as important in cities has been riparian areas of streams. Following the model of landscape function that emerged from agricultural landscapes, city policy makers transferred to their management tool kit the rural approach that riparian zones would help clean urban streams. However, detailed studies of Baltimore streams documented that the capacity of urban riparian zones to reduce nitrate pollution was severely impaired by streambed erosion and isolation of the floodplains from the groundwater table. Consequently, upstream areas and their vegetated components such as trees and pervious areas were recognized to be functionally important in controlling stormwater amount and quality.[29] Thus, if there is to be an ethical consideration, even from an instrumental point of view, of urban riparian zones, it is not sufficient to view them as isolated green patches. Rather, riparian function is something that has a more extensive distribution throughout broader urban patch mosaics. The ecology *of* the city exposes unexpected functional connections, and hence suggests that the targets of ethical concern should not be isolated to biologically dominated patches.

The paradigm of ecology *of* cities must therefore result in a different approach to an urban land ethic. Rather than focus on isolated, island-like ecotopes or green patches, the ecology of cities suggests attending to the biophysical aspects throughout the urban region. Membership in the urban land community—the urban ecosystem—brings with it the ethical consideration of numerous things, including:

- organisms, wherever they exist or move in the urban matrix;
- biogeochemical processes, those that process so-called wastes as well as those that support resources used by people;
- heterogeneous patch mosaics that permit coexistence of

different species and social arrangements, and that support
diverse ecological functions;
- biophysical amenities that provide cultural services as well
as those that directly affect human well-being.

In other words, the existence value, the intrinsic value, the building of
human virtue, and the duty to protect ecological structures and processes are among the motivations for ethical consideration of all parts
of the urban ecosystem. And the urban land ethic recognizes social justice and equity, embracing its complexity and diversity of meanings. *But
from my words you will have reached the conclusion that the real Beren-
ice is a temporal succession of different cities, just and unjust. But what I
wanted to warn you about is something else: all the future Berenices are
already present in this instant, wrapped one within the other, confined,
crammed, inextricable.*[30]

It is unfortunate that an environmental ethic has been so little explored in the context of urban systems. The land ethic is traditionally
applied in wild lands, rural landscapes, and in areas where biological
conservation values are paramount. This brief discussion suggests that
there can be a land ethic for urban systems. This would complement the
well-developed ethic of social justice and social equity that exists already
for urban systems. And there is no denying the significance and efficacy
of this social view in areas of environmental justice, both in terms of the
distribution of biophysical goods, services, and hazards, and in the just
civic and institutional procedures for allocating those benefits and burdens. But what of the ethics of the use and abuse of the biophysical components of urban ecosystems? This question is modestly investigated
or acted upon. What is the ethics of the ecology of *all* urban patches,
even those that are not obviously "green"? The rubric of sustainability is one attempt to bring environment into the normative fold, of
course. Because sustainability is a civic and democratic set of goals that
by definition embraces environmental, economic, and social outcomes,
it suggests that an ethical treatment must exist in all three constituent
realms and in their interaction. What this means is an open frontier of
scholarship and civic dialog for which we have only questions at this
time. We might rephrase Leopold's question about the land ethic for the

urban situation: "How can we share a lived place without ruining it?" Who shares, including individuals, groups, biota, fluxes, and structures? What is the implication of an urban land ethic for planning, design, intervention, and restoration? What are the just procedures and outcomes of inclusive environmental justice in urban systems? How might a sense of place and the recognition that urban areas are ecosystems in whole and in part influence the articulation and application of an urban land ethic? These are ethical questions that will help guide a patch dynamics approach toward equitable and resilient futures for our emerging metacities.

Notes

ONE The Baltimore School of Urban Ecology

1. S. T. A. Pickett, W. R. Burch Jr., and S. Dalton, "Integrated Urban Ecosystem Research," *Urban Ecosystems* 1, no. 4 (1997): 183–84; N. B. Grimm, J. M. Grove, Steward T. A. Pickett, and C. L. Redman, "Integrated Approaches to Long-term Studies of Urban Ecological Systems Present Multiple Challenges to Ecologists—Pervasive Human Impact and Extreme Heterogeneity of Cities, and the Need to Integrate Social and Ecological Approaches," *BioScience* 50, no. 7 (2000): 571–84.

2. M. L. Cadenasso and S. T. A. Pickett, "Urban Principles for Ecological Landscape Design and Management: Scientific Fundamentals," *Cities and the Environment (CATE)* 1, no. 2 (2008): 1–16; S. T. A. Pickett and J. M. Grove, "Urban Ecosystems: What Would Tansley Do?" *Urban Ecosystems* 12 (2009): 1–8.

3. A. G. Tansley, "The Use and Abuse of Vegetational Concepts and Terms," *Ecology* 16 (1935): 284–307.

4. G. E. Machlis, J. E. Force, and W. R. Burch Jr., "The Human Ecosystem, Part I: The Human Ecosystem as an Organizing Concept in Ecosystem Management," *Society and Natural Resources* 10 (1997): 347–67.

5. J. A. Wiens, "Ecological Heterogeneity: An Ontogeny of Concepts and Approaches," in *Ecological Consequences of Habitat Heterogeneity,* ed. M. J. Hutchings, E. A. John, and A. J. A. Stewart (Malden, Mass.: Blackwell, 2000), 9–31.

6. M. L. Cadenasso and S. T. A. Pickett, "Three Tides: The Development and State of the Art of Urban Ecological Science," in *Resilience in Ecology and Urban Design: Linking Theory and Practice for Sustainable Cities,* ed. S. T. A. Pickett, M. L. Cadenasso, and B. P. McGrath (New York: Springer New York, 2013), 29–46.

7. R. T. T. Forman, "Some General Principles of Landscape and Regional Ecology," *Landscape Ecology* 10, no. 3 (1995): 133–42.

8. J. Wu and O. L. Loucks, "From Balance of Nature to Hierarchical Patch Dynamics: A Paradigm Shift in Ecology," *Quarterly Review of Biology* 70 (1995): 439–66.

9. G. D. Jenerette and J. Wu, "Analysis and Simulation of Land-Use Change in the Central Arizona–Phoenix Region, USA," *Landscape Ecology* 16, no. 7 (2001): 611–26.

10. Cadenasso and Pickett, "Three Tides"; G. D. Shane, *Recombinant Urbanism: Conceptual Modeling in Architecture, Urban Design, and City Theory* (Chichester, U.K.: John Wiley and Sons, 2005).

11. M. L. Cadenasso, S. T. A. Pickett, and J. M. Grove, "Dimensions of Ecosystem Complexity: Heterogeneity, Connectivity, and History," *Ecological Complexity,* no. 3 (2006): 1–12.

12. J. A. Wiens, "Landscape Mosaics and Ecological Theory," in *Mosaic Landscapes and Ecological Processes,* ed. L. Hansson, L. Fahrig, and G. Merriman (New York: Chapman and Hall, 1995), 1–26; H. Li and J. F. Reynolds, "On Definition and Quantification of Heterogeneity," *Oikos* 73 (1995): 280–84.

13. Li and Reynolds, "On Definition and Quantification of Heterogeneity."

14. V. Ahl and T. F. H. Allen, *Hierarchy Theory: A Vision, Vocabulary, and Epistemology* (New York: Columbia University Press, 1996); J. M. Grove and W. R. Burch Jr., "A Social Ecology Approach and Applications of Urban Ecosystem and Landscape Analyses: A Case Study of Baltimore, Maryland," *Urban Ecosystems* 1, no. 4 (1997): 259–75; R. R. Chowdhury, K. Larson, J. M. Grove, C. Polsky, and E. Cook, "A Multi-scalar Approach to Theorizing Socio-ecological Dynamics of Urban Residential Landscapes," *Cities and the Environment* 4, no. 1 (2011).

15. C. S. Holling and L. H. Gunderson, "Resilience and Adaptive Cycles," in *Panarchy: Understanding Transformations in Human and Natural Systems,* ed. L. H. Gunderson and C. S. Holling (Washington, D.C.: Island, 2002), 25–62.

16. M. L. Cadenasso, S. T. A. Pickett, and J. M. Grove, "Integrative Approaches to Investigating Human-Natural Systems: The Baltimore Ecosystem Study," *Natures, Sciences, Societies,* no. 14 (2006): 4–14.

17. Cadenasso, Pickett, and Grove, "Dimensions of Ecosystem Complexity."

18. Ibid.

19. Machlis, Force, and Burch, "The Human Ecosystem, Part I."

20. R. K. Merton, *Social Theory and Social Structure,* rev. ed. (New York: Free Press, 1968).

21. Ibid., 39.

22. Ibid.

23. S. T. A. Pickett, K. T. Belt, M. F. Galvin, P. Groffman, J. M. Grove, D. C. Outen, R. Pouyat, W. P. Stack, and M. Cadenasso, "Watersheds in Baltimore, Maryland: Understanding and Application of Integrated Ecological and Social Processes," *Journal of Contemporary Water Research and Education* 136 (June 2007): 44–55.

24. D. E. Stokes, *Pasteur's Quadrant—Basic Science and Technological Innovation* (Washington, D.C.: Brookings Institution Press, 1997). Figure is adapted from original.

TWO Standing on the Shoulders of Giants

1. G. E. Likens and O. Kinne, *The Ecosystem Approach: Its Use and Abuse* (Oldendorf/Luhe, Germany: Ecology Institute, 1992).

2. R. T. T. Forman and M. Godron, *Landscape Ecology* (New York: John Wiley and Sons, 1986).

3. R. E. Park, E. W. Burgess, and R. D. McKenzie, *The City: Suggestions for the Investigation of Human Behavior in the Urban Environment* (Chicago: University of Chicago Press, 1925).

4. D. Ross, *The Origins of American Social Science* (Cambridge: Cambridge University Press, 1991).

5. J. M. Grove, "The Relationship Between Patterns and Processes of Social Stratification and Vegetation of an Urban-Rural Watershed" (Ph.D. diss., School of Forestry and Environmental Studies, Yale University, 1996); J. S. Light, *The Nature of Cities: Ecological Visions and the American Urban Professions, 1920–1960* (Baltimore: Johns Hopkins University Press, 2009).

6. R. E. Park, "The City: Suggestions for the Investigation of Human Behavior in the Urban Environment," in *The City: Suggestions for the Investigation of Human Behavior in the Urban Environment,* ed. R. E. Park, E. W. Burgess, and R. D. McKenzie (Chicago: University of Chicago Press, 1925), 1–46.

7. E. W. Burgess, "The Growth of the City: An Introduction to a Research Project," in Park, Burgess, and McKenzie, *The City,* 47–62. Figure courtesy of University of Chicago Press.

8. C. D. Harris and E. L. Ullman, "The Nature of Cities," *Annals of the American Academy of Political and Social Science,* no. 242 (1945): 7–17.

9. R. D. McKenzie, "The Ecological Approach to the Study of the Human Community," in Park, Burgess, and McKenzie, *The City,* 63–79; R. D. McKenzie, "The Scope of Human Ecology," *American Sociological Society of America* 20 (1925): 141–54.

10. A. H. Hawley, *Human Ecology: A Theoretical Essay* (Chicago: University of Chicago Press, 1986).

11. W. Firey, "Sentiment and Symbolism as Ecological Variables," *American Sociological Review* 10 (April 1945): 140–48.

12. M. Gottdiener and R. Hutchison, *The New Urban Sociology,* 4th ed. (Boulder, Colo.: Westview, 2011).

13. Hawley, *Human Ecology.*

14. L. Wirth, "Human Ecology," *American Journal of Sociology* 50 (May 1945): 483–88.

15. Firey, "Sentiment and Symbolism."

16. Ibid.

17. Hawley, *Human Ecology.*

18. Ibid.

19. Gottdiener and Hutchison, *New Urban Sociology.*

20. S. Kostof, *The City Shaped: Urban Patterns and Meanings Through History* (London: Thames and Hudson, 1991).

21. E. Shevky and W. Bell, *Social Area Analysis: Theory, Illustrative Application and Computational Procedure* (Stanford: Stanford University Press, 1955).

22. Gottdiener and Hutchison, *New Urban Sociology.*

23. B. J. L. Berry, "A New Urban Ecology?" *Urban Geography* 22 (2001): 699–701.

24. M. V. Melosi, "The Historical Dimension of Urban Ecology: Frameworks and Concepts," in *Understanding Urban Ecosystems: A New Frontier for Science and Education,* ed. A. R. Berkowitz, C. H. Nilon, and K. S. Hollweg (New York: Springer-Verlag, 2003), 187–200.

25. Ibid.

26. I. McHarg, *Design with Nature* (Garden City, N.J.: Doubleday/Natural History Press, 1969); A. W. Spirn, *The Granite Garden: Urban Nature and Human Design* (New York: Basic Books, 1984).

27. S. W. Havlick, *The Urban Organism* (New York: Macmillan, 1974).

28. D. Harvey, *Spaces of Hope* (Berkeley: University of California Press, 2000).

29. K. Lynch, *The Image of the City* (Cambridge, Mass.: MIT Press, 1960).

30. T. R. Detwyler and M. G. Marcus, *Urbanization and Environment: The Physical Geography of the City* (Belmont: Duxbury, 1972).

31. W. Cronon, *Nature's Metropolis: Chicago and the Great West* (New York: Norton, 1991).

32. G. D. Shane, *Recombinant Urbanism: Conceptual Modeling in Architecture, Urban Design, and City Theory* (Chichester, U.K.: John Wiley and Sons, 2005).

33. E. Mayr, *The Growth of Biological Thought: Diversity, Evolution, and Inheritance* (Cambridge, Mass.: Harvard University Press, 1982).

34. M. Hough, *City Form and Natural Process: Towards a New Urban Vernacular* (New York: Van Norstrand Reinhold, 1984).

35. S. T. A. Pickett, M. L. Cadenasso, J. M. Grove, C. H. Nilon, R. V. Pouyat, W. C. Zipperer, and R. Costanza, "Urban Ecological Systems: Linking Terrestrial Ecological, Physical, and Socioeconomic Components of Metropolitan Areas," *Annual Review of Ecology and Systematics* 32 (2001): 127–57.

36. A. H. Hawley, *Human Ecology: A Theory of Community Structure* (New York: Ronald, 1950).

37. L. F. Schnore, "Social Morphology and Human Ecology," *American Journal of Sociology* 63 (May 1958): 620–24, 629–34; O. D. Duncan, "Human Ecology and Population Studies," in *The Study of Population,* ed. P. M. Hauser and O. D. Duncan (Chicago: University of Chicago Press, 1959), 687–716; O. D. Duncan, "From Social System to Ecosystem," *Sociological Inquiry* 31 (1961): 140–49; O. D. Duncan, "Social Organization and the Ecosystem," in *Handbook of Modern Sociology,* ed. R. E. L. Faris (Chicago: Rand McNally, 1964), 37–82; W. Firey, *Man, Mind and Land* (Middleton, Wis.: Social Ecology, 1999).

38. B. J. L. Berry, "Cities as Systems Within Systems of Cities," *Papers in Regional Science* 13 (1964): 146–63.

39. M. L. Cadenasso, S. T. A. Pickett, and J. M. Grove, "Dimensions of Ecosystem Complexity: Heterogeneity, Connectivity, and History," *Ecological Complexity,* no. 3 (2006): 1–12.

THREE Expanding the Landscape

1. S. T. A. Pickett and K. Rogers, "Patch Dynamics: The Transformation of Landscape Structure and Function," in *Wildlife and Landscape Ecology: Effects of Pattern and Scale*, ed. J. A. Bissonette (New York: Springer-Verlag, 1997), 101–27.

2. M. Gottdiener and R. Hutchison, *The New Urban Sociology*, 4th ed. (Boulder, Colo.: Westview, 2011).

3. S. E. Kingsland, *Modeling Nature: Episodes in the History of Population Ecology* (Chicago: University of Chicago Press, 1985).

4. R. Levins, "The Strategy of Model Building in Population Biology," *American Scientist* 54 (1966): 421–31.

5. E. Mayr, *This Is Biology: The Science of the Living World* (Cambridge, Mass.: Harvard University Press, 1997).

6. R. P. McIntosh, "Concept and Terminology of Homogeneity and Heterogeneity," in *Ecological Heterogeneity*, ed. J. Kolasa and S. T. A. Pickett (New York: Springer-Verlag, 1991), 24–46.

7. J. A. Wiens, "Ecological Heterogeneity: An Ontogeny of Concepts and Approaches," in *Ecological Consequences of Habitat Heterogeneity*, ed. M. J. Hutchings, E. A. John, and A. J. A. Stewart (Malden, Mass.: Blackwell, 2000), 9–31.

8. S. T. A. Pickett and M. L. Cadenasso, "Vegetation Succession," in *Vegetation Ecology*, ed. E. van der Maarel (Malden, Mass.: Blackwell, 2005), 172–98.

9. J. A. Wiens, "Population Responses to Patchy Environments," *Annual Review of Ecology and Systematics* 7 (1976): 81–120.

10. S. T. A. Pickett, M. Cadenasso, and C. G. Jones, "Generation of Heterogencity by Organisms: Creation, Maintenance, and Transformation," in *Ecological Consequences of Habitat Heterogeneity*, ed. M. J. Hutchings, E. A. John, and A. J. A. Stewart (Malden, Mass.: Blackwell, 2000), 33–52.

11. S. A. Levin, "Population Dynamic Models in Heterogeneous Environments," *Annual Review of Ecology and Systematics* 7 (1976): 287–310; S. T. A. Pickett and P. S. White, *The Ecology of Natural Disturbance and Patch Dynamics* (New York: Academic, 1985).

12. Pickett and Rogers, "Patch Dynamics."

13. M. P. Austin and T. M. Smith, "A New Model for the Continuum Concept," *Vegetatio* 83 (1989): 35–47.

14. H. A. Gleason, "The Structure and Development of the Plant Association," *Bulletin of the Torrey Botanical Club* 44 (1917): 463–81.

15. P. M. Vitousek and P. A. Matson, "Gradient Analysis of Ecosystems," in *Comparative Analyses of Ecosystems: Patterns, Mechanisms, and Theories*, ed. J. Cole, G. M. Lovett, and S. Findlay (New York: Springer-Verlag, 1991), 287–98.

16. R. H. Whittaker, *Communities and Ecosystems* (New York: Macmillan, 1975).

17. Pickett and Rogers, "Patch Dynamics."

18. J. Wu, *Modeling the Landscape as a Dynamics Mosaic of Patches: Some Computational Aspects* (Ithaca, N.Y.: Cornell Theory Center, 1993).

19. W. P. Sousa, "Disturbance and Patch Dynamics on Rocky Intertidal Shores,"

in *The Ecology of Natural Disturbance and Patch Dynamics,* ed. S. T. A. Pickett and P. S. White (Orlando: Academic, 1985), 101–24.

20. J. M. Facelli and E. Facelli, "Interactions after Death: Plant Litter Controls Priority Effects in a Successional Plant Community," *Oecologia* 95 (1993): 277–82.

21. Wiens, "Population Responses."

22. P. S. White, "Pattern, Process, and Natural Disturbance in Vegetation," *Botanical Review* 45 (1979): 229–99.

23. Pickett and White, "Ecology of Natural Disturbance"; M. L. Cadenasso, S. T. A. Pickett, K. C. Weathers, S. S. Bell, T. L. Benning, M. M. Carreiro, and T. E. Dawson, "An Interdisciplinary and Synthetic Approach to Ecological Boundaries," *BioScience* 53 (2003): 717–22; L. Fahrig, "When Is a Landscape Perspective Important?" in *Issues and Perspectives in Landscape Ecology,* ed. J. A. Wiens and M. R. Moss (New York: Cambridge University Press, 2005), 3–10.

24. J. Jacobs, *The Death and Life of Great American Cities* (New York: Vintage Books, 1961); K. Lynch, *Good City Form* (Cambridge, Mass.: MIT Press, 1981); M. Batty, "The Size, Scale, and Shape of Cities," *Science* 319, no. 8 (2008): 769–71.

25. United Nations Population Fund, *State of World Population, 2007: Unleashing the Potential of Urban Growth* (New York: United Nations Population Fund, 2007), www .unfpa.org/swp/2007/english/introduction.html.

26. G. E. Likens and O. Kinne, *The Ecosystem Approach: Its Use and Abuse* (Oldendorf/Luhe, Germany: Ecology Institute, 1992); S. T. A. Pickett and M. L. Cadenasso, "Ecosystem as a Multidimensional Concept: Meaning, Model and Metaphor," *Ecosystems* 5, no. 1 (2002): 1–10.

27. K. Jax, C. Jones, and S. T. A. Pickett, "The Self-Identity of Ecological Units," *Oikos* 82 (1998): 253–64; K. Jax, "Ecological Units: Definitions and Application," *Quarterly Review of Biology* 81 (2006): 237–58.

28. A. G. Tansley, "The Use and Abuse of Vegetational Concepts and Terms," *Ecology* 16 (1935): 284–307.

29. L. Von Bertalanffy, *General System Theory: Foundations, Development, Applications* (New York: George Braziller, 1968).

30. T. F. H. Allen and T. W. Hoekstra, *Toward a Unified Ecology: Complexity in Ecological Systems* (New York: Columbia University Press, 1992).

31. N. B. Grimm, L. J. Baker, and D. Hope, "An Ecosystem Approach to Understanding Cities: Familiar Foundations and Uncharted Frontiers," in *Understanding Urban Ecosystems: A New Frontier for Science and Education,* ed. A. R. Berkowitz, C. H. Nilon, and K. S. Holweg (New York: Springer-Verlag, 2003), 95–114.

32. C. J. Krebs, *Ecology: The Experimental Analysis of Distribution and Abundance* (San Francisco: Benjamin Cummings, 2001).

33. G. E. Machlis, J. E. Force, and W. R. Burch Jr., "The Human Ecosystem, Part I: The Human Ecosystem as an Organizing Concept in Ecosystem Management," *Society and Natural Resources* 10 (1997): 347–67; E. Ostrom, *Understanding Institutional Diversity* (Princeton: Princeton University Press, 2005).

34. Tansley, "Use and Abuse."

35. S. T. A. Pickett and J. M. Grove, "Urban Ecosystems: What Would Tansley Do?" *Urban Ecosystems* 12 (2009): 1–8.

36. Machlis, Force, and Burch, "Human Ecosystem Part I."

37. M. V. Melosi, *The Sanitary City: Urban Infrastructure in America from Colonial Times to the Present* (Baltimore: Johns Hopkins University Press, 2000).

38. Pickett and Cadenasso, "Ecosystem as Multidimensional Concept."

39. Jax, "Ecological Units."

40. S. T. A. Pickett, J. Kolasa, and C. Jones, *Ecological Understanding: The Nature of Theory and the Theory of Nature,* 2nd ed. (Boston: Academic, 2007).

41. K. Lynch, *The Image of the City* (Cambridge, Mass.: MIT Press, 1960); G. D. Shane, *Recombinant Urbanism: Conceptual Modeling in Architecture, Urban Design, and City Theory* (Chichester, U.K.: John Wiley and Sons, 2005).

42. W. E. Rees, "Eco-Footprint Analysis: Merits and Brickbats," *Ecological Economics* 32 (2000): 371–74.

43. Grimm, Baker, and Hope, "Ecosystem Approach to Understanding"; P. Clergeau, J. Jokimäki, and R. Snep, "Using Hierarchical Levels for Urban Ecology," *Trends in Ecology and Evolution* 21 (2006): 660–61; E. Shochat, P. S. Warren, S. H. Faeth, N. E. McIntyre, and D. Hope, "From Patterns to Emerging Processes in Mechanistic Urban Ecology," *Trends in Ecology and Evolution* 21 (2006): 186–91.

44. W. R. Effland and R. V. Pouyat, "The Genesis, Classification, and Mapping of Soils in Urban Areas," *Urban Ecosystems* 1 (1997): 217–28; R. V. Pouyat, I. D. Yesilonis, J. Russell-Anelli, and N. K. Neerchal, "Soil Chemical and Physical Properties That Differentiate Urban Land-Use and Cover Types," *Soil Science of America Journal* 71, no. 3 (2007): 1010–19.

45. P. J. Craul, "A Description of Urban Soils and Their Characteristics," *Journal of Arboriculture* 11 (1985): 330–39.

46. B. H. Wilkinson, "Humans as Geologic Agents: A Deep-time Perspective," *Geology* 33 (2005): 161–64.

47. C. H. Nilon and L. W. Vandruff, "Analysis of Small Mammal Community Data and Applications to Management of Urban Greenspaces," in *Integrating Man and Nature in the Metropolitan Environment,* ed. L. W. Adams and D. L. Leedy (Columbia, Md.: National Institute of Urban Wildlife, 1987), 53–59; Shochat et al., "Patterns to Emerging Processes."

48. Shane, *Recombinant Urbanism*; D. G. Shane, "Urban Patches: Granulation, Patterns and Patchworks," in *Designing Patch Dynamics,* ed. B. McGrath, V. Marshall, M. L. Cadenasso, J. M. Grove, S. T. A. Pickett, R. Plunz, and J. Towers, *New Urbanisms* (New York: Columbia, Graduate School of Architecture, Planning, and Preservation, 2007), 94–103.

49. B. McGrath and D. Thaitakoo, "Tasting the Periphery: Bangkok's Agri- and Aquacultural Fringe," *Architectural Design* 75 (2005): 43–51.

50. K. Olson, "Old West Baltimore: Segregation, African-American Culture, and the Struggle for Equality," in *The Baltimore Book: New Views on Local History,* ed. E. Fee (Philadelphia: Temple University Press, 1991), 57–80.

51. S. H. Olson, *Baltimore: The Building of an American City* (Baltimore: Johns Hopkins University Press, 1997).

52. G. Clay, *Close Up: How to Read the American City* (New York: Praeger, 1973).

53. E. C. Ellis, R. G. Li, L. Z. Yang, and X. Cheng, "Long-term Change in Village-Scale Ecosystems in China Using Landscape and Statistical Methods," *Ecological Applications* 10, no. 4 (2000): 1057–73.

54. H. Sukopp and P. Werner, *Nature in Cities: A Report and Review of Studies and Experiments Concerning Ecology, Wildlife, and Nature Conservation in Urban and Suburban Areas* (Strasbourg: Council of Europe, 1982).

55. M. L. Cadenasso, S. T. A. Pickett, K. C. Weathers, and C. G. Jones, "A Framework for a Theory of Ecological Boundaries," *Bioscience*, no. 53 (2003): 750–58; M. L. Cadenasso and S. T. A. Pickett, "Boundaries as Structural and Functional Entities in Landscapes: Understanding Flows in Ecology and Urban Design," in McGrath et al., *Designing Patch Dynamics*, 116–31.

56. McGrath et al., *Designing Patch Dynamics*.

57. E. W. B. Russell, *People and the Land Through Time* (New Haven: Yale University Press, 1997).

58. C. S. Smith, *Urban Disorder and the Shape of Belief: The Great Chicago Fire, the Haymarket Bomb, and the Model Town of Pullman* (Chicago: University of Chicago Press, 1995).

59. A. R. Troy, J. M. Grove, J. P. M. O'Neil-Dunne, S. T. A. Pickett, and M. L. Cadenasso, "Predicting Opportunities for Greening and Patterns of Vegetation on Private Urban Lands," *Environmental Management* 40 (2007): 394–412.

60. C. G. Boone and A. Modarres, *City and Environment* (Philadelphia: Temple University Press, 2006).

61. S. T. A. Pickett, J. Kolasa, J. J. Armesto, and S. L. Collins, "The Ecological Concept of Disturbance and Its Expression at Various Hierarchical Levels," *Oikos* 54, no. 2 (1989): 129–36.

62. R. J. Sampson, J. D. Morenoff, and T. Gannon-Rowley, "Assessing 'Neighborhood Effects': Social Processes and New Directions in Research," *Annual Review of Sociology* 28 (2002): 443–78.

63. J. R. Borchert, "Major Control Points in American Economic Geography," *Annals of the Association of American Geographers* 68 (1978): 214–32.

64. Pickett and White, "Ecology of Natural Disturbance."

65. E. J. Rykiel, "Towards a Definition of Ecological Disturbance," *Australian Journal of Ecology* 10 (1985): 361–65.

66. C. E. Colten, *An Unnatural Metropolis: Wrestling New Orleans from Nature* (Baton Rouge: Louisiana State University Press, 2005).

67. J. M. Barry, *Rising Tide: The Great Mississippi Flood of 1927 and How It Changed America* (New York: Simon and Schuster, 1997).

68. National Research Council, *Facing Hazards and Disasters: Understanding Human Dimensions* (Washington, D.C.: National Academies Press, 2006).

69. S. Winchester, *A Crack in the Edge of the World: America and the Great California Earthquake of 1906* (New York: Harper Collins, 2005).

70. G. Plafker, L. R. Mayo, and U. S. Geological Survey, *Tectonic Deformation, Subsequent Slides and Destructive Waves Associated with the Alaskan March 27, 1964 Earthquake: An Interim Geologic Evaluation* (Menlo Park, Calif.: U.S. Geologic Survey, 1965).

71. S. Winchester, *Karakatoa: The Day the World Exploded: August 27, 1883* (New York: Harper Collins, 2003).

72. S. L. Cutter, *American Hazardscapes: The Regionalization of Hazards and Disasters* (Washington, D.C.: Joseph Henry, 2001).

73. Barry, *Rising Tide.*

74. S. J. Pyne, *Fire: A Brief History* (Seattle: University of Washington Press, 2001).

75. Olson, *Baltimore.*

76. E. Klinenberg, *Heat Wave: A Social Autopsy of Disaster in Chicago* (Chicago: University of Chicago Press, 2003).

77. Ibid., 116.

78. Ibid., 127.

79. T. S. Chapin, "Sports Facilities as Urban Redevelopment Catalysts," *Journal of the American Planning Association* 70 (2004): 193–209.

80. J. R. Borchert, "American Metropolitan Evolution," *Geographical Review* 57 (1967): 301–32.

81. S. Berling-Wolff and J. Wu, "Modeling Urban Landscape Dynamics: A Review," *Ecological Research* 19, no. 1 (2004): 119–29.

82. D. J. Nowak, "Historical Vegetation Change in Oakland and Its Implications for Urban Forest Management," *Journal of Arboriculture* 19 (1993): 313–19; M. L. McKinney, "Urbanization, Biodiversity, and Conservation," *BioScience* 52, no. 10 (2002): 883–91.

83. A. W. Spirn, "Constructing Nature: The Legacy of Frederick Law Olmsted," in *Uncommon Ground: Toward Reinventing Nature,* ed. W. Cronon (New York: Norton, 1995), 91–113.

84. R. Solnit, "The Uses of Disaster: Notes on Bad Weather and Good Government," *Harper's Magazine* 311, no. 1865 (2005): 31–37.

85. Barry, *Rising Tide.*

86. D. J. Bain and G. S. Brush, "Placing the Pieces: Reconstructing the Original Property Mosaic in a Warrant and Patent Watershed," *Landscape Ecology* 19 (2004): 843–56.

87. C. Boone, "An Assessment and Explanation of Environmental Inequity in Baltimore," *Urban Geography* 23, no. 6 (2002): 581–95.

88. W. Kornblum, *Blue Collar Community* (Chicago: University of Chicago Press, 1974).

89. Ibid., 15.

90. Ibid., 228.

91. Cadenasso and Pickett, "Boundaries as Structural and Functional Entities."

92. J. Wu and J. L. David, "A Spatially Explicit Hierarchical Approach to Modeling

Complex Ecological Systems : Theory and Applications," *Ecological Modelling* 153 (2002): 7–26.

93. J. Wu and O. L. Loucks, "From Balance of Nature to Hierarchical Patch Dynamics: A Paradigm Shift in Ecology," *Quarterly Review of Biology* 70 (1995): 439–66; Pickett, Cadenasso, and Jones, "Generation of Heterogeneity."

94. Cadenasso et al., "Interdisciplinary and Synthetic Approach"; Cadenasso and Pickett, "Boundaries as Structural and Functional Entities."

95. Lynch, *Image of the City.*

96. F. Oswald and P. Baccini, *Netzstadt* (Basel: Springer, 2003).

97. R. T. T. Forman, "Corridors in a Landscape: Their Ecological Structure and Function," *Oecologia* 2, no. 4 (1983): 375–87.

98. R. T. T. Forman, "Interaction Among Landscape Elements: A Core of Landscape Ecology," in *Perspectives in Landscape Ecology: Proceedings of International Congress Organized by Netherlands Society for Landscape Ecology, Veldhoven, the Netherlands, April 6–11, 1981,* ed. S. P. Tjallingii and A. A. de Veer.

99. K. Easterling, *Organization Space: Landscapes, Highways and Houses in America* (Cambridge, Mass.: MIT Press, 1999).

100. M. V. Melosi, *The Sanitary City: Urban Infrastructure in America from Colonial Times to the Present* (Baltimore: Johns Hopkins University Press, 2000).

101. P. Groffman, N. L. Law, K. T. Belt, L. E. Band, and G. T. Fisher, "Nitrogen Fluxes and Retention in Urban Watershed Ecosystems," *Ecosystems* 7, no. 4 (2004): 393–403; M. Cadenasso, S. T. A. Pickett, P. Groffman, L. E. Band, G. S. Brush, M. F. Galvin, J. M. Grove, et al., "Exchanges Across the Land-Water-Scape Boundaries in Urban Systems," *Annals of New York Academy of Sciences,* no. 1134 (2008): 213–32.

102. Cadenasso et al., "Framework for a Theory."

103. Cadenasso and Pickett, "Boundaries as Structural and Functional Entities."

104. J. R. Anderson, E. E. Hardy, J. T. Roach, and R. E. Witmer, *Land Use and Land Cover Classification Systems for Use with Remote Sensor Data* (Washington, D.C.: U.S. Government Printing Office, 1976).

105. A. DiGregorio and L. J. M. Jansen, "FAO Land Cover Classification: A Dichotomous, Modular-Hierarchical Approach," in *Food and Agriculture Organization of the United Nations* (Rome, 1996).

106. Cadenasso and Pickett, "Boundaries as Structural and Functional Entities."

107. Maryland Department of Planning, *Multi-resolution Land Characteristics, Maryland Property View* (Annapolis: Maryland Department of Planning, 1999).

108. Claritas, *PRIZM Cluster Snapshots: Getting to Know the 62 Clusters* (Ithaca, N.Y.: Claritas, 1999).

109. J. M. Grove, A. R. Troy, J. P. M. O'Neil-Dunne, W. R. Burch Jr., M. L. Cadenasso, and S. T. A. Pickett, "Characterization of Households and Its Implications for the Vegetation of Urban Ecosystems," *Ecosystems* 9, no. 4 (2006): 578–97.

110. P. E. Green, C. S. Tull, and G. Albaum, *Research for Marketing Decisions,* 5th ed. (Englewood Cliffs, N.J.: Prentice-Hall, 1988).

111. Gottdiener and Hutchinson, *New Urban Sociology.*

112. Jacobs, *Death and Life of Great American Cities*; S. Johnson, *Emergence: The Connected Lives of Ants, Brains, Cities, and Software* (New York: Scribner, 2001).

113. N. E. Golubiewski, "Urbanization Increases Grassland Carbon Pools: Effects of Landscaping in Colorado's Front Range," *Ecological Applications* 16 (2006): 555–71.

114. J. E. Force and G. E. Machlis, "The Human Ecosystem, Part II: Social Indicators for Ecosystem Management," *Society and Natural Resources* 10 (1997): 369–82.

115. M. E. Hayward and C. Belfoure, *The Baltimore Rowhouse* (New York: Princeton Architectural Press, 1999).

116. Gottdiener and Hutchinson, *New Urban Sociology*.

117. R. Plunz, "Apropos 'Patch Dynamics': Notes on Indeterminacy as Operational Philosophy in Design," in McGrath et al., *Designing Patch Dynamics*, 42–53; Shane, "Urban Patches."

118. W. H. Lucy and D. L. Phillips, "Suburban Decline: The Next Urban Crisis," *Issues in Science and Technology* 27, no. 1 (2000): 55–62.

119. P. Clergeau, S. Croci, J. Jokimäki, M.-L. Kaisanlahti-Jokimäki, and M. Dinetti, "Avifauna Homogenisation by Urbanisation: Analysis at Different European Latitudes," *Biological Conservation* 127, no. 3 (2006): 336–44; N. B. Grimm, S. H. Faeth, N. E. Golubiewski, C. L. Redman, J. Wu, X. Bai, and J. M. Briggs, "Global Change and the Ecology of Cities," *Science* 319, no. 8 (2008): 756–60.

120. Boone and Modarres, *City and Environment*.

FOUR From Baltimore to Bangkok

1. A. Perrin, "Fancy a Swim? The Lethal Problem with Bangkok's Canals," *Time*, November 17, 2003.

2. S. T. A. Pickett and R. S. Ostfeld, "The Shifting Paradigm in Ecology," in *A New Century for Natural Resources Management*, ed. R. L. Knight and S. F. Bates (Washington, D.C.: Island, 1995), 375.

3. D. N. Wear, "Challenges to Interdisciplinary Discourse," *Ecosystems* 2, no. 4 (1999): 299–301; S. T. A. Pickett, W. R. Burch Jr., and J. M. Grove, "Interdisciplinary Research: Maintaining the Constructive Impulse in a Culture of Criticism," *Ecosystems* 2, no. 4 (1999): 302–7.

4. P. Silltoe, "Interdisciplinary Experiences: Working with Indigenous Knowledge in Development," *Interdisciplinary Science Reviews* 29, no. 1 (2004): 6–23.

5. C. H. Jakobsen, T. Hels, and W. J. McLaughlin, "Barriers and Facilitators to Integration Among Scientists in Transdisciplinary Landscape Analysis: A Cross-Country Comparison," *Forest Policy and Economics* 6, no. 1 (2002): 15–31.

6. G. L. A. Fry, "Multifunctional Landscapes—Towards Transdisciplinary Research," *Landscape and Urban Planning* 57, no. 3 (2001): 159–68; W. Morse, M. Nielsen-Pincus, J. D. Wulfhorst, and J. E. Force, "Bridges and Barriers to Developing and Conducting Integrated Team Research: Lessons Learned from a NSF IGERT Experience," unpublished MS, 2005.

7. B. Tress, G. Tress, and G. Fry, "Integrative Studies on Rural Landscapes: Policy

Expectations and Research Practice," *Landscape and Urban Planning* 70, nos. 1–2 (2005): 177–91.

8. Jakobsen, Hels, and McLaughlin, "Barriers and Facilitators."

9. D. Stokols, J. Fuqua, J. Gress, R. Harvey, K. Phillips, and L. Baesconde-Garbanati, "Evaluating Transdisciplinary Science," *Nicotine and Tobacco Research* 5, no. 1 (2003): S21–S39.

10. G. C. Daily and P. R. Ehrlich, "Managing Earth's Ecosystems: An Interdisciplinary Challenge," *Ecosystems* 2, no. 4 (1999): 277.

11. A. Bruce, "Interdisciplinary Integration in Europe: The Case of the Fifth Framework Programme," *Futures* 36 (2004): 457–70.

12. Tress, Tress, and Fry, "Integrative Studies."

13. M. G. Turner and S. R. Carpenter, "Tips and Traps in Interdisciplinary Research," *Ecosystems* 2, no. 4 (1999).

14. Silltoe, "Interdisciplinary Experiences."

15. Fry, "Multifunctional Landscapes"; Morse et al., "Bridges and Barriers."

16. Pickett, Burch, and Grove, "Interdisciplinary Research."

17. Jakobsen, Hels, and McLaughlin, "Barriers and Facilitators."

18. Turner and Carpenter, "Tips and Traps"; Pickett, Burch, and Grove, "Interdisciplinary Research."

19. L. E. Benda, L. N. Poff, C. Tague, M. A. Palmer, J. Pizzuto, S. Cooper, E. Stanley, and G. Moglen, "How to Avoid Train Wrecks When Using Science in Environmental Problem Solving," *Bioscience* 52, no. 12 (2002); K. A. Poiani, B. D. Richter, M. G. Anderson, and E. Holly, "Biodiversity Conservation at Multiple Scales: Functional Sites, Landscapes, and Networks." *Bioscience* 50, no. 2 (2000): 133–46.

20. Daily and Ehrlich, "Managing Earth's Ecosystems," 280.

21. R. J. Naiman, "A Perspective on Interdisciplinary Science," *Ecosystems* 2, no. 4 (1999): 292–95.

22. Tress, Tress, and Fry, "Integrative Studies."

23. Pickett, Burch, and Grove, "Interdisciplinary Research"; Stokols et al., "Evaluating Transdisciplinary Science."

24. Stokols et al., "Evaluating Transdisciplinary Science."

25. Daily and Ehrlich, "Managing Earth's Ecosystems," 279.

26. R. W. Kates and the National Academy of Sciences Committee on Facilitating Interdisciplinary Research, *Facilitating Interdisciplinary Research* (Washington, D.C.: National Academies Press, 2004).

27. S. T. A. Pickett, M. Cadenasso, J. M. Grove, C. H. Nilon, R. Pouyat, W. C. Zipperer, and C. Costanza, "Urban Ecological Systems: Linking Terrestrial, Ecological, Physical, and Socioeconomic Components of Metropolitan Areas," *Annual Review of Ecology and Systematics,* no. 32 (2001): 127–57.

28. A. H. Hawley, *Human Ecology: A Theoretical Essay* (Chicago: University of Chicago Press, 1986); G. E. Machlis, *Usable Knowledge: A Plan for Furthering Social Science and the National Parks* (Washington, D.C., 1996); Pickett et al., "Urban Ecological Systems."

29. J. C. Collins, A. Kinzig, N. Grimm, W. Fagan, D. Hope, J. Wu, and E. Borer, "A New Urban Ecology," *American Scientist* 88, no. 5 (2000): 416–25.

30. L. Mumford, *The City in History: Its Origins, Its Transformations, and Its Prospects* (San Diego: Harcourt, 1968).

31. R. Masters, *Fortune Is a River: Leonardo Da Vinci and Niccolo Machiavelli's Magnificent Dream to Change the Course of Florentine History* (New York: Penguin Putnam, 1999).

32. W. R. Catton Jr., *Overshoot: The Ecological Basis of Revolutionary Change* (Urbana: University of Illinois Press, 1982).

33. W. E. Rees, "Eco-Footprint Analysis: Merits and Brickbats," *Ecological Economics* 32 (2000): 371–74.

34. M. Alberti, J. M. Marzluff, E. Shulenberger, G. Bradley, C. Ryan, and C. Zumbrunnen, "Integrating Humans into Ecology: Opportunities and Challenges for Studying Urban Ecosystems," *Bioscience* 53, no. 12 (2000): 1171.

35. N. Grimm, J. M. Grove, S. T. A. Pickett, and C. L. Redman, "Integrated Approaches to Long-term Studies of Urban Ecological Systems," *Bioscience* 50, no. 7 (2000): 571–84.

36. G. E. Machlis, J. E. Force, and W. R. Burch Jr., "The Human Ecosystem, Part I: The Human Ecosystem as an Organizing Concept in Ecosystem Management," *Society and Natural Resources* 10 (1997): 347–67.

37. Ibid.

38. Pickett, Burch, and Grove, "Interdisciplinary Research."

39. J. M. Grove and W. R. Burch Jr., "A Social Ecology Approach and Applications of Urban Ecosystem and Landscape Analyses: A Case Study of Baltimore, Maryland," *Urban Ecosystems* 1, no. 4 (1997): 259–75.

40. Pickett, Burch, and Grove, "Interdisciplinary Research."

41. T. F. H. Allen and T. W. Hoekstra, *Toward a Unified Ecology: Complexity in Ecological Systems* (New York: Columbia University Press, 1992).

42. Bruce, "Interdisciplinary Integration."

43. C. E. Lindblom, *Usable Knowledge: Social Science and Problem Solving* (New Haven: Yale University Press, 1979); Machlis, *Usable Knowledge.*

44. G. E. Machlis, D. J. Forester, and J. E. McKendry, *Biodiversity Gap Analysis: Critical Challenges and Solutions,* contribution no. 736 (Moscow: University of Idaho Press, 1995).

45. Daily and Ehrlich, "Managing Earth's Ecosystems."

46. C. L. Redman, J. M. Grove, and L. H. Kuby, "Integrating Social Science into the Long-term Ecological Research (LTER) Network: Social Dimensions of Ecological Change and Ecological Dimensions of Social Change," *Ecosystems* 7, no. 2 (2004): 161–71.

47. Pickett and Ostfeld, "Shifting Paradigm in Ecology."

48. Allen and Hoekstra, *Toward a Unified Ecology.*

49. J. Wu and O. L. Loucks, "From Balance of Nature to Hierarchical Patch Dynamics: A Paradigm Shift in Ecology," *Quarterly Review of Biology* 70 (1995): 439–66; J. Wu and J. L. David, "A Spatially Explicit Hierarchical Approach to Modeling Complex Ecological Systems: Theory and Applications," *Ecological Modelling* 153 (2002): 7–26.

50. L. H. Gunderson and C. S. Holling, *Panarchy: Understanding Transformations in Human and Natural Systems* (Washington, D.C.: Island, 2002).

51. M. Heemskerk, K. Wilson, and M. Pavo-Zuckerman, "Conceptual Models as Tools for Communication Across Disciplines," *Conservation Ecology* 7, no. 3 (2003): 8.

52. Machlis, Force, and Burch, "Human Ecosystem, Part I."

53. Grove and Burch, "Social Ecology."

54. Pickett et al., "Urban Ecological Systems."

55. Allen and Hoekstra, *Toward a Unified Ecology,* 9.

56. P. A. Langley, *Geographic Information Systems and Science* (New York: John Wiley and Sons, 2001); M. N. Demers, *Fundamentals of Geographic Information Systems* (New York: John Wiley and Sons, 2002).

57. I. McHarg, *Design with Nature* (Garden City, N.J.: Doubleday / Natural History, 1969).

58. J. E. McKendry, "The Influence of Map Design on Resource Management Decision Making," *Cartographica* 37, no. 2 (2000): 13–27.

59. Redman, Grove, and Kuby, "Integrating Social."

60. Machlis, Force, and Burch, "Human Ecosystem, Part I."

61. Grove and Burch, "Social Ecology."

62. E. R. Tufte, *The Visual Display of Quantitative Information* (Cheshire, Conn.: Graphic, 1983); E. R. Tufte, *Envisioning Information* (Cheshire, Conn.: Graphics, 1990).

63. M. Monmonier, *How to Lie with Maps* (Chicago: University of Chicago Press, 1991); M. Monmonier, *Mapping It Out: Expository Cartography for the Humanities and Social Sciences* (Chicago: University of Chicago Press, 1993).

64. M. Gottdiener, C. C. Collins, and D. R. Dickens, *Las Vegas: The Social Production of an All-American City* (Malden, Mass.: Blackwell, 1999).

65. Ibid.

66. J. H. Kunstler, *The City in Mind: Notes on the Urban Condition* (New York: Free Press, 2001).

67. Ibid.

68. Gottdiener, Collins, and Dickens, *Las Vegas.*

69. M. Davis, *Dead Cities* (New York: Free Press, 2002).

70. Kunstler, *City in Mind,* 143.

FIVE Pixels, Plots, and Parcels

1. N. B. Grimm, S. H. Faeth, N. E. Golubiewski, C. L. Redman, J. Wu, X. Bai, and J. M. Briggs, "Global Change and the Ecology of Cities," *Science* 319, no. 8 (2008): 756–60; M. J. McDonnell and A. Hahs, "Comparative Ecology of Cities and Towns: Past, Present and Future," In *Ecology of Cities and Towns: A Comparative Approach,* ed. M. J. McDonnell, A. Hahs, and J. Brueste (New York: Cambridge University Press, 2009), 71–89.

2. T. M. Lillesand and R. W. Kiefer, *Remote Sensing and Image Interpretation,* 2nd ed. (New York: John Wiley and Sons, 1987).

3. D. Unwin, *Introductory Spatial Analysis* (New York: Methuen, 1981).

4. J. Mennis, "Generating Surface Models of Population Using Dasymetric Mapping*," *Professional Geographer* 55 (2003): 31–42; C. G. Boone, "Improving Resolution of Census Data in Metropolitan Areas Using a Dasymetric Approach: Applications for the Baltimore Ecosystem Study," *Cities and the Environment* 1, no. 1 (2008): 1–25.

5. M. J. Fortin and M. Dale, *Spatial Analysis: A Guide for Ecologists* (Cambridge: Cambridge University Press, 2005), 365; A. R. Troy, "Geodemographic Segmentation," in *Encyclopedia of Geographical Science,* ed. S. Shenkar (New York: Springer-Verlag, 2008).

6. J. M. Grove, M. Cadenasso, W. R. Burch Jr., S. T. A. Pickett, J. P. M. O'Neil-Dunne, K. Schwarz, M. Wilson, A. R. Troy, and C. Boone, "Data and Methods Comparing Social Structure and Vegetation Structure of Urban Neighborhoods in Baltimore, Maryland," *Society and Natural Resources* 19, no. 2 (2006): 117–36; M. L. Cadenasso, S. T. A. Pickett, and J. M. Grove, "Integrative Approaches to Investigating Human-Natural Systems: The Baltimore Ecosystem Study," *Natures, Sciences, Societies,* no. 14 (2006): 4–14.

7. A. R. Troy, J. M. Grove, J. P. M. O'Neil-Dunne, S. T. A. Pickett, and M. L. Cadenasso, "Predicting Opportunities for Greening and Patterns of Vegetation on Private Urban Lands," *Environmental Management* 40 (2007): 394–412; W. Zhou, A. Troy, and J. M. Grove, "Modeling Residential Lawn Fertilization Practices: Integrating High Resolution Remote Sensing with Socioeconomic Data," *Environmental Management* 41, no. 5 (2008): 742–52.

8. J. M. Grove, A. R. Troy, J. P. M. O'Neil-Dunne, W. R. Burch Jr., M. L. Cadenasso, and S. T. A. Pickett, "Characterization of Households and Its Implications for the Vegetation of Urban Ecosystems," *Ecosystems* 9, no. 4 (2006): 578–97.

9. O. L. Loucks, "Sustainability in Urban Ecosystems: Beyond an Object of Study," in *The Ecological City: Preserving and Restoring Urban Biodiversity,* ed. R. H. Platt, R. A. Rowntree, and P. C. Muick (Amherst: University of Massachusetts Press, 1994), 48–65.

10. C. Boone, G. Buckley, J. M. Grove, and C. Sister, "Parks and People: An Environmental Justice Inquiry in Baltimore, Maryland," *Annals of the Association of American Geographers* 99, no. 4 (2009): 767–87; C. H. Lord and K. Norquist, "Cities as Emergent Systems: Race as a Rule in Organized Complexity," *Environmental Law* 40 (2010): 551–97; G. B. Buckley and C. G. Boone, "To Promote the Material and Moral Welfare of the Community: Neighborhood Improvement Associations in Baltimore, Maryland, 1900–1945," in *Environmental and Social Justice in the City: Historical Perspectives,* ed. R. Rodger and G. Massard-Guilbaud (Cambridge: White Horse, 2011), 43–65.

11. C. L. Merse, G. L. Buckley, and C. G. Boone, "Street Trees and Urban Renewal: A Baltimore Case Study," *Geographical Bulletin* 50 (2009): 65–81.

12. S. Johnson, *The Ghost Map: The Story of London's Most Terrifying Epidemic and How It Changed Science, Cities, and the Modern World* (New York: Riverhead Books, 2006).

13. Ibid.

14. Ibid.

15. Lord and Norquist, "Cities as Emergent Systems."

16. S. R. Carpenter, "The Need for Large-Scale Experiments to Assess and Predict

the Response of Ecosystems to Perturbation," in *Successes, Limitations, and Frontiers in Ecosystem Science*, ed. M. L. Pace and P. M. Groffman (New York: Springer, 1998), 287–312. Figure is adapted from original.

17. G. E. Likens, *Long-term Studies in Ecology: Approaches and Alternatives* (New York: Springer, 1989).

18. J. M. Grove and W. R. Burch Jr., "A Social Ecology Approach and Applications of Urban Ecosystem and Landscape Analyses: A Case Study of Baltimore, Maryland," *Urban Ecosystems* 1, no. 4 (1997): 259–75; W. M. Cook., D. G. Casagrande, D. Hope, P. M. Groffman, and S. L. Collins, "Learning to Roll with the Punches: Adaptive Experimentation in Human-Dominated Systems," *Frontiers in Ecology and the Environment* 2 (2004): 467–74.

19. J. M. Grove, "Cities: Managing Densely Settled Social-Ecological Systems," in *Principles of Ecosystem Stewardship: Resilience-Based Natural Resource Management in a Changing World*, ed. F. S. Chapin III, G. Kofinas, and C. Folke (New York: Springer-Verlag, 2009), 281–94.

six Cholera in London and Urban Tree Canopy in Baltimore

1. E. R. Tufte, *Visual Explanations: Images and Quantities, Evidence and Narrative* (Cheshire, Conn.: Graphic, 1997); S. Johnson, *The Ghost Map: The Story of London's Most Terrifying Epidemic and How It Changed Science, Cities, and the Modern World* (New York: Riverhead Books, 2006).

2. Map of Broad Street pump cholera outbreak of 1854, John Snow site, Department of Epidemiology, UCLA, www.ph.ucla.edu/epi/snow.html.

3. Map of Index case, adapted from John Snow site, Department of Epidemiology, UCLA, www.ph.ucla.edu/epi/snow.html.

4. Johnson, *Ghost Map*, 113.

5. F. H. Bormann and G. Likens, *Patterns and Processes in a Forested Ecosystem* (New York: Springer-Verlag, 1979); S. T. A. Pickett, K. T. Belt, M. F. Galvin, P. Groffman, J. M. Grove, D. C. Outen, R. Pouyat, W. P. Stack, and M. Cadenasso, "Watersheds in Baltimore, Maryland: Understanding and Application of Integrated Ecological and Social Processes," *Journal of Contemporary Water Research and Education* 136 (June 2007): 44–55.

6. P. M. Groffman, N. J. Boulware, W. C. Zipperer, R. V. Pouyat, L. E. Band, and M. F. Colosimo, "Soil Nitrogen Cycle Processes in Urban Riparian Zones," *Environmental Science and Technology* 36, no. 4547–52 (2002); P. M. Groffman and M. K. Crawford, "Denitrification Potential in Urban Riparian Zones," *Journal of Environment Quality* 32 (2003): 1144–49; P. M. Groffman, D. J. Bain, L. E. Band, K. T. Belt, G. S. Brush, J. M. Grove, R. V. Pouyat, I. C. Yesilonis, and W. C. Zipperer, "Down by the Riverside: Urban Riparian Ecology," *Frontiers in Ecology* 1, no. 6 (2003): 315–21.

7. Pickett et al., "Watersheds in Baltimore"; M. Cadenasso, S. T. A. Pickett, P. Groffman, L. E. Band, G. S. Brush, M. F. Galvin, J. M. Grove, et al., "Exchanges Across the Land-Water-Scape Boundaries in Urban Systems," *Annals of New York Academy of Sciences*, no. 1134 (2008): 213–32.

8. S. Raciti, M. F. Galvin, J. M. Grove, J. P. M. O'Neil-Dunne, A. Todd, and S. Clagett, *Urban Tree Canopy Goal Setting: A Guide for Chesapeake Bay Communities* (Annapolis, Md.: U.S. Department of Agriculture, Forest Service, Northeastern State & Private Forestry, Chesapeake Bay Program Office, 2006).

9. J. M. Grove, M. Cadenasso, W. R. Burch Jr., S. T. A. Pickett, J. P. M. O'Neil-Dunne, K. Schwarz, M. Wilson, A. R. Troy, and C. Boone, "Data and Methods Comparing Social Structure and Vegetation Structure of Urban Neighborhoods in Baltimore, Maryland," *Society and Natural Resources* 19, no. 2 (2006): 117–36; A. R. Troy, J. M. Grove, J. P. M. O'Neil-Dunne, M. Cadenasso, and S. T. A. Pickett, "Predicting Patterns of Vegetation and Opportunities for Greening on Private Urban Lands," *Environmental Management,* no. 40 (2007): 394–412; W. Zhou, A. Troy, J. M. Grove, and J. C. Jenkins, "Can Money Buy Green? Demographic and Socioeconomic Predictors of Lawn-Care Expenditures and Lawn Greenness in Urban Residential Areas," *Society and Natural Resources* 22, no. 8 (2009): 744–60; C. G. Boone, M. L. Cadenasso, J. M. Grove, K. Schwarz, and G. L. Buckley, "Landscape, Vegetation Characteristics, and Group Identity in an Urban and Suburban Watershed: Why the 60s Matter," *Urban Ecosystems* 13, no. 3 (2010): 255–71.

10. Grove et al., "Data and Methods"; Grove et al., "Characterization of Households"; Boone et al., "Landscape, Vegetation Characteristics, and Group Identity."

11. J. I. Nassauer, Z. Wang, and E. Dayrell, "What Will the Neighbors Think? Cultural Norms and Ecological Design," *Landscape and Urban Planning* 92 (2009): 282–92; D. Mustafa, T. A. Smucker, F. Ginn, R. Johns, and S. Connely, "Xeriscape People and the Cultural Politics of Turfgrass Transformation," *Environment and Planning D: Society and Space* 28 (2010): 600–617.

12. C. H. Lord and K. Norquist, "Cities as Emergent Systems: Race as a Rule in Organized Complexity," *Environmental Law* 40 (2010): 551–97.

13. S. T. A. Pickett, C. G. Boone, B. P. McGrath, M. L. Cadenasso, D. L. Childers, L. A. Ogden, M. McHale, and J. M. Grove, "Ecological Science and Transformation to the Sustainable City," *Cities* 32 (2013): S10–S20; E. S. Zeemering, *Collaborative Strategies for Sustainable Cities: Economy, Environment, and Community in Baltimore* (New York: Routledge, 2014), 159.

14. D. H. Locke, J. M. Grove, M. Galvin, J. P. M. O'Neil-Dunne, and C. Murphy, "Applications of Urban Tree Canopy Assessment and Prioritization Tools: Supporting Collaborative Decision Making to Achieve Urban Sustainability Goals," *Cities and the Environment* 6, no. 1 (2013): 7.

15. Ibid.

16. M. Romolini, J. M. Grove, C. Ventriss, C. Koliba, and D. Krymkowski, "Adaptive Governance for 21st Century Sustainable Cities: Comparing Stewardship Networks in Baltimore and Seattle" (Ph.D. diss., University of Vermont, 2013); M. Romolini, J. M. Grove, and D. H. Locke, "Assessing and Comparing Relationships Between Urban Environmental Stewardship Networks and Land Cover in Baltimore and Seattle," *Landscape and Urban Planning* 120 (December 2013): 190–207. See also foundational work on organizational networks in Baltimore in S. E. Dalton, "The Gwynns Falls Watershed: A

Case Study of Public and Non-profit Sector Behavior in Natural Resource Management" (Ph.D. diss., Johns Hopkins University, 2002).

SEVEN Metacities and an Urban Land Ethic

1. H. Lefebvre, *The Production of Space* (Oxford: Blackwell, 1991).

2. J. Jacobs, *The Death and Life of Great American Cities* (New York: Vintage Books, 1961).

3. A. W. Spirn, *The Granite Garden: Urban Nature and Human Design* (New York: Basic Books, 1984); M. Hough, *City Form and Natural Process: Towards a New Urban Vernacular* (New York: Van Norstrand Reinhold, 1984).

4. C. S. Holling and L. H. Gunderson, "Resilience and Adaptive Cycles," in *Panarchy: Understanding Transformations in Human and Natural Systems*, ed. L. H. Gunderson and C. S. Holling (Washington, D.C.: Island, 2002), 25–62; R. Biggs, F. R. Westley, and S. R. Carpenter, "Navigating the Back Loop: Fostering Social Innovation and Transformation in Ecosystem Management," *Ecology and Society* 15 (2010): article 9; C. Folke, S. R. Carpenter, B. Walker, M. Scheffer, F. S. Chapin III, and J. Rockstrom, "Resilience Thinking: Integrating Resilience, Adaptability and Transformability," *Ecology and Society* 15 (2012): 20; S. T. A. Pickett, C. G. Boone, B. P. McGrath, M. L. Cadenasso, D. L. Childers, L. A. Ogden, M. McHale, and J. M. Grove, "Ecological Science and Transformation to the Sustainable City," *Cities* 32 (2013): S10–S20.

5. Lefebvre, *Production of Space*.

6. K. Lynch, *The Image of the City* (Cambridge, Mass.: MIT Press, 1960).

7. J. I. Nassauer, "The Appearance of Ecological Systems as a Matter of Policy," *Landscape Ecology* 6 (1992): 239–50; J. L. Nassauer and R. C. Corry, "Using Normative Scenarios in Landscape Ecology," *Landscape Ecology* 19 (2004): 343–56.

8. M. L. Cadenasso, S. T. A. Pickett, and J. M. Grove. "Dimensions of Ecosystem Complexity: Heterogeneity, Connectivity, and History," *Ecological Complexity*, no. 3 (2006): 1–12.

9. G. E. Likens and O. Kinne, *The Ecosystem Approach: Its Use and Abuse* (Oldendorf/Luhe, Germany: Ecology Institute, 1992); M. L. Cadenasso and S. T. A. Pickett, "Urban Principles for Ecological Landscape Design and Management: Scientific Fundamentals," *Cities and the Environment* 1, no. 2 (2008): 1–16; S. T. A. Pickett and J. M. Grove, "Urban Ecosystems: What Would Tansley Do?" *Urban Ecosystems* 12 (2009): 1–8.

10. G. C. Daily, "Introduction: What Are Ecosystem Services?" in *Nature's Services: Societal Dependence on Natural Ecosystems*, ed. G. C. Daily (Washington, D.C.: Island, 1997), 1–10.

11. L. F. Schnore, "Social Morphology and Human Ecology," *American Journal of Sociology* 63 (May 1958): 620–24, 629–34; O. D. Duncan and L. F. Schnore, "Cultural, Behavioral and Ecological Perspective in the Study of Social Organizations," *American Journal of Sociology* 65 (1959): 132–46; W. Firey, *Man, Mind and Land* (Middleton, Wis.: Social Ecology, 1999).

12. W. N. Adger, "Vulnerability," *Global Environmental Change* 16 (2006): 268–81.

13. P. Todorovich and S. Vallabhajosyula, "Northeast Megaregion 2050: A Common Future," in *Regional Plan Association* (New York, 2007); T. Metaxas and M. Tsavdariou, "From 'Blue Banana' to 'Red Octopus' and the Development of Eastern and Southern European Cities: Warsaw and Lisbon," *Regional and Sectoral Economic Studies* 13 (2013): 15–31.

14. D. N. Laband, B. G. Lockaby, and W. C. Zipperer, *Urban-Rural Interfaces: Linking People and Nature* (Madison, Wis.: American Society of Agronomy, Crop Science Society of America, and Soil Science Society of America, 2012).

15. I. Calvino, *Invisible Cities* (New York: Random House, 1974).

16. Ibid., 27.

17. Ibid., 108.

18. Ibid., 121.

19. B. P. McGrath and S. T. A. Pickett, "The Metacity: A Conceptual Framework for Integrating Ecology and Urban Design," *Challenges* 2, no. 4 (2011): 55–72; B. P. McGrath and D. G. Shane, "Metropolis, Megalopolis and the Metacity," in *The Sage Handbook of Architectural Theory*, ed. C. G. Crysler, S. Cairns, and H. Heynen (London: Sage, 2012); S. T. A. Pickett, B. P. McGrath, M. L. Cadenasso, and A. J. Felson, "Ecological Resilience and Resilient Cities," *Building Research and Information* 42, no. 2 (2014): 143–57.

20. C. G. Boone, C. L. Redman, H. Blanco, J. Koch, S. Lwasa, H. Nagendra, S. Pauleit, S. T. A. Pickett, K. C. Seto, and M. Yokohari, "Group 4: Reconceptualizing Urban Land Use," in *Rethinking Urban Land Use in a Global Era*, ed. K. C. Seto and A. Reenberg (Cambridge, Mass.: MIT Press, 2014), 313–32.

21. Calvino, *Invisible Cities*, 138.

22. Pickett et al., "Ecological Science and Transformation."

23. Calvino, *Invisible Cities*, 135.

24. Ibid., 150.

25. A. Leopold, *A Sand County Almanac* (New York: Oxford University Press, 1949); J. B. Callicott, "Aldo Leopold's Metaphor," in *Ecosystem Health: New Goals for Environmental Management*, ed. R. Costanza, B. G. Norton, and B. D. Haskell (Washington, D.C.: Island, 1992), 42–56.

26. R. Rozzi, "Bicultural Ethics: Recovering the Vital Links Between the Inhabitants, Their Habits, and Habitats," *Environmental Ethics* 34 (2012): 27–50.

27. Leopold, *Sand County Almanac*.

28. Millennium Ecosystem Assessment, *Ecosystems and Human Well-Being: A Framework for Assessment* (Washington, D.C.: Island, 2003).

29. M. Cadenasso, S. T. A. Pickett, P. Groffman, L. E. Band, G. S. Brush, M. F. Galvin, J. M. Grove, et al., "Exchanges Across the Land-Water-Scape Boundaries in Urban Systems," *Annals of New York Academy of Sciences*, no. 1134 (2008): 213–32.

30. Calvino, *Invisible Cities*, 161.

Further Readings

Readers may seek greater depth in some of the ideas and topics identified in this book. We provide the following readings, organized by topic and then in chronological order. We also list *The BES Urban Lexicon*. As we note in chapter 4, interdisciplinary projects benefit from developing and formalizing a shared vocabulary. *The BES Urban Lexicon* is such an example for urban ecology research. Updated on an ad hoc basis, it is freely available to anyone who wants to use it and open to contributions outside of BES. We welcome additons that you might have to offer in this endeavor to further the goal of nurturing a larger urban ecology community.

Urban Ecology Lexicon

Baltimore Ecosystem Study LTER. *The BES Urban Lexicon.* http://besur banlexicon.blogspot.com/.

Urban Design

Olmsted Brothers. *Report upon the Development of Public Grounds for Greater Baltimore.* 1904. Reprint, Baltimore: Friends of Maryland's Olmsted Parks & Landscapes, 1987.

Spirn, A. W. *The Granite Garden: Urban Nature and Human Design.* New York: Basic Books, 1984.

Shane, G. D. *Recombinant Urbanism: Conceptual Modeling in Architec-*

ture, Urban Design, and City Theory. Chichester, U.K.: John Wiley and Sons, 2005.

Steiner, F. R., ed. *The Essential Ian McHarg: Writings on Design and Nature.* Washington, D.C.: Island, 2006.

Cadenasso, M. L., and S. T. A. Pickett. "Urban Principles for Ecological Landscape Design and Management: Scientific Fundamentals." *Cities and the Environment* 1, no. 2 (2008): 1–16.

Steiner, F. *Design for a Vulnerable Planet.* Austin: University of Texas Press, 2011.

McGrath, B. P., and D. G. Shane. "Metropolis, Megalopolis and the Metacity." In *The Sage Handbook of Architectural Theory,* edited by C. G. Crysler, S. Cairns, and H. Heynen, 641–57. London: Sage, 2012.

Spirn, A. W. *Ecological Urbanism: A Framework for the Design of Resilient Cities* (2012). http://www.annewhistonspirn.com/pdf/Spirn-Eco Urbanism-2012.pdf.

Pickett, S. T. A., M. L. Cadenasso, and B. McGrath, eds. *Resilience in Ecology and Urban Design: Linking Theory and Practice for Sustainable Cities.* New York: Springer, 2013.

Pickett, S. T. A., B. McGrath, M. L. Cadenasso, and A. J. Felson. "Ecological Resilience and Resilient Cities." *Building Research and Information* (2013): 1–15.

Urban Ecology and Equity

Boone, C. "An Assessment and Explanation of Environmental Inequity in Baltimore." *Urban Geography* 23, no. 6 (2002): 581–95.

Heynen, N., M. Kaika, and E. Swyngedouw, eds. *In the Nature of Cities: Urban Political Ecology and the Politics of Urban Metabolism.* New York: Routledge, 2006.

Boone, C. G., G. L. Buckley, J. M. Grove, and C. Sister. "Parks and People: An Environmental Justice Inquiry in Baltimore, Maryland." *Annals of the Association of American Geographers* 99, no. 4 (2009): 767–87.

Lord, C. H., and K. Norquist. "Cities ad Emergence Systems: Races as a Rule in Organized Complexity," *Environmental Law* 40 (2010): 551–97.

Rodger, R., and G. Massard-Guilbaud, eds. *Environmental and Social Justice in the City: Historical Perspectives,* Cambridge: White Horse, 2011.

Boone, C. G., and M. Fragkias. *Urbanization and Sustainability: Linking Urban Ecology, Environmental Justice and Global Environmental Change.* New York: Springer, 2012.

Land Use and Land Cover

Cadenasso, M. L., S. T. A. Pickett, and K. Schwarz. "Spatial Heterogeneity in Urban Ecosystems: Reconceptualizing Land Cover and a Framework for Classification." *Frontiers in Ecology and Environment* 5 (2007): 80–88.

Seto, K. C., and A. Reenberg, eds. *Rethinking Urban Land Use in a Global Era.* Cambridge, Mass.: MIT Press, 2014.

Perspectives on Theory, Theoretical Perspectives

Jacobs, J. *The Death and Life of Great American Cities: The Failure of Town Planning.* New York: Random House, 1961.

Johnson, S. *Emergence: The Connected Lives of Ants, Brains, Cities, and Software.* New York: Scribner, 2001.

Gottdiener, M., and L. Budd. *Key Concepts in Urban Studies.* London: Sage, 2005.

Boone, C. G., and A. Modarres. *City and Environment.* Philadelphia: Temple University Press, 2006.

Pickett, S. T. A., J. Kolasa, and C. Jones. *Ecological Understanding: The Nature of Theory and the Theory of Nature.* 2nd ed. Boston: Academic, 2007.

Gottdiener, M., and R. Hutchison. *The New Urban Sociology.* 4th ed. Boulder, Colo.: Westview, 2011.

Batty, M. *The New Science of Cities.* Cambridge, Mass.: MIT Press, 2013.

Dillon, M. *Introduction to Sociological Theory: Theorists, Concepts, and Their Applicability to the Twenty-first Century.* 2nd ed. Malden, Mass.: Wiley Blackwell, 2014.

Meaning, Models, and Metaphors

Pickett, S. T. A., M. L. Cadenasso, and J. M. Grove. "Resilient Cities: Meaning, Models and Metaphor for Integrating the Ecological,

Socio-economic, and Planning Realms." *Landscape and Urban Planning* 69 (2004): 369–84.

Musacchio, L. R. "Pattern:Process Metaphors for Metropolitan Landscapes." In *Ecology of Cities and Towns: A Comparative Approach*, edited by M. J. McDonnell, A. Hahs, and J. Breuste, 484–502. New York: Cambridge University Press, 2009.

Larson, B. *Metaphors for Environmental Sustainability: Redefining Our Relationship with Nature.* New Haven: Yale University Press, 2011.

Progress in Contemporary Urban Ecology

McDonnell, M. J., and S. T. A. Pickett. *Humans as Components of Ecosystems: The Ecology of Subtle Human Effects and Populated Areas.* New York: Springer-Verlag, 1993.

Pickett, S. T. A., W. R. Burch Jr., and S. Dalton. "Integrated Urban Ecosystem Research." *Urban Ecosystems* 1, no. 4 (1997): 183–84.

Collins, J. C., A. Kinzig, N. Grimm, W. Fagan, D. Hope, J. Wu, and E. Borer. "A New Urban Ecology." *American Scientist* 88, no. 5 (2000): 416–25.

Grimm, N., J. M. Grove, S. T. A. Pickett, and C. L. Redman. "Integrated Approaches to Long-term Studies of Urban Ecological Systems." *Bioscience* 50, no. 7 (2000): 571–84.

Marzluff, J. M., E. Schulenberger, W. Endlicher, M. Alberti, G. Bradley, C. Ryan, U. Simon, and C. ZumBrunne, eds. *Urban Ecology: An International Perspective on the Interaction Between Humans and Nature.* New York: Springer, 2008.

McDonnell, M. J., and A. Hahs. "Comparative Ecology of Cities and Towns: Past, Present and Future." In *Ecology of Cities and Towns: A Comparative Approach*, edited by M. J. McDonnell, A. Hahs, and J. Breuste, 71–89. New York: Cambridge University Press, 2009.

McDonnell, M. J. "The History of Urban Ecology: An Ecologist's Perspective." In *Urban Ecology: Patterns, Processes, and Applications*, edited by J. Niemela, 5–13. New York: Oxford University Press, 2011.

Pickett, S. T. A., M. L. Cadenasso, J. M. Grove, C. G. Boone, P. M. Groffman, E. Irwin, S. S. Kaushal, V. Marshall, B. P. McGrath, C. H. Nilon, R. V. Pouyat, K. Szlavecz, A. Troy, and P. Warren. "Urban Ecological

Systems: Scientific Foundations and a Decade of Progress." *Journal of Environmental Management* 92, no. 3 (2011): 331–62.

Wu, J. "Urban Ecology and Sustainability: The State-of-the-Science and Future Directions." *Land* 125 (2014): 209–21.

Approaches to Urban Ecology Research

McDonnell, M. J., and S. T. A. Pickett. "Ecosystem Structure and Function Along Urban-Rural Gradients: An Exploited Opportunity for Ecology." *Ecology* 71 (1990): 1232–37.

Cadenasso, M. L., S. T. A. Pickett, and J. M. Grove. "Dimensions of Ecosystem Complexity: Heterogeneity, Connectivity, and History." *Ecological Complexity*, no. 3 (2006): 1–12.

Pickett, S. T. A., and M. L. Cadenasso. "Advancing Urban Ecological Studies: Frameworks, Concepts, and Results from the Baltimore Ecosystem Study." *Australian Ecology*, no. 31 (2006): 114–25.

Grove, J. M., S. T. A. Pickett, A. Whitmer, and M. L. Cadenasso. "Building an Urban LTSER: The Case of the Baltimore Ecosystem Study and the D.C./B.C. ULTRA-Ex Project." In *Long Term Socio-ecological Research: Studies in Society: Nature Interactions Across Spatial and Temporal Scales,* edited by J. S. Singh, H. Haberl, M. Chertow, M. Mirtl, and M. Schmid, 369–408. New York: Springer, 2013.

Index

Page numbers in italic type refer to illustrations